VIGILANTES TO VERDICTS

⬅——————➡

Stories from a Texas District Court

With Introduction
By
Judge Donald R. Jones
266th Judicial District Court

VIGILANTES TO VERDICTS

◄─────────►

Stories from a Texas District Court

by

Sherri Knight

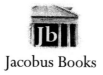

Jacobus Books

Copyright © 2009 by Sherri Knight. All rights reserved.

Published by
Jacobus Books
P. O. Box 1587
Stephenville, Texas 76401

All rights reserved. No part of this publication may be reproduced, stored in a retrieval system, or transmitted, in any form or by any means, electronic, mechanical, photocopying, recording, or otherwise, without the written prior permission by the author.

ISBN 13: 978-0-9841857-0-2
ISBN 10: 0-9841857-0-4

First Edition

Book sales for North America and International:
Jacobus Books

Cover: -The noose on the front cover is the one that was used to hang Tom Wright and is located at the Stephenville Museum. The lynching cartoon at the top of the noose is from *Frank Leslie's Illustrated Newspaper*, Nov. 12, 1881. Photo of jury courtesy of Stephenville Museum.

Cover Design: Julie Moeller
www.LegaseeKeepsakes.com

Printed in the United States of America

Table of Contents

Author's note	i
Introduction by District Judge Donald R. Jones	iii
Preface	v

Part One – The Court Organizes	1
Jack of Many Trades –	1
Texas Sheriffs in the Nineteenth Century	
Forced Accommodations—The County Jail	7
Court Life	14
A Citizen' Obligation – Jury Duty	19
Seat of Justice – The County Courthouse	24

Part Two – Early Justice	31
Judge Lynch in Erath County	31
The Lower Brazos Reserve Indians Massacre	37
Drink as Much Whiskey as You Want –	44
The Fount Arnold Gang	
A Tragedy of Frontier Insanity –	48
The James M. McCarty Story	

Part Three – The Court Deliberates	53
A Wrong Move on the Texas Frontier –	53
The Parks Crenshaw Story	
An Overland Stagecoach Overturns –	57
The Dulany Family Story	
Taking the Edge Off – I. W. Lacy Case	62
Charged with Murder – The James Taylor Story	66
Marital Bliss – The Court Steps In	70

Part Four – The Court Grows Up	77
A Woman in a Man's World – The Phebe Haws Story	77
Bigamy Leads To Murder—The W. F. Holland Story	83
Attempted Citizens' Arrest Ends in Deadly Force –	88
The Dr. W. M. Barry, S. O. Berry, and John Shelby Story	
Three Views to a Killing – The John Wesley Hardin Story	91

The Bad Luck Horse Thieves –	103
The C. E. Aiken & A. B. James Story	
What's Yours Is Mine –The Jasper Reynolds Story	107
Revenge – The Morg McInturf Story	112
Murder Near Rat Row –The Harry Barrett Story	117
A Traveling Murder Case –The David Kemp Story	122
Infanticide – The Anna Williamson Story	129
Road Work – The John Henning Story	133
Murder After Dark –	138
The Monroe Coldiron and Brink Favors Story	
Part Five – The Court Takes Control	145
Moral of the Murder – The Tom Putty Story	145
A Hate Crime – The Tom Lauderdale Story	149
A Knifing in the Side Room – The Tom Wood Story	155
When Adultery Leads to Perjury – The John Hull Story	160
Sable King – The Frank Lewis Story	167
'They Have My Boy in That Damned Hell Hole' –	173
The T. J. Wilson Story	
'Promise Me That You Will Let Liquor Alone' –	178
The Tom Wright & Frank Leslie Story	
Part Six – District Court Judges	197
Nicholas William Battle	197
Wilson Yandell McFarland	199
Richard Coke	201
Thomas Harrison	203
John J. Good	205
A. B. Norton	207
John Patterson Osterhout	210
James Richard Fleming	213
Thomas Lewis Nugent	216
Charles Keith Bell	219
John Smith Straughan	221
End Notes	223
Index	233
Author's Biography	244

Author's Note

The impetus for researching/writing this volume came from a conversation with District Judge Donald R. Jones of the 266th Judicial District. I had turned to him for advice in understanding legal procedures when writing my first book—*Tom P's Fiddle, A True Texas Tale*. During one of our discussions, the judge reflected that little was known about the district judges who had preceded him—especially from the nineteenth century—in Erath County. I offered to research the topic and quickly found myself mentally pulled back into a bygone time.

Digging through the files and minutes of the District Court of Erath County yielded a rich goldmine of information and material. Hidden among the dusty, rarely viewed volumes was information reflecting the judicial impact on the lives of men and women who lived in a Texas frontier county in the nineteenth century. Intertwined within the legalese used to record important matters that came before the court was evidence that provided a window into the human drama that took place twice a year as traveling district judges arrived to administer the "law of the land." These stories—both fascinating and thought-provoking—are brought back to life in this volume.

Many thanks are given to those who daily work and record the legal matters that come before the district court. Erath County is blessed because so much of the court records and files from the nineteenth century are still extant and available for researchers. District Court Coordinator Candy Perry and District Clerk Wanda Pringle along with Susan Culpepper, Jan Brown, Kristie Montgomery, and Melissa Ibarra were unfailingly supportive in my quest for information.

For early local newspapers and county court records the Dick Smith Library at Tarleton State University proved invaluable. Sandy Dennis was very helpful plus willing to walk over to the "dungeon" several times so that old document books such as the Sheriff's Docket could be retrieved for perusal. Also located at the Smith Library are the *Stephenville Empire* archives. Librarian Glenda Stone was instrumental in looking up obscure information.

Tony Black and Laura Saegert at the archives of the Texas State Library were patient with my requests and welcoming when I traveled to Austin to research the records on court proceedings at the appellate level plus the penitentiary archives from Huntsville and Rusk.

Local researcher James Pylant, author of *Sins of the Pioneers*, supplied needed information on Erath County history. Much appreciated was his willingness to share the family photos and information about Sheriff J. C. Gilbreath.

This project could not have been completed without the editing work of Arden Knight and readers—James Pylant, Cindy Shipman and Glenda Stone. Their input proved invaluable!

The cover of this volume reflects the many talents of Julie Moeller, a wiz where Photoshop is concerned. I appreciate her effort and hours of working and reworking the graphics.

Last but certainly not least is the assistance given by District Judge Donald R. Jones. Much appreciated are the hours of discussion on law and court procedure from the nineteenth century.

—Sherri Knight

Photo Credits except those noted on photos:

Stephenville Museum: Pages 1, 3, 4, 7, 10, 19, 25, 29, 30, 49, 77, 88, 157, 160, 169, 188, 194, 213, 221; James Pylant: p. 1; Pat Sharp; p. 32; Mike Cox: p. 38; DMEC online: p. 91; *Biographical Encyclopedia of Texas* (1880) Pages 197, 203; *Belton Illustrated*, p. 210; Wikimedia online: p. 201; *Life Work of T. L. Nugent*: p. 216.

Author's Personal Collection: Pages 17, 47, 62, 68, 86, 105, 111, 120, 123, 131, 133, 141, 152

Introduction

The title tells the story. In *Vigilantes to Verdicts*, Sherri Knight has done an astonishing amount of in-depth research, giving the reader an overview not only of the law and legal system as it developed in Erath County, but also of life in the mid to late nineteenth century for the new settlers and frontiersmen in this area of the relatively new State of Texas.

The book begins with the early origin of law and establishment in 1858 of the first district court in Erath County, moves through the development of the court in the setting of the times and ends at the turn of the century. Throughout this journey the development of the county and the law in Erath County is illustrated by anecdotal historical short stories with actual dialogue and narrative straight out of newspaper articles and official court records of the times.

The book is not dry—it is not boring. Instead, it is an interesting and true history that will be of special benefit to anyone wanting more information on early Texas laws and their enforcement, and the evolution of both law and society from the rigors of frontier life in the mid-1800s to a more civilized justice system in the county by the beginning of the 1900s.

The reader will learn about—life on the district court circuit; the location, disputes and construction of early courthouses in Stephenville; early law enforcement personalities; jury duty; and methods of dealing with those who were alleged to have violated the law—all through a series of true historical stories that have been extensively researched by an extremely talented research writer. The final part of the book contains a short and interesting biographical sketch of each of the individuals who served as district judge for the various districts in which Erath County found itself from 1858 through 1900 with actual photographs of most.

Whether you are a history buff interested in early pioneer life in the newly organized counties of Texas or a person interested in the development of the rule of law in Erath County in the late nineteenth century, upon completion of this book you will feel as though you have a true and accurate sense of "how it was." As a lifelong resident of Erath County and as the presiding judge of the current district court of this county, I found this book to be a well-documented history of both, illustrated by fascinating stories of the actual lives and events which make up our colorful past.

> Donald R. Jones
> District Judge
> 266th District Court of
>   Erath County, Texas

Preface

In the nineteenth century Texas was impacted by many course-changing events. Going from a Mexican province to a republic then on to statehood was traumatic enough but added to the mix was the Civil War and later Radical Reconstruction. This was plenty to digest, but settlers in the frontier counties were also challenged by an unforgiving landscape along with Indians who attacked and harassed those encroaching on their territory.

Life was difficult enough without the added burden of outlaws bent on taking what few possessions these pioneers brought with them or managed to accumulate. How men dealt with crime showed an ingrained and strong sense of right and wrong.

Judicial history—often ignored by historians except for sensational crimes—is full of human drama and affords the researcher a window on past events that affected more than just those involved in litigation or prosecution. A society's mores and values are reflected in the type of crimes committed and the severity of punishments meted out by judges and juries.

The Texas Legislature scrambled to keep the legal system organized then reorganized as emigrants poured over the Texas borders—many having "good" reasons for sudden exits from their previous homes. While each county was allowed several inferior courts such as county courts, municipal courts and justice of the peace courts, district courts had jurisdiction over more serious crimes and civil cases.

Problems arose on several fronts. The elected district judge visited counties with small populations only twice a year in the nineteenth century. Waiting for justice to be administered was many times untenable for the local populace seeking relief from these lawbreakers. Thrown into the mix was the chaos generated by the Civil War and its aftermath.

Erath County, located in the western edge of north central Texas, experienced a suspicious fire in 1866 when the courthouse was located on the east side of the square rather than in the middle of the downtown square. All county and district court records were destroyed. No notation was recorded as to the cause of the fire, but interesting is the fact that it happened so soon after the end of the Civil War and victory for the Unionists. Counties went without district court sessions for a whole year at times. This happened in Erath County in 1868 and 1870.

Without benefit of legal means to dispose of criminal activity, settlers turned to tried and true methods of dealing with unwanted outlaws—vigilantism. Rarely carried out in broad daylight or documented, these "night courts" used the services of men willing to summarily dispatch criminals, using the closest convenient tree. Born of necessity, these nocturnal attempts at justice allowed those accused little or no time to protest their innocence.

As events settled down and Texans took back control of their own state government in the mid-1870s, district courts also began turning the wheels of justice with a little more regularity. No longer on the district bench were Yankee-appointed judges not trusted by locals. Slowly, but surely, people turned to the government through the courts to solve legal problems—both because the state insisted on it—but also because settlers knew vigilantism had a built in anarchy component that could easily wreak havoc if allowed to go unchecked.

Ironically, by the end of the nineteenth century the Twenty-Ninth Judicial District Court of Erath County had firm control over judicial matters but closed out the century by "legally" condemning a man to be hung—Tom Wright. So from illegal hangings to a government sanctioned one, this volume travels along the judicial trail. Although many more stories were available than space allowed, the ones included were chosen either for their impact or uniqueness. Two cases were included from outside of Erath County—the Dulany runaway stagecoach incident from McLennan County and the John Wesley Hardin murder trial from Comanche County—but in both instances, the district judge dispensing justice also sat on the bench at the same time in Erath County. All the stories can be seen as a progression from people taking matters into their own hands to the imposition of law and order; i. e.—*Vigilantes to Verdicts*.

"We have a criminal jury system which is superior to any in the world; and its efficiency is only marred by the difficulty of finding twelve men every day who don't know anything and can't read."
~Mark Twain

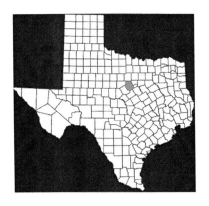

Map of Erath County, Texas

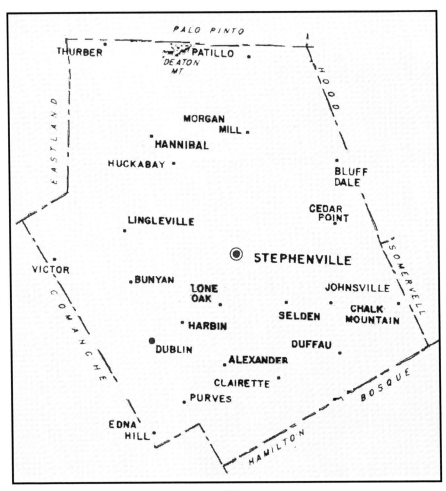

Part One – The Court Organizes

Jack of Many Trades
Texas Sheriffs in the Nineteenth Century

While keeping law and order was considered the cornerstone of a county sheriff's job description, the fine print would yield evidence that the man elected to this position had to be capable of juggling many assignments from both the state and county officials.

Sheriffs in Texas were elected for two-year terms in the nineteenth century. Being a good politician was necessary. Knowing the "pulse" of the local population and using it to keep the peace was essential.

Besides keeping an eye out for wrongdoers, the county lawman was expected to go after fugitives who had managed to elude facing justice for their actions. Often the sheriff or the local district attorney would send an appeal to the governor for funds in order to pay for expeditions to track these wanted men, many of whom took off to New Mexico or Indian Territory (Oklahoma). With or without state funds, one Erath County lawman during the 1880s, J. C. Gilbreath, took

Sheriff J. C. Gilbreath

it as his personal responsibility to track down fugitives. If necessary, he was willing to cross state lines to nab a wanted man.[1]

The sheriff's day got a lot longer during the weeks when district court was being held. He was responsible for summoning prospective grand and petit jurors. During court, he had to make sure that the jurors were fed. He also tracked down citizens who did not show up for jury duty.

Taking care of the district court's official business in the form of delivering subpoenas for witnesses and court documents was expected. During the Criminal Docket, the sheriff hauled defendants to and from jail, which seemed like a simple task except that Erath did not have a sturdy jail in the early decades of its existence. This meant that those charged with serious crimes had to be taken to other counties for housing. Erath used the Comanche and Waco jails and sometimes Fort Worth. The new jail for Erath County was finished by 1879.

Besides summoning jurors, the peace officer was expected to watch over an impaneled jury. This presented problems when a jury was sequestered and one or more members took it upon themselves to leave the group. Not only could the juror get into trouble but so could the sheriff. In May 1897 District Judge J. S. Straughan fined Sheriff Frank Freeman $100 for contempt of court for not sufficiently guarding the jury.[2]

The sheriff was also expected to be on hand during trial proceedings, ever ready to do the judge's bidding. This included becoming a purchasing agent for the court. In one notation of the Erath County district minutes, the sheriff was instructed to purchase "four sets of rawhide bottomed chairs for use of jurors and lawyers."[3] The chief lawman found himself responsible for the maintenance on the courthouse. In 1874 after receiving complaints, the commissioners' court ordered the sheriff to secure the doors and windows of the courthouse at the end of each day to prevent misuse.

On the other side of trials the sheriff was expected to enforce court rulings and take those convicted of crimes into custody until they paid their fines. If the conviction included prison time, the sheriff had to take the convict to Huntsville or Rusk State Penitentiary unless a prison contractor was available.

It was not unusual to receive papers from other counties for the sheriff to deliver or serve. He also had to keep a vigil for fugitives from other parts of Texas, capturing and holding them until authorities could arrive to take them back to their home counties.

Added to the peace officer's duties was the responsibility of the county jail. He had to hire guards, purchase food, and arrange for medical care for prisoners. He had the daily duty in the winter of procuring wood for both the jail and the courthouse. Noted in the *Minutes of the District Court* of Erath County for April 1879 is a request from the grand jury to District Judge J. R. Fleming asking that the "cleanings and filth" from the jail should be buried in trenches or removed at a greater distance from the jail. This type chore fell to the sheriff to accomplish. Not sure was whether the grand jurors were concerned for the jail inmates or more worried about the "deposits" being thrown in front of the Baptist Church located close by the jail.[4]

Sheriff Nathan Shands

When someone was found guilty of a lesser crime entailing a fine and/or jail time, the sheriff leased the inmates out to interested parties or sent them to work at the county poor farm. Usually, "working" girls fell into this category if they were convicted of "vagrancy." Interestingly, Sheriff Nathan Shands employed Sophie Pierce, a known prostitute, in 1896 as a cook. Not noted is whether this employment was an effort to get honest work for her or if she was simply "working off" a fine.[5]

The sheriff's wife usually ended up helping by being the main cook at the jail. One story told in Sheriff Shands' family concerned his wife Rebecca. One day at mealtime a group of prisoners believed they had an opening for an escape while she was serving a meal. Realizing the situation, Rebecca Shands used her own gun to order the men back into their cell. One look at her determined expression and no nonsense demeanor convinced them to comply.[6]

The sheriff's children often lived in the family quarters inside the jail facility. Some were born there. *The Stephenville Empire* in the April 11, 1885, issue took note—

> *One day this week a stranger appeared at the county jail, and it was all Dr. Ritchie could do to prevent Sheriff Gilbreath from putting her in a cell, and turning the keys. Mr. Gilbreath was indignant because his girl was not a boy. He now smiles muchly.*

The county's lawman was also the ex officio tax collector. He was responsible for traveling throughout the county and knowing all the residents, their comings and goings. He also had the unenviable task of holding delinquent tax auctions on real estate as directed by the district court.

R. T. Long, Erath sheriff in 1879

As county administrator and tax collector, the sheriff was also expected to keep tabs on saloonkeepers and peddlers who had to obtain licenses to operate within the county. A peddler's license was for a specific amount of time. Some professionals, such as doctors and lawyers, also had to obtain a license to operate within the county. The sheriff made sure those who solicited local business were registered, or he arrested them for noncompliance.

Hiring deputies to help shoulder the load was also important. The sheriff had to find men willing to work for fairly low pay and yet have good reputations. The actions of the deputies could come home to haunt a sheriff come re-election time. In 1870 Erath Sheriff Fell Ross hired Light Nowlin as a deputy. A year later, Ross was chagrined when Nowlin was arrested for playing cards in a saloon as well as other misdemeanors.[7]

The commissioners' court expected the peace officer to attend their meetings and carry out their directives. In a fit of ire during Reconstruction, the commissioners' court fined Sheriff Ross $100 for not attending their meetings and for not keeping the courthouse in decent order.[8] Most of the time the court relied on the chief lawman's knowledge of the location of where people lived. The sheriff was consulted on routes for roads to be laid out in the county.

For obvious reasons, being a sheriff or even a deputy sheriff was a dangerous profession. Being attacked or shot at from time to time was considered a part of the job. Compounding the danger, sheriffs and deputies could not wear a gun, according to town ordinances, except when on official duty. In some counties this left the lawmen as unarmed targets for those with a grudge to settle.

The public was not always sympathetic with the sheriff trying to carry out his official duties. Sheriff R. T. Long met with resistance when he served a warrant on J. E. Thompson in 1878 for assault with intent to murder. Although the grand jury brought an additional indictment against Thompson, the petit jury showed their thoughts on the matter when they found Thompson guilty but only fined him $1.00.

James Mastin was the only sheriff to die in the line of duty in Erath County. Attempting to arrest a suspect proved fatal. Monday, June 25, 1877, Sheriff Mastin rode three miles out of Stephenville with Deputies Handsel and Cozby to the residence of a Mr. Wolfe. Mastin's object was Bonaparte (Bone) Wilson from Palo Pinto County, a known horse thief. After being allowed to search inside the house, Mastin stepped outside to survey the area. Wilson stepped out from behind the house and shot the sheriff who died instantly. The deputies in turn fired at Wilson, but he was able to get away.

Wilson's days were numbered. The death of a sheriff killed in the line of duty was considered to be a particularly heinous crime. Wilson headed west. The Texas Rangers, stationed in Runnels County and led by Captain John Sparks, followed not far behind. They finally located Wilson's encampment close to Snyder, Texas. The plan was to shoot Wilson's horse out from under him and then bring about an arrest, but the outlaw, instead of surrendering, ducked behind his horse and kept firing. The surprised Rangers had no choice but to kill him. A barrage of bullets accomplished the goal. The body was hauled all the way back to Stephenville, including changing conveyances in order to get across a swollen creek.

Ranger Noah Armstrong recalled the killing of Wilson and the taking back of his body to Erath to collect the $1000 reward plus some land that was being offered. The Rangers put Wilson's body on a wagon but had to switch to a hack in order to get across some of the creeks. Armstrong stated that Gus Young got the land and decided to live on it.[9] Erath County Commissioners later voted to pay Willie Harris and Temus Williamson $3.00 each to dig a grave for Bone Wilson in the West End Cemetery in Stephenville.[10]

Fearless men came forward to serve as lawmen in Texas. Without their determination many of these counties along the frontier would have been at the mercy of rustlers and outlaws. These courageous men kept the wheels of justice rolling in the right direction.

Sheriffs of the Nineteenth Century, Erath County			
1856	John Maloney	1872	A. L. Kirk
1857	Sam Hicks	1873	W. G. Waller
1860	John Waller	1874	James Mastin
1862	David Thornton	1878	H. M. Henderson
1864	William Skipper	1879	R. T. Long
1866	R. M. Whiteside	1880	W. B. Slaughter
1867	A. Brown	1882	J. C. Gilbreath
1868	John Brumley	1886	N. J. Shands
1869	G. W. Keith	1896	Frank Freeman
1870	Fell Ross	1898	Robert Tutt Hume

Forced Accommodations
The County Jail

Settlers in Erath understood the need for a place to hold rowdy merrymakers along with more serious criminals. Various nicknames for the county accommodations included calaboose, hoosegow, bucket, pokey, lockup, hole, along with many others. It all meant the same for those forced to stay there – loss of freedom.

Like county courthouses, jails usually reflected the extent to which a county meant business with lawbreakers. Early Texas jails were many times primitive wooden affairs—not meant to hold serious outlaws bent on leaving at the earliest opportunity.

The first official jail for Erath County was built close to downtown. A two-story board and batten building, this jail was 24' square and used a double course of heavy timber, much sturdier than its appearance gave. Prisoners were kept on the second floor that could only be reached by using an outside ladder. One small window allowed for light and air.

First jail in Erath County

A description of how prisoners were kept appeared in the June 10 1921 issue of the *Stephenville Empire Tribune*—

> ...prisoners were carried up the outside, dropped through a trap door in the ceiling to the prison below. In the center of this dungeon an enormous ring anchored deep in the floor protruded, to which the prisoner was chained if he was regarded as a "bad man."

Only one anecdotal story has survived concerning a break from the earliest jail in Erath County on an unremembered date. A wife was allowed to visit her husband. Unseen, as she climbed the stairs, because it was hidden among the many folds of her petticoats, was a steel file to which the prisoner made good use. He effectively departed when no one was keeping a good eye on him.

Judge John Osterhout in 1871 noted in the *Minutes of the District Court* that Erath did not have a jail where prisoners could be kept to serve out short sentences. He ordered the sheriff to take these men to the McLennan County jail in Waco until their fines and costs were discharged and/or they had served out their time. Outlaws charged with serious crimes were also taken to other county jails for safekeeping in the early decades after the Civil War. Hood, Comanche, and even Tarrant County jails were all used by Erath County at one time.

Unfortunately, placing the convicted in other county jails was not very cost effective. The commissioners were constantly having to approve the payment of the medicine, room and board for these men, being held accountable for breaking the laws in Erath. The commissioners started planning for a new jail shortly after the Civil War, but the lack of funds prevented these plans from going forward. At one point they called for sealed bids and in 1871 accepted the offer of B. F. Allen and F. Kimbell to build a new jail for $2200. Toward the end of the decade the new edifice was finally built.[1]

The completed three-story stone jail boasted a cupola on the top. Measuring forty feet by seventy-two feet, the jail's bottom floor was devoted to offices and living quarters for the sheriff and his family. The second floor had iron cages built to hold about twenty inmates. The third floor was the jury room. Both the second and third floors had narrow windows, which allowed in only a minimum of light and air. The building had the appearance of a fortress.

Almost immediately, complaints started pouring in but surprisingly not from those forced to stay in the new county accommodations. Living near the new jail seemed to have had a negative effect. The grand jury on April 16, 1879, through their foreman, L. E. Gillett, wrote into the *Erath County District Court Minutes*, Book C:

> *There is one thing however that the Grand Jury would like through Your Honor to call the attention of the County Court Commissioners, and that is the removal of the cleanings and filth from the County Jail to a great distance from the jail, and the residence and places of Public worship in that vicinity; We find that deposits are thrown out immediately in front of the Baptist Church and near the residences of those living in the community and that a stench arises from it that floats in the air for several blocks distant that is nauseating and disgusting to the Human senses. We would most respectfully recommend that the proper authorities take the necessary steps and remove this nuisance, either by having the filth carried to a greater distance from the jail or by preparing the necessary pits into which it may be thrown and the necessary disinfectants used.*

Refuse notwithstanding, grand juries after disposing of the bi-annum indictments also reviewed the county's poor farm as well as the jail facility. The *Stephenville Empire* usually printed their findings. While some reports tended to gloss over the problems related to holding men in close confinement, other reports were critical, noting crowded conditions, insufficient light, lingering smoke from lanterns, hindered ventilation, along with other concerns. Most reports though stated all the problems were unavoidable.

In an effort to alleviate the crowded conditions, many county jails started "farming" out convicts who were doing their time locally. Farmers and businessmen paid the county a nominal sum of about fifty cents a day toward the convict's accumulated fines in return for the labor of these convicted men. The sheriff formed chain gangs, which pulled the men out of the jail during the day to work on local roads and other public projects. A few of those working off fines were allowed to live at the county poor farm to help with the farming and other chores the very poor were unable to complete.

The new Erath County Jail had its share of attempted escapes. An inmate, George Boucher, attempted to make a break for his freedom in 1882. Although he made it to the outside of the jail, he was recaptured a short time later. The first official notation of a successful escape in the Sheriff's Docket Book was for Bob Ford on August 3, 1883. The clerk wrote, "absconded without leave." 1884 turned out to be a banner year for attempted jailbreaks. The first one came in February when Sheriff J. C. Gilbreath learned that prisoners had contraband. Confronted, the jailmates admitted to having some items but were reluctant to turn them over. The sheriff simply informed the defiant men that they were going on a bread and water diet until they changed their minds. One day later the jailmates caved and turned over to Gilbreath a large cross-cut file, two bars of iron, two pocket knives and two billets of wood to be used for prizing off the iron bolts of the cells after the heads had been filed. The sheriff immediately ordered a big pot of coffee for the men.[2]

Stone jail built in Erath County in the 1870s.

Another escape plot was reported in the *Stephenville Empire* on May 17, 1884. The prisoners cut up their boots, making long strings.

The makeshift rope was lowered out the narrow window where an accomplice waited. Three British Bulldog pistols were tied so that the inmates could haul them up. Before the plot could move forward, which included killing the jailors, the sheriff caught wind of it and confronted the plotters.

In the jail for stock theft, Tom Davidson bragged that he financed the operation. He had been tracked down previously by Sheriff Gilbreath in Hearne, Texas, and had a special grudge against the lawman. Anytime the sheriff appeared on the second floor of the jail, Davidson commenced to cursing and calling the sheriff vile names. Gilbreath pretty much ignored the disgruntled inmate. The sheriff was relieved when the prison contractor arrived to collect Davidson and others who were headed for Huntsville. At the foot of the stairs from the second floor accommodations, the twenty-one-year-old Davidson, heavily shackled, spotted the sheriff. Along with one last burst of profanity, the convict threatened, "When I get out of the pen, I am going to kill you."

Months later Sheriff Gilbreath took a lone prisoner to Huntsville. He heard a convict calling his name. Turning, Gilbreath was surprised, not so much that the convict was Davidson, but because of what the man had to say, "Gilbreath, I never was so glad to see anyone. As long as I was in Jail, you treated me like I was a white man . . . I wish I could go back to serve out my time with you."[3]

A July 4, 1891 jailbreak brought down some public criticism on R. H. Dunn, special deputy jailor. Stung by what he considered an unjust censure, Dunn went to the newspaper. The *Stephenville Empire*, July 25, 1891, published his account of what really happened. According to Dunn, he went into the run-around outside the cells at the end of exercise time and ordered the inmates back behind bars. Four retired to the back cell while two went into the front cage. As Dunn threw the sliding switch to close the iron doors, a prisoner hung a blanket at the edge of the back cell, preventing Dunn from having a full view of the back door. Hitting the blanket, the cell door rebounded slightly. The dead bolt then slid to the inside and did not lock.

Dunn, believing the men were secure, ambled down the corridor to pick up the breakfast pans still sitting on the floor. As he bent over, one of the men rushed him, knocking Dunn into the tin pans. The men threatened Dunn with severe bodily harm if he did not stay quiet. Two of the inmates slipped the outside bolt and escaped while some decided to stay behind.

Two of the escapees were Jack Kimmell, accused horse thief, and Phil Roberts, in jail for assault and rape. They struck out for freedom but had a major problem—only one pair of boots between the two of them. The escapees took turns wearing the boots. Trudging through the hills northwest of Stephenville, they made it to Strawn where Kimmell caught a train to Colorado City. Fear of capture caused him to walk along the Colorado River, keeping out of sight. Luck was not with the wanted man. He was caught by the Coke County sheriff. Kimmel's painful feet guaranteed he was not going to try for freedom again anytime soon. Roberts successfully disappeared.

Perhaps the most unusual jailbreak was orchestrated by an odd couple. The brains of the operation, Jack Hollis, was armless and charged with the unlikely occupation of stock thief in October 1881. Erath Sheriff William Slaughter decided the cellblock area was too confining for the seemingly physically disabled outlaw. So, he allowed Hollis to stay in the run-around corridor that surrounded the cells. Slaughter then assigned a slow-witted convicted felon to assist Hollis.

Later, Hollis was heard to say that he planned the escape, because he could not stand the bad water in the jail. He convinced the other inmate that between his brawn and Hollis' brains, they could make a break for it. At Hollis' direction the other young man dug around one of the heavy cut stones, finally pulling it out. The two men went through the opening to freedom.

The escapees made their way to Indian Territory (Oklahoma), a favorite refuge of those traveling on the wrong side of the law. Jack Hollis had a twenty-dollar bill given to him by a friend. Not long after crossing the Red River, Hollis became ill while camped at a good distance from a town. Realizing he needed medicine, Hollis gave his companion the money and exacted a promise to return. He did not. Hollis was finally found barely alive. The authorities were notified and Sheriff Slaughter, a bit wiser as to Hollis' abilities, traveled to Indian Territory to retrieve his missing prisoner. Hollis' companion went unapprehended.[4]

Many of the sheriffs in Erath moved their families into the quarters on the first floor. This meant that children often ran up and down the corridors. Older boys soon learned they could make a little extra cash running errands for the inmates. Henry Jones Gilbreath, the son of Sheriff J. C. Gilbreath, spent several years growing up at the jail. He recounted, "I was nearly always called on to run the errands. Whiskey was $1.00 per quart, and when they used the whiskey I got the bottle and sold it for five cents. Bill Dawson ran the saloon and had orders to let me have the whiskey."[5]

Toward the end of the nineteenth century, people began agitating for a new jail for Erath. Leading the group was Sheriff Nath Shands. He had a great way of convincing folks a new jail was needed. He invited visiting farmers, when court was not in session, to sleep on the third floor where the jury room was located. While the visitors appreciated the free accommodations, they could not help but get a whiff of the stale dank air from the second floor. Whether that did the trick or not, the demand increased until the county commissioners placed a bond for a new $75,000 jail on the ballot in 1905. It carried by a good majority.[6]

Erath not only welcomed a new century but also a new detention facility. Sheriff Shands did not stay in office long enough to live in the new jail. As for the men incarcerated, their lack of freedom was still their biggest concern.

Court Life

Carved out of Bosque County in late 1855, Erath was considered to be on the edge of the Texas frontier. Besides Erath, other counties were rapidly being formed, organized, and incorporated into the legal and political structure of the State of Texas. State legislators scrambled to create new districts for court purposes. In November 1857, they created the Nineteenth Judicial District, composed of the counties of McLennan, Bosque, Erath, Palo Pinto, Buchanan [later renamed Stephens], Comanche, Coryell, and Bell. Erath was in six different districts during the nineteenth century.

Applying laws and directives from the state and national government, especially during Reconstruction, fell to a county's local officials. Compliance to these directives many times depended on local interpretation by county officials, including sheriffs, judges, commissioners, and finally the district judge who may or may not have been a local resident, since his district covered several counties. A judge's politics and personal inclinations were more likely to have great influence as he sat on the bench in each county. People tended to respect the judge's position and the power he had over court proceedings.

Life on the district court circuit could be entertaining, because attorneys many times traveled the same route as the district judge. Once in a county the attorneys offered their services to the citizens. These attorneys came to know each other well. In county seats they stayed with local attorneys or at boarding houses or inns. If the weather was good, they slept under the stars to save on expenses or for personal reasons.

Many times these weary travelers preferred not to stay in public accommodations. The meals were not always appetizing. District Judge John J. Good described in a letter to his wife, Sue, that supper consisted of "clammy cornbread, pale muddy coffee, and tainted fat bacon..."[1] A longing for the home fires surely loomed large for these men.

If a bad meal was all they had to contend with, perhaps life on the road would have been bearable, but sleeping quarters hid lurking enemies that could not be hauled into court for their nefarious activities. John Good's letter to his wife continued with "At night [I was] shown to a filthy bed where forty thousand bed bugs and at least the same number of ...fleas were laying in an ambush for me."[2]

A young man striving to become a legal counsel during this time could do so by learning from someone who had already been admitted to practice through the local bar. While classes at a university could be taken, being an apprentice to a local attorney seemed almost to be a requirement. To receive a law license, the young man would apply through his mentor to the district court which then appointed three local attorneys to examine (question) said applicant as to his knowledge of the law. Their verdict decided the professional fate of the applicant. An anecdotal story was passed down that the local bar in Erath County expected applicants to know the law, but they also expected these applicants to be willing to attend a drinking party with the other attorneys. To eschew doing so jeopardized "passing the bar." It was reported that one teetotaling applicant struggled but finally managed to down a glass of beer, ensuring his fate as a future district judge.[3]

Without juries the district court's business could not take place. Wheels started turning toward holding court in the county thirty days ahead of time. It was the duty of the district and county clerks to draw names of possible jurors. Qualifications going back to 1858 included being: male, at least twenty-one years old; a legal voter; and either a "freeholder" in the state; or a "householder" in the county. Notices were sent out thirty days prior to the commencement of court week to ensure delivery and to allow the men to make arrangements to be in town for duty. Jurors who did not show up could be and usually were fined and even jailed until the fine was paid.

Because of complaints made by Unionist men, Circular Order No. 13 was signed into law April 1867. It was called the Test Oath for Jurors. This order basically barred from jury duty men who had participated on the side of the South in the Civil War. District judges found themselves faced with a dilemma, not enough white jurors and a populace not ready to use Freedmen. Judge Good tried to hold court but was adamantly against the use of Negro jurors. Like other judges, he felt former slaves were not qualified according to the rules that had been set up by the State of Texas in 1858 and not specifically negated by Order No. 13. Many times the judge simply could not adjudicate cases requiring a jury. The *Dallas Weekly Herald* reported on October 5, 1867, that Judge Good left Cleburne (Johnson County) without holding court after three days of unsuccessfully trying to find enough jurors. Ultimately, the oath was rescinded, but the episode led to the majority of district judges, including Judge Good, being dismissed from the bench by the military governor for "being an impediment to Reconstruction."[4]

The local sheriff also played an important and vital role during court week. He was expected to attend all proceedings and to carry out the orders of the judge. He brought defendants into court, served papers, and rounded up more jurors if the jury pool proved insufficient. The sheriff was the one person who traveled the county enough to pretty much know who all the residents were.

Some sheriffs did not hold with the rules coming down from appointed state officials during Radical Reconstruction. Many ignored directives that they believed were not in the best interests of the local population. They knew, unless totally flagrant, that what went on at the local level in these frontier outposts like Erath County was not enough to send in the troops for noncompliance.

When they could not ignore Reconstruction directives that went against the grain, sheriffs simply resigned. R. M. Whiteside of Erath County stepped down during Judge Good's tenure. Ironically, he was called for jury duty and served as foreman during the next term of court.

Accused criminals also had trials to face, both in the courtroom and out. Most small frontier counties did not have a sufficient jail. Defendants many times found themselves handcuffed to posts and railings. One sheriff who did not have a sturdy jail handcuffed an accused felon to the post at the end of his bed in order to keep an eye on him.

Waiting to be tried had suspects facing an uncertain future. If the local population were stirred up enough, defendants did not last to have their fate decided in court but were sentenced by "Judge Lynch" in short order. While some sheriffs tried to protect these accused outlaws, many times they did not stand in the way of vigilante justice such as with the notorious Fount Arnold and his gang. Often a judge ordered a defendant removed to a larger town such as Waco or Fort Worth for safekeeping, both for the outlaw's sake and to lessen the chances of a jailbreak.

If the locals allowed a defendant to make it to court, he was assured of counsel. The state passed a provision that everyone was entitled to a legal defense. On the negative side, court appointed attorneys rarely had more than a day or two to prepare a defense for their clients.

If the court did not allow for bail or if a defendant could not come up with the necessary funds, he had to stay in jail. Unfortunately, none of the time spent "cooling his heels" went toward any time assessed by a jury who brought back a guilty verdict for a felony.

Even so, neither the judge nor attorneys could predict what juries might do in the case of someone they were forced to convict of a crime. Men in the mid-nineteenth century tended to be harsher on those who stole livestock, especially horses, than those who took the life of another.

Sometimes juries took matters into their own hands. In the case of *State of Texas v Riley Major*, the jury was surprised when the defendant decided to plead guilty to the simple assault for which he was accused. Evidence showed that they were leaning in his favor by the fact that they voted on a punishment of a fine for one cent.[5] Major was not the only defendant to get a one-cent fine in the district court for Erath County.

State v Jesse Hollis. Minutes of the District Court, Erath County, Texas, Dec. 1871 showing a punishment of a one-cent fine.

Without the cooperation and efforts of many different people, district court could not be held or run smoothly. Radical Reconstruction placed a strain on an already delicate dance in which all these different players participated. Notwithstanding, district courts did manage to do the work put before them though at times in a haphazard but still basically effective manner.

A Citizen's Obligation
Jury Duty

Stephen F. Austin brought more than colonists into Texas. These Anglo-Americans arrived from the United States, importing their sense of what a judicial system should be. Although they preferred the English system, these early settlers had to adapt to the Mexican government's rules, which did not always include the right to a jury trial. This caused friction between the Tejas province and central Mexico.

The years as a republic and the provisions of the Texas Constitution of 1845 established the use of the ancient concept of both the grand and petit juries, along with the use of male citizens to fulfill the duty of serving on juries in the counties where they lived.

County seats took on a festive atmosphere during district court week due to the increased numbers of visitors and possible jurors in town. Friends and family reconnected, as businesses enjoyed booming sales. The saloons filled to capacity. Many flocked to the courthouse to watch trials—most of which were considered entertainment and a good source for local gossip.

Erath County Jury for District Court - 1886

Many men harbored ambivalence toward jury duty. While most applauded the system, especially when they were in need of it, few really wanted to serve, as it meant they had to turn away from any economic endeavor in which they were participating. Farmers had to travel to the county seat, which could be close to thirty miles away, and then figure out where to stay overnight—sometimes for a full week.

A certain element of the population was what the newspapers called "permanent jurors." These men hung around the courthouse, hoping to be called in when the court ran short which happened when not enough of the regular venire showed up or the list was exhausted in the lawyers' efforts to seat a jury. The *Galveston News* in 1869 stated that attorneys knew these men so well that certain ones could be depended on to vote a certain way while in the jury room.[1] *The Dallas Weekly Herald* stated, "such men are a nuisance to the law officers, bar and community."[2] Ten years later the *Herald* went farther by stating their belief that these courthouse "loungers" could be and had been bribed to vote a certain way in criminal cases.[3] While the state legislature wrote into the record that courts should not rely on these "professional jurors," county courts continued to use any qualified male they could snatch outside the courtroom in order to complete the number needed.

While the *San Antonio Express* in 1871 bemoaned jury duty as being unconstitutional in the summer time when the heat and tedious lawyers equaled "cruel and unusual punishment," other editorials bemoaned the extent to which some men went to avoid jury duty or made efforts to get exempt from it.[4] Women were excluded from jury duty until the 1950s in Texas, three decades after earning the right to vote.

Reconstruction brought its own set of challenges as courts passed from being run by elected officials to judges and district attorneys being appointed by the military government. Defeated rebels in Texas refused to register to vote, thinking it would exempt them from jury duty. Several newspaper articles appeared informing citizens that not registering would not exempt them or lessen their chances of being called up.[5]

For a short period of time during Radical Reconstruction, the defeated rebels *were* left out of the jury pools if they could not take the Test Oath, a proclamation stating that they did not aid or participate on the side of the South during the war. District judges found themselves without enough whites to serve. While many Freedmen were qualified, most district judges were reluctant to use them in cases involving the fate of a white defendant.

Reconstruction also proved to be frustrating for district judges who had to travel a large circuit. Many times they arrived to hold court in a hostile atmosphere. In the fall of 1866 in Erath County not enough grand jurors showed up on the first day of court. District Judge Thomas Harrison sent Sheriff R. M. Whiteside out to get the five more needed to complete the panel. Six potential jurors were fined $25 each for not showing up for duty.[6]

John O'Neal in 1867 was fined $10 because he "positively refused to appear" for jury duty. When confronted with the judgment of the court, Mr. O'Neal had a change of heart. He traveled to Stephenville where he made an appearance before District Judge John Good. The judge reduced the fine to $2.50 but ordered the sheriff to convey the Erath resident to jail until the fine was paid.[7]

Because of the lack of a large pool of jurors, judges used the same petit jurors for a variety of cases for the full judicial week. Those who did serve were paid fifty cents a day. Showing they were in no mood for some cases or in an effort to show defiance toward the appointed judicial officers, juries found defendants guilty but assessed only small fines. In the case of *State of Texas v Thomas Edwards* in 1873 in Erath County, the charge was for assault, and the defendant decided to plead guilty. The jury assessed Edwards' punishment - a five-cent fine.[8]

In the fall of 1868 newly appointed District Judge A. B. Norton arrived in Erath to hold court. To his dismay and anger, the judge found no one available to help him hold court. No *venire* of possible jurors for either the grand or petit juries had been called for duty. To make matters worse, Sheriff John Brumley, responsible for rounding up jurors, had left the county just prior to the arrival of the district judge. In a rage Judge Norton fined the sheriff $300 for contempt of court and for interfering with orderly court proceedings. Norton stripped Brumley of his position and appointed a new sheriff for Erath County.[9]

Becoming a juror was actually the end of a process, which started weeks before each court session was set to begin. The job of selecting citizens eligible for jury duty fell to the commissioners' court. The Constitution of 1876 and the Texas Legislature adopted the guidelines to be used. Twice a year the county judge and three selected jury commissioners met to draw names from a box of those eligible to serve during the next session of district court (grand and petit jurors) and for the following six months of county court. This was done thirty days prior to the opening day of court so that those selected could make provisions to be away from home in order to arrive in Stephenville on the day listed on their summons. The district lists for grand and petit juries were sealed separately with the jury commissioners' names across each seal. The envelopes were then delivered to the district clerk for processing.

Qualifications to be a juror included being a legal voter, a citizen of Texas, a freeholder of Texas or a householder in his home county, of sound mind, and good moral character. Lack of literacy was a reason for a challenge. Any male who had been convicted or indicted for a felony was not eligible, unless the governor had restored full citizenship to him.

With thirty days notice of jury duty, most prospective jurors for the criminal docket had time to find out what cases would be coming up for trial. In a county with a small population like Erath, the citizens widely discussed the defendants under indictment. Occasionally, this led to accusations of some jurors having arrived at the court with their minds made up as to the guilt or innocence of certain accused men.

Jury misconduct often was the road for a defense attorney to travel to get a jury's verdict overturned. In the 1891 Erath County case *State of Texas v Tom Wood*, Juror J. P. Silar was accused of telling two men prior to sitting on the jury that Wood should have his "damned neck broke." The district attorney had to scramble to get affidavits from all the remaining jurors. They all supported Silar and stated their belief that he acted in a fair, unbiased manner.[10]

Juror misconduct was not limited to having already formed an opinion. Jurors were admonished to stay with the other jurors throughout the court's proceedings and not discuss the case before them. In *State of Texas v Anna Williamson* (1881), juror John Zimmerman was accused of having expressed his belief in the guilt of the defendant who was accused of killing her newborn child, but another juror, Thomas Murphy, left the other jurors sequestered for the night. The sheriff found him imbibing in the Hyatt & Watts Saloon in downtown Stephenville. Murphy explained that he left to get a little liquid libation. Not amused, the judge slapped a fine on the tippler. The *coup de grâce* came when Judge Nugent learned that jurors were seen holding conversations through open windows with people standing outside the courthouse during court. More jurors were fined, and the judge had no choice but to grant a new trial to the defendant.[11]

The case of *The State of Texas v Tom Wright* showed an example of a juror's deliberate withholding of information, which ultimately affected the outcome. I. A. Griffith had sat on the jury that convicted Wright of arson in 1891. He was called up and placed on a jury for Wright's murder trial in 1897. He did not tell the attorneys that he had served before. It was only after the trial that his omission came to light. Wright's attorneys failed to make an objection in time for the Texas Court of Criminal Appeals to consider this omission as a reversible error. Wright's conviction and execution were upheld.[12]

Of course, the jury system, even with its flaws and problems, remained a cornerstone of the judicial system. People often complained about the time and effort it took to serve but also knew if they did not heed the call, the judge had the power to enforce a fine or imprisonment for noncompliance. This duty was (and still is) a citizen's obligation.

Seat of Justice
The County Courthouse

Justice had no better symbol than the county courthouse. The importance of being the county seat where the courthouse was located cannot be over-estimated. Settlers gravitated first toward the county seat when moving to the frontier. Businesses vied to be located around the square, knowing that settlers would come to town on a regular basis to vote, purchase supplies, go to church, visit other citizens, get the news, and attend court.

In Erath County John M. Stephen donated a portion of his land for a town to become the county seat. Stephenville was officially named on July 4, 1855. Property was set aside for a courthouse to be built in the center of the square, but the earliest structure used to conduct the county's legal business was actually on the east side of the square. Finished in 1857, the courthouse operated as a safe-haven for the settlers when Indians went on the warpath. Women and children slept on the courthouse floor while the men took turns standing guard.[1]

Records show that a fire in the clerk's office incinerated all the county's legal documents in 1866. The Texas Legislature noted in November 1866 the demise of these records and passed an act that provided money to help Erath County reconstitute deed records necessary to reestablish land ownership.[2]

What was not clear was the extent of the damage to the building used as the courthouse at that time. Even so, some clues were found in the early *County Commissioners' Minutes*. Book C of the minutes showed that an order was made to sell at private auction the courthouse building in 1867, but the minutes did not note if a sale actually took place.[3]

The commissioners did start planning for a new courthouse to be built—this time in the middle of the square. An ad valorem tax was levied to secure repairs of the existing courthouse and jail but also to start a fund for a new courthouse. Lots belonging to the town were sold with the proceeds going to the courthouse and jail fund. The lack of wealth in the county slowed the process down. By 1870 the county records showed only $225.75 in the building fund.

The commissioners decided the need for a good sturdy jail was a priority and should be built first. Finally, in 1874 the notice for sealed bids for a 50' square two-story courthouse made of stone was published in the newspapers for Stephenville and Waco. The county rented rooms from various businessmen around the square so that both the county and district court business could continue uninterrupted.[4]

The notice was placed for twenty days in the *Stephenville Westward Empire* for the sale of the old courthouse and lot located on the east side of the square in January 1875. The sale was done at a public auction. While waiting for the old courthouse and lot to be sold, the commissioners accepted the bid by J. D. Parnell and J. J. Porter to build the new courthouse for $11,890. The contract stipulated that the building would be completed within sixteen months from November 1875.

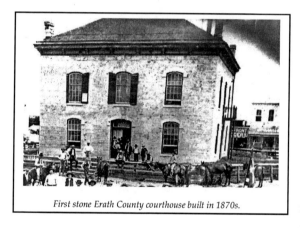

First stone Erath County courthouse built in 1870s.

The first story of the building was quickly completed by March 1876, but the records show that Parnell and Porter asked the county commissioners to release them from completing the contract. The minutes do not note the reasons, but the commissioners did agree to pay Parnell and Porter for the portion of the building they did complete.

Left with a half-built project, the commissioners called once again for sealed bids to move the project forward. Walker and White received the contract in November 1876. The revised plans reflected the addition of a fireproof vault. The new contract totaled $8750. The commissioners approved the placement of lightning rods on the roof of the newly erected courthouse, paying S. E. Moss to do the project.

Fire once again caused a chain of events that affected the courthouse square and was a catalyst for a political firestorm when Dublin, a neighboring town located in southwestern Erath County, made a concerted bid to become the county seat. The fire broke out on January 29, 1891, on the west side of the courthouse square in Stephenville. The alarm bells were rung, but many citizens decided not to respond. A rumor had been circulating that a lynching party was due to arrive from Comanche to fetch an outlaw named W. H. Frizzell who had been lodged in the Erath County Jail for safekeeping. He was being held on a murder charge, arriving in Stephenville from Comanche on January 24th. Some townspeople believed the alarm they heard was a diversionary tactic by the expected lynchers, so they did not respond in a timely manner.[5]

Unfortunately, the fire spread rapidly, and the lack of volunteers severely hampered efforts to contain the devastation. Some quick-thinking residents who did respond to the alarm threw water on the roof of the stone courthouse to prevent blowing embers from catching hold. Most of the businesses to the west of the courthouse were not so lucky.

To everyone's horror another fire broke out on the south side of the square three months later. Alarmed, R. T. Long, the county clerk, loaded the document books out of the courthouse and took them to his home for safekeeping. The fireproof vault must not have been large enough to house all the significant document books. Just like the west side, the south side of the square was decimated.

In June 1891 a petition signed by two-thirds of the voters of Erath "to build a comodius [sic] courthouse sufficient for all the needs of the county" was presented to the Erath County Commissioners who agreed, making the decision that the population of the county had grown enough to support a larger more imposing courthouse to serve the judicial needs of the citizens. They approved a budget for the project at $80,000.[6]

Sensing an opportunity to vault their town into prominence, the businessmen of Dublin quickly circulated a petition, forcing a countywide referendum on where the county seat would be located. Why would Dublin have the audacity to call for such an election? With a population of over a thousand more citizens than Stephenville, the residents of Dublin felt they had a decent chance of winning this election and reaping the rewards of being the county seat.⁷

Dublin's rapid population growth was due to the arrival of the Texas Central Railroad. Although Stephenville tried very hard to be the first to get the rails, Alexander was selected as the first railroad depot for Erath County. The tracks were then extended to Dublin not Stephenville. To use the modern conveyance, citizens of Stephenville had to travel twelve miles. Many believed that Stephenville might fade away while Alexander and Dublin, like other rail towns, would prosper due to increased commerce and travel through their locations. Businessmen of Stephenville made a valiant effort by organizing wagon trains to haul goods to and from Alexander until rails could be secured through the county seat.

Sensing a possible victory, several businessmen of Dublin quickly gathered the 250 signatures necessary to force an election to take place. County Judge H. H. Harbin set the voting date for July 28, 1891. The rivalry between the two towns reached a fever pitch as the newspapers reported that prominent citizens from both burgs traveled around the county promoting their towns. Retired District Judge T. L. Nugent was very vocal in his support for Stephenville. In his speeches he reminded people that Stephenville had been the county seat for forty years and was located near the center of the county while Dublin was near the southwestern county line.

Articles in the *Dublin Progress* debated the virtues of a new county seat being located there. The paper argued that Dublin was conveniently situated and that "with all due respect to Stephenville and her citizens, it is our candid opinion that, as a town she is as dead as a last year's bird nest."⁸

Stephenville shot back, arguing that all the major roads would have to be changed and that the capital outlay would be high because of the new bridges that would have to be built. Dublin answered by offering to raise the $80,000 needed to build the new courthouse. Feeling pretty confident, the Dublin newspaper announced—

When the smoke of battle has cleared away and the Stephen-

*ville fellows are caring for their sick and burying their dead, the busy hum of saw and hammer in the city of business will apprise the inquisitive of the fact that the courthouse is being built in Dublin.*⁹

Not timid about trading barbs, the *Stephenville Empire* in their July 18, 1891 issue took Dublin to task for using Mr. Eager, a recent emigrant from Kansas, as their spokesperson at gatherings. The paper scoffed that no true ex-Confederate would call their fellow brethren "Rebels." In another article in the same issue entitled "The County Seat Question," the newspaper implied that Dublin citizens were thinking about "breaking away" from Erath and forming their own county. This article stated emphatically that according to the law that a new county could not be created out of Erath territory.

If the election had strictly been between Stephenville and Dublin, the outcome would probably have been easy to predict, but fifteen other polling stations within the county also had a say in the contest for supremacy. Although several polling stations voted in favor of Dublin, the majority did not. The *Stephenville Empire* reported that the election had some controversy. Fraudulent tickets (votes) were printed, and a few men spread out across the county to try to use them. In one instance they approached voters who could not read and tried to substitute a "For Removal of Depot" for a "Remain at the Center" ticket. Whiskey was also offered, but Sheriff Nath Shands put a stop to that according to the newspaper.

Old Erath chastiseth Dublin, because, like Washington, she "wouldn't tell a lie."

Political Cartoon in <u>Dublin Progress</u> August.1, 1891

The official returns known on August 1, 1891, gave Stephenville the edge with 2269 votes to Dublin's 950. The *Dublin Progress* opined, "We have met the enemy, and we are their'n."[10]

With a sigh of relief the county commissioners turned their attention to the task of getting the new courthouse built. The old courthouse had to be dismantled first. The Erath County Commissioners Court leased space on the second floor of a building owned by John and Ruth Frey for a period of two years.

Tragedy struck while Henry Wilkins was engaged in prizing out a stone from one of the interior walls of the old courthouse. The masonry gave way. Wilkins tried to retreat but was caught in the falling debris. His body was bent almost double, and his skull was crushed. He lived only a few minutes before dying. Though not from Stephenville, Wilkins was buried there.[11]

The courthouse design by J. Riely Gordon was accepted. His fame as an architect grew rapidly from the time he was an apprentice to W. C. Dodson, who designed several Texas county courthouses including Parker and Hood, until Gordon was a highly sought after architect in his own right. He was also responsible for public buildings, such as the courthouses for Ellis and McLennan counties. Gordon was already known in Stephenville, because he designed the First National Bank in 1889. Later he designed Crow's Opera House in 1892.

Second stone courthouse being built in 1891.

S. A. Tomlinson from Fort Worth submitted the winning bid of $65,073 to build the new courthouse using Gordon's architectural plans. To pay for the structure, the commissioners' court issued 144 bonds at $500 each. The Stephenville Masonic Lodge hosted a formal ceremony for the laying of the cornerstone on December 3, 1891.

Tomlinson used Pecos sandstone in the construction of the new temple of justice along with native limestone quarried from the Leon River to grace the exterior. The marble used in the interior was imported and trimmed with East Texas pine. Cast and wrought iron completed the stairways.

Erath County Courthouse completed in 1892.

Finished, the new courthouse soared over the other buildings of downtown Stephenville. Erath had an imposing venue for Texas justice to play out in the courtroom on the second floor. This courthouse stands today as a tribute to the past of Erath County.

Part Two – Early Justice

'Judge Lynch' In Erath County

Early legal justice in Erath County was a cumbersome, uncertain affair. Prior to the creation of the Nineteenth Judicial District, Erath citizens were required to take legal matters to the courtrooms of Coryell or Bosque counties where court met under the leadership of Judge R.E.B. Baylor. For locals who felt the need for immediate justice, or, at least action, it seemed at times to be more expedient to administer their own brand of swift and sure retribution for those perceived to be murderers or livestock thieves. Men worked in small groups. Citizens whispered about these activities but rarely talked openly about them. Some locals called them "nightriders," as justice was often administered under the cloak of the evening hours.

Few records exist that document the activities of vigilante groups, but anecdotal evidence suggests that such swift justice did indeed reign prior to Judge N. W. Battle's election to the Nineteenth Judicial District in 1858. The activities of these vigilante groups did not end with the election of the judge. Living in Waco put almost a hundred miles between him and the events of Erath and other frontier counties in his district and the twice a year visits the jurist made to take care of legal matters. Even when court was in session, far too many who ran afoul of the law were acquitted when a "friendly" juror was in place or when the jury was too frightened of retribution if it brought back a conviction.

In between court dockets the locals dealt with crime by helping the sheriff keep the peace and the activities of outlaws at a minimum so that settlers could go about their daily existence. Regardless of how western movies portray cattle rustlers and thieves, most of the real-life outlaws on the Texas frontier were hard to pick out of the crowd. A contemporary description of these outlaws pointed out—

> As a rule, they did not get drunk, and shoot up the town, like the cowboys. Many of them, to all outward appearances,

seemed to be quiet, peaceful and inoffensive citizens, and it was sometimes hard for honest men to know who they were. They would frequently steal whole herds of horses or cattle, and run them out of the country, before being discovered.[1]

In the Anniversary Edition (January 1936) of the *Stephenville Empire Tribune* several articles mentioned the administering of swift but sure frontier justice. One article, "Pioneer Days in Erath County," had a subtitled section – "Notorious Outlaw Killed," which was a reprint from the *Texas Baptist* newspaper -

Jan. 2, 1859 – It is stated that the company that killed the friendly Indians in Palo Pinto County on Dec. 27, 1858, afterwards hunted up the notorious outlaw and horse thief, Joe Walker, so well known on the western frontier, and killed him.

The Weekly Telegraph out of Houston carried a report in their August 21, 1860 issue under "Texas Items." They cited as their source the *Fort Worth Chief* newspaper. The story told about a horse thief named Robert Parker, who was taken by a group of vigilantes from Erath County. He was believed to be one of eight men in a ring of thieves working out of the county. Parker was apprehended while waiting for a companion to show up. He had in his possession several horses taken from area farms and ranches. The paper stated, "The people have, at last, determined to administer the law themselves to these vermin."

The above mentioned article from the paper matches up with a story Maurice and Gary Sharp's grandfather told

Gary and Maurice Sharp

them when they were youngsters. The Owen and Keith families settled along Cow Creek in southwest Erath County. John Thomas Owen (the Sharps' great grandfather) was very young but helped chase after a horse thief who came through with a string of horses taken from various farms. Following the trail, the posse caught up with the thief on the north side of Stephenville. The culprit was told he would be hung. The only allowance the posse gave him was to be able to pick the person who would run the horse out from under him. The doomed man chose John Thomas, not yet a teenager. Refusing to allow his young son to be the executioner, the boy's father, John Owen, stepped in and proceeded to "dispatch" the outlaw.[2]

Another story involved a man named Dalton. The retelling appeared in the July 9, 1950 issue of the *Stephenville Empire Tribune*. Dalton lived along the Bosque River a few miles from Stephenville. Toward the end of the Civil War, officials arrested Dalton for the murder of his wife. Arriving in town, the posse found many of the citizens there to greet them and the accused man they brought in for the killing. A local "court" was hastily convened without the benefit of an "official" judge. Finding Dalton guilty, the citizens were instructed to stand on one side or the other of a line drawn in the dirt to decide if the murderer should be hung. With most moving to the guilty choice, Dalton's fate was sealed. The crowd moved the condemned man swiftly to a hanging tree close to the town square.

Swift justice did not end with the culmination of the Civil War. During Reconstruction many Texans did not trust the judicial system since the court officers, including the district judge, were appointed by federal military authorities and then later by the Radical Reconstruction governor, Edmund Davis. The vigilante activities in Erath and Comanche counties came to the attention of Governor Davis when Adjutant General and Chief of State Police F. L. Britton filed a report highlighting two different lynchings involving "nightriders." The report was dated December 4, 1872.

The first lynching involved T. D. Reynolds who was arrested for murder by Dr. J. D. Windham of Brown County. Reynolds was taken first to the Comanche County Jail. Two more men named Mason and Roberts were arrested at this time for horse theft and placed in the custody of Windham who told the sheriff he was taking the men to the Stephenville Jail for safekeeping.

Was the Comanche sheriff a bit suspicious when Windham arrived with several men at midnight to start the trip? Was the thirty-six feet of new rope in the back of the wagon where the accused men were placed a clue? Maybe the fact that many of the "guards" were under the influence of whiskey should have been a signal that all was not as it should have been.

About six miles north of Comanche the prisoners were hung. At the inquest Dr. Windham and his special deputies reported that they were overpowered by a "mob," who took the prisoners and hung all three together on the same branch which had to be propped up by a huge forked stick to sustain the weight. No indictments came out at the inquest.

History repeated itself that same October of 1872 when James Latham and J. B. McDow were arrested for horse theft and brought before John D. St. Clair, Justice of the Peace for Precinct 3 of Erath County. He appointed several men to guard the prisoners. Three more—Fayette Latham, Noble Hardin, and James Coats—were rounded up for the same crime. A "mob" led by Mose Hurley, according to Britton's report, seized all the prisoners. They were taken just across the line into Comanche County. Britton's report indicated that James Latham died, attempting to escape, but later court documents indicate he survived. James Coats did manage to escape by jumping from his horse and scrambling into the darkness.

The other three men were not so fortunate. They were hung. Bent on administering their brand of justice and hoping for a confession of being part of a livestock theft ring, the "mob" cut Fayette Latham down more than once. Each time they revived him, the men promised to spare Latham's life if he would just confess, but Fayette Latham steadfastly proclaimed his innocence. The last time they strung him up, Latham managed to catch hold of the noose with his teeth to prevent strangulation. Being at the end of the branch where the other two were hung helped Latham, since the weight bent the limb down enough for him to touch the ground with his toes. With the mob gone, he managed to retrieve a knife from his pocket and cut himself down.

He was not able to save any of the other men. Not trusting his luck in Erath County, Latham took off for Austin to tell his tale. His testimony led the governor to send Captain Asa Collinsworth Hill with a force of Negro police to Erath to investigate.

Governor Davis also sent his brother-in-law, Captain F. L. Britton, along with Lieutenant J. A. Wright and the Minute Men of Company D, who managed to round up and arrest several "nightriders" and turned them over to the sheriff of Comanche County. Britton was promised that these men would be put on trial, and justice would be served.

Later Britton admitted to the governor that he had no hope of getting the grand jury of Comanche County to indict or convict those involved in the nocturnal lynchings, but he did get Fayette Latham to name those he believed were involved. Many of the men he named came from well-known and respected families of Erath County such as the Turnbows, Barbees, Hurleys and Martins. One of those named, J. C. Gilbreath, was later elected sheriff of Erath. Britton's written words revealed his frustration over the incident—

> *I talked to many of the citizens of both Erath and Comanche counties; also to the district judge of that district, who unanimously gave it as their opinion that a jury could not be empaneled [sic] under the present jury system of this State, in either of these counties, that would convict the members of these mobs, no matter how strong the evidence; and while, without doubt, there is a great number of the citizens of Comanche and Erath counties who sympathize with the mob, I must do them the justice to state that there is a considerable portion of them who regret the shameful deeds. . . but under the present reign of terror, no citizen, however much he may oppose this mob violence, will voluntarily come forward and give evidence against the mob, for fear it will be his time next (as they term it) to 'feed the wolves.'*[3]

While some locals applauded the work of the "mob," others lived in fear of retribution from these vigilantes. In a 1936 interview Owen

West, an early resident of Tolar when it was still a part of Erath County, was quoted as saying, "If you couldn't tell exactly where you had been and exactly where you were going and exactly what you were doing here, you were liable to get strung up in record time."[4] He explained that mob law prevailed in this section. No one was concerned about allowing the law to take care of things—the local mob did. Mr. West related how some men were hung without even being allowed to answer questions.

How many of these anecdotal stories are accurate can be debated. Except for Britton's report, official records neither confirm nor deny the oral and newspaper accounts. For obvious reasons the participants did not leave written evidence authenticating such stories. Did they even happen? So many retellings would lead one to believe that plenty of vigilante justice did indeed take place. Having to wait for the twice a year official term of district court was probably untenable to these frontiersmen who had a strong sense of what was right or wrong. Survival in Texas' growing settlements depended on both earlier and new arrivals being able to keep their livestock and few possessions from being stolen. Lynching horse thieves, murderers, or those accused of serious charges may have seemed simply a matter of expediency. Guarding such desperate men associated with vile crimes while waiting for the court system to catch up may not have been an option local citizens, who set their own standards of justice, were willing to follow.

W. H. Fooshee, who served as district clerk for Erath County from 1876 to 1885, did not admit to participating in any nocturnal activities. In his memoirs he did, however, have this to say about such events—

> *This method of dealing out summary justice to such offenders had a salutary effect in decreasing the amount of offenders of horse and cattle stealing in the frontier counties of Texas.*[5]

So for many, seemingly by necessity, Texas justice on the frontier was best found in the court of "Judge Lynch." Gradually, the gavel did overcome the rope and the gun as a way to bring peace to a turbulent and at times unforgiving landscape of the early Texas frontier.

The Lower Brazos Reserve Indians Massacre

Luring emigrants to the newly created county of Erath would have been easy with the fertile soil and inexpensive land except for one prevailing fact – Indians also laid claim to the North Central Texas countryside. Settlers arrived and regularly left, with a few hardy folks staying, willing to tough it out against the hostile actions of Indians still roaming the rolling terrain. The loss of life and property proved too much for some—even hearty frontier settlers.

The Texas State Legislature faced the dilemma of how to control the ingrained Indians whose attacks on pioneers increased. Tales of atrocities reached Austin, and the state governing body finally made the decision to move the Indians onto reserves (reservations) starting in February 1854. One of the reserves was set aside for Comanches, considered to be the most hostile. The location selected was at Camp Cooper on the Clear Fork of the Brazos River, seven miles north of Fort Griffin in south central Throckmorton County, while the other two reserves held more docile tribes including the Caddos, Anadarkos, Wacos, Tonkawas and others. Many of the "friendly" natives were sent to the Lower Brazos Reserve located twelve miles from Fort Belknap in Young County.

Life for settlers who came to Erath County remained uncertain to downright miserable at times. Renegade Indians, not easily corralled, continued to visit and harass and kill Cross Timbers pioneers. J. T. Deshield stated the following in his account found in Wilbarger's *Indian Depredations in Texas* —

> During the spring, summer and fall of 1858, Indian raids into Erath, Comanche, and Brown counties were as frequent and regular as the full and change of the moon, and to preserve life and save property required constant vigilance and continuous scouting, and with all that could be done, hundreds of men in the counties embraced in these articles lost by Indian raids their entire stock of horses, amounting in many cases to several hundred head.[1]

Anger and frustration caused citizens to turn to John R. Baylor, a former agent with the Upper Comanche Reserve who had been dismissed from the service in May 1857. Baylor not only believed Indians should be placed on reservations but also that those reservations should be anywhere but Texas. Baylor traveled along the frontier counties amassing large audiences wherever he went. He gave impassioned speeches about the inability of the state government to provide for the safety of the citizens. Baylor argued that the reserves provided cover for Indians to carry out "hit and run" raids. He cited that many stolen horses had been recovered on the reserves and urged locals to organize for defense. Petitions, demanding action, were often circulated to receptive audiences during Baylor's speeches.[2]

Texas Ranger John 'Rip' Ford

In the meantime Governor Hardin Runnels, in an effort to calm the settlers nerves and provide some governmental protection, gave a special assignment to John "Rip" Ford in November 1858 to protect that portion of the frontier from the unfriendly renegade Indians. Ranger Ford set up his home base, Camp Leon, at the junction of Mercer Creek and the South Leon River in northern Comanche County. He later stated that he had to work with mostly raw young recruits among the one hundred men he took with him but soon toughened them up for the rigors of life in the saddle chasing unrepentant natives.[3]

Far from being intimidated, the Comanches became adept at their raids where they struck mostly at night and then quickly put distance between themselves and their victims. The prairies where they liked to roam were just west of Erath County. There they could readily lose those who pursued them. John M. Stephen, Stephenville's founder, was not immune, as he had horses stolen from him in the winter of 1857.

In far western Erath close to the Eastland County border a meeting was held close to Jameson Peak in an effort to organize a local militia to head off Indian depredations. Peter Garland was elected the captain of the group who called themselves the Erath County Rangers. The newly organized band vowed to kill any Indians who traveled south of Cedar Creek, a tributary of the Brazos River. The local citizens agreed to collect a special tax so that the men could be paid $28 per month for their duties.[4]

On December 27, 1858, twenty of the Erath County Rangers, under Garland's leadership, struck out for the Lower Brazos Reserve. U. S. Indian Agent Shapley Ross met with the group when they arrived at the reserve bearing arms. He later named several men including Garland, Dr. W. W. McNeill, James Waller, and William Motheral as being among the Erath Rangers that day. Reports conflict as to whether or not through compromise Ross convinced the band to leave or the decision was made by Garland when entrance was denied. For whatever reason the men left, heading back to Erath. They stopped outside the small settlement of Golconda (later named Palo Pinto), telling some residents that they would be heading home the next morning.

An individual told Peter Garland privately that a band of Indians was encamped a few miles from Golconda. Not clear was whether or not Garland was told that this was a group of friendly Indians made up of mostly Anadarkos and Caddos. Led by Choctaw Tom, this group of friendly Indians had permission to be off the reserve for a week to help the locals hunt for bear. They camped beside the Ioni Creek. Choctaw Tom returned to the Lower Brazos Reserve, while some of the Indians stayed in the area at the invitation of the local citizens.

Garland and his men were led to the encampment close to dawn. With no knowledge of who the occupants of the wigwams were, they attacked almost immediately, even though it was not yet daylight.

When the melee was over, four male and three female Indians were dead with four others wounded. One of Garland's men, Samuel W. Stephen, the son of John M. Stephen, lay dead, reportedly from "friendly" fire, while George Hardin was severely wounded. John Stephen later traveled to Golgonda to retrieve his fallen son, burying him in the West End Cemetery in Stephenville.[5]

A firestorm of controversy erupted as Garland's raiders arrived back in their home county. The citizens busied themselves in preparation for a retaliation they believed would come from the Indians. Palo Pinto residents distanced themselves by publishing a letter in the newspaper that specified they had no role in the attack, hoping this would prevent a retaliatory excursion from the reserve Indians.[6] George B. Erath led a group to the reserve to avert any retaliation and met with some success with the agent and Indians located there.

As reports started showing up in the *Dallas Herald* and other newspapers, sides were drawn, ranging from being shocked at the seemingly senseless murder of sleeping Indians to believing that frontiersmen had been pushed to their limit of endurance by the almost daily incursion of hostile natives bent on harassing settlers. Dr. McNeill sent a letter of defense to Ranger John Ford with a conflicting version of events. The raiders alleged they had been on the trail of Indian horse thieves that led to the camp they attacked.[7]

When word reached District Judge Nicholas Battle, he made the decision to prosecute Garland and his followers. He strongly believed that the attack was led by a violent element of lawlessness, which had to be stamped out. It was within his jurisdiction as district judge of the Nineteenth Judicial District, and he meant to mete out justice with bench warrants for the arrests of the men involved. The decision was easier to make than carry out. He found resistance in Palo Pinto County by those he thought would indict these "murderers." They did not. Instead, the grand jury indicted the Anadarko chief, José Maria, for horse stealing and issued a report stating that the reserves were a nuisance. Undaunted, Judge Battle pressed forward by appointing E. J. Gurley, a Waco attorney, as special prosecutor. Evidence was gathered against Garland and his followers.[8]

At first glance this situation would seem to have no impact on

Texas Ranger Ford or his assignment to "protect" settlers as best he could. His focus had been on convincing Governor Runnels and the federal government to shift their policy toward hostile Indians from passive resistance to active pursuit and engagement on the frontier west of the Cross Timbers. When Ford heard of the events of December 27th, he decided to take a trip to Austin to consult with the governor. He wanted to know what the official position of the Texas Rangers should be over the incident. While there, Ford also consulted with Indian Agent Robert Neighbors, promising his co-operation if civil authorities requested Ranger assistance.

Arriving back at Camp Leon, Ford was surprised to find Special Prosecutor E. J. Gurley waiting for him. Gurley informed the Ranger that he had papers to give to Ford that deputized him to enter those counties necessary to arrest Peter Garland and his band. Ranger Ford refused to recognize the deputation given to him, stating that the matter was largely a civil one over which he, as a military officer, had no jurisdiction. He suggested that local civil officers (the sheriffs) should carry out the writs. When Gurley pressed the matter, Ford informed him that under the circumstances only the governor could order him to interfere. Returning to Waco, Gurley sent a strongly worded protest to Governor Runnels concerning Ford's refusal and behavior.

Governor Runnels responded by sending a message to Ford in early March that ordered him to assist in the arrest of Peter Garland, et al, while at the same time, also forwarding a strongly worded statement to Erath County settlers chastising them for their acts of violence that reflected badly on them and the whole state. Ford again refused to accept the deputation. He sent a private letter to Runnels explaining that he was simply protecting the governor's reputation, as he was sure any action on his part would cause a clash between the Texas Rangers and the citizens, a potential embarrassment. He went on to say that while he agreed to assist, he did not believe he should be the substitute for local authorities. Although there were veiled threats that Ford and his men would be dismissed over the matter, Ford stood his ground. The governor backed down.[9]

Although Judge Battle had eyewitness accounts and plenty of evidence to bring the Erath County Rangers to trial, he lacked the essential legal ingredients necessary to carry the case forward. Judge Battle told the *Waco Southerner* in April that he would take no further steps to bring Garland to Waco for trial.[10] With no support from local authorities or citizens willing to indict, along with the refusal of the military (Texas Ranger Ford) to enter the counties to arrest the culprits, the matter gradually died for want of prosecution.

Ranger Ford later defended his actions in the April 30, 1859 issue of the *Texas State Gazette*. He revealed correspondence between himself, the governor, Indian Agent Neighbors, Gurley, and Judge Battle. Less than complimentary to the judge, Ford reiterated that Judge Battle and Special Prosecutor Gurley's actions were illegal and would have brought about a civil war. Incensed, Gurley replied with his own version of events in the May 21st issue of the same newspaper.[11] After his company was decommissioned, John Ford successfully returned to politics.

Peter Garland moved to Hood County where he served as County Treasurer. James Waller was elected Erath County Sheriff. None of the Erath County Rangers were ever prosecuted successfully, even though Judge Battle tried.

The Lower Brazos Reserve Indian massacre did serve as a catalyst. The Indians, both friendly and cooperating Comanches, were removed from North Texas by federal troops to the Choctaw Reservation in Indian Territory (Oklahoma) less than a year later. Indian Agent Robert Neighbors accompanied the Indians across the Red River to their destination, and then he returned to Texas. Without provocation or a known reason, Ed Cornett, a local resident at Fort Belknap, shot Agent Neighbors who had just arrived at Fort Belknap west of Jacksboro. The agent had his back turned and was talking to another man when the shot rang out. Neighbors' assassin was not publicly tried, but he met his fate when John Cochran and Ben Milam along with some "Minute Men" tracked Cornett to Salt Creek between Jacksboro and Graford in April 1860.[12]

However, for residents of Erath County, Indian raids continued. In a letter to the editor of the *Dallas Herald* dated July 25, 1866, H. L. Ray of Erath complained that the Indian raids were worse than ever and that most of them were now using six-shooters rather than bows and arrows. Hostile Indian forays slowed down after 1874 when the Texas Rangers were brought back after the end of Reconstruction in Texas.

Judge Nicholas Battle served as district judge for Erath and other counties in the Nineteenth Judicial District for four years before he resigned to serve the South in the Civil War. Though none of the court's documents for Erath County remain from that time period due to the fire in the county clerk's office in 1866, other sources reveal that Judge Battle continued to speak out against the Erath County Rangers, both from the bench and privately.

Perhaps the following quote—

> *They, the leaders of mobocracy—they would have made a Jeffries of me! They would have transformed the courts of a peaceful State, into the bloody assizes of two centuries ago! But I defied their threats on the one hand and scorned their blandishments on the other, as I despised the cowards who did their beck and bidding!*[13]—

in the *Biographical Encyclopedia of 1880* attributed to Judge Battle best illustrated his sentiments about the whole affair.

Drink As Much Whiskey As You Want
The Fount Arnold Gang

Erath County at the end of the Civil War was located along the edge of the settled Texas frontier. With so many of the men away fighting for the Southern cause, both hostile Indians and scheming outlaws took advantage, making life miserable for those on the home front. Indians tended to use hit and run tactics, but some of the bolder outlaws took up residence in the county, seemingly daring the local populace to interfere with their shady activities.

The population of Stephenville in 1865 was small, made smaller by those who decided they had had enough, pulling up stakes and moving on. Will Conine, who lived in Stephenville in 1867, estimated only about 200 citizens made up the town. He stated in his memoir that there were two mercantile stores, one owned by Morrison and Powers—the other by John Frey. A good business for Morrison and Powers was supplying alcohol. They hauled barrels of whiskey into town where they poured it into quart jars for sale.[1]

Well-organized, the Fount Arnold gang moved about the county freely. Few interfered as Arnold usually had fifteen to twenty relatives and hired guns with him at all times. On Saturdays Arnold brought his men into town for a little fun on a regular basis. When citizens saw them coming in on horses, riding single file like Indians and wearing red blankets, they would hurry their children indoors to wait out the booze-induced noise and ruckus soon to come.

Fount Arnold usually chose Morrison and Powers to patronize. The gang waited outside while the boss entered to tell the proprietors to get the whiskey out. Arnold would then go to the door and invite the men in to drink as much whiskey as they wanted. Before long, shots would ring out as the revelers ripped into having a good time. Often, if buffalo hunters were in town, they would join in the merry-making. Behind closed doors citizens wanted no part of any "dust-ups" that might happen. This did not keep them from peering out through windows and cracked doors in anticipation and speculation.

Will Conine remembered watching Fount Arnold riding around

the courthouse square shooting off his six-gun, scattering other cowboys and raising dust in his wake. Several times the outlaw showed off to his comrades (and those peering behind doors and windows) by pitching his whiskey bottle up into the air and then catching it while riding at full speed on his horse. Others joined Fount in the lively antics; each cowboy trying to outdo the others in stunts and marksmanship.

Few citizens were willing to confront the gun-toting Arnold, including the lawmen, but one who did, according to Conine, was Jim Cage. An argument between the two men led to a tense confrontation. Taking advantage of an opportunity, Cage managed to snatch Arnold's six-shooter. A tense quiet fell over the two men and those observing. Calmly, Fount Arnold faced down his adversary and told Cage that he could shoot if he wanted to do so, as he had the advantage. For whatever reason Cage handed the gun back but, determined to be fearless, continued to stare at Arnold. Finally, the outlaw nodded, turned and walked away.

Once the dust settled at the end of the Civil War and Texas went about initiating the Presidential Reconstruction Plan, Thomas Harrison was elected District Judge of Erath and other counties in June. With so many courts to hold, October 1866 rolled around before Harrison made his way to Stephenville. Once there, he was faced with a fire that decimated the county records stored in the county clerk's office. Starting over, the judge ordered Sheriff Whiteside to get enough men together to have a grand jury. This took two days to accomplish.

The first to feel the weight of indictments was Fount Arnold. According to the first two indictments passed down from the grand jury, Arnold had engaged in the theft of both cattle and horses. It was whispered among citizens that the Arnold gang had a ranch west of Erath County where they herded their ill-gotten livestock to hold prior to selling them.

Arnold was taken into custody at the same time three more indictments against him were passed down. Judge Harrison set bail at $1000 plus adding the requirement of having two men willing to act as sureties at $250 for each indictment. Arnold's attorneys, Coleman and Evans, convinced Judge Harrison to give Arnold ten days to get the necessary bail money and sureties. The sheriff was told to allow Arnold the freedom to move about to get this accomplished but to stay close by so that the notorious Arnold stayed in custody of the law.

Judge Harrison, as a precaution or because he believed that Arnold would not come up with the requirements to get out of jail, put into the record that if Arnold was unable to pull together the bail or the sureties that the sheriff was to take Arnold to the Tarrant County Jail in Fort Worth for safekeeping. One has to wonder if this was for Arnold's safety or to deter a jailbreak by his gang. Regardless, Arnold was able to secure the bail with J. D. McKenzie and D. W. Self coming forward to act as sureties.

Two of the many indictments against Fount Arnold were brought to trial. He was found "Not Guilty." Many believed the jurors were too intimidated to convict. His attorneys managed a delaying tactic on the other pending indictments by requesting that certain witnesses – William Hitson and William Fowler – be brought in for the defense. Although orders were sent to the Palo Pinto and Kaufman County sheriffs, these men were never served, but it did allow the cases to be continued from docket to docket while Arnold still roamed freely in Erath County.[2]

Will Conine wrote that at one point he remembered the U. S. Army coming through Stephenville because of so many reports of Indian depredations and outlaw activity. They stayed the winter, but when they left the soldiers took Fount Arnold with them to the jail in Weatherford. The residents of Erath hoped it was the last they would see of the outlaw, but by the spring of 1868 Arnold was back. No one seemed to know how he was able to get out of jail, but he did. It was not long before Arnold and his gang were again up to their old ways, including horse and cattle rustling.

By the fall of 1868 a group of citizens, infuriated that the law and the courts could not do anything about Arnold, decided to take matters into their own hands. Former Rangers and Indian fighters joined the vigilante gathering. When word was received that Arnold and his men were seen driving a large herd of horses west, the group went into action. Overtaking the outlaws, the vigilance group engaged in battle. Fount Arnold was killed along with several of his men.

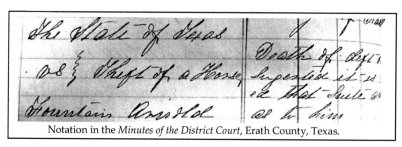
Notation in the *Minutes of the District Court*, Erath County, Texas.

A couple of gang members, including Baylor Thurman, were taken into custody and back to Stephenville, but tempers were running high. These outlaws were quickly taken to the edge of town and shot. It was also reported that angry citizens went out to the Arnold Ranch and killed Fount Arnold's father. Though arguably outside the legal realm, the actions of the vigilantes brought to an end the activities of the Fount Arnold gang in Erath County. Any survivors assuredly beat a hasty retreat to parts unknown.[3]

A penciled notation into the *Erath County District Court Minutes* serves as a postscript to the Arnold tale. It read - *"Oct 20th 1868 – Death of defendant suggested, suit abated."*

A Tragedy of Frontier Insanity
The James M. McCarty Story

Living on the edge of settlement and a good distance from large towns posed many problems for emigrants to Texas. Much has been written about the struggle these hearty folk waged just to keep food on the table and Indians from stealing what little they did have. Few had time to worry about those relatives who were losing touch with reality, nor did they know what to do when clear signs of insanity were being manifested in one of their own.

James M. McCarty, Jr. and his wife, Martha, seemed to be model settlers. Nearing thirty-five years of age, the young farmer had an "irreproachable character for industry, sobriety and integrity."[1] Several said that it was well known how hard James Jr. worked to make his small holding close to Duffau Creek prosperous. His land was along the line between Bosque and Erath counties. His father, James McCarty, Sr., had a farm about five miles away also along Duffau Creek. Many families lived close together wherever they could. Besides being able to socialize, these families also had a ready-made work-pool for busy times of the year or for when one family was in great need of help.

James Jr. started acting strangely a few months before his mental delusions erupted into violence. His family noticed but hoped it was connected to being overworked and tired. Farming was indeed a backbreaking enterprise but generally not one to cause a person to go crazy. No one felt the young man was heading for a total psychopathic breakdown.[2]

The day before the trouble began in September 1869, James Jr. announced to Martha that he wanted to be baptized immediately by Henry Hurley. This unusual request came at the beginning of the very busy harvest season. The crops had to be harvested, sold or prepared for winter storage. Did Martha see or feel the difference in her husband's behavior or demeanor?

Regardless, James Jr. left his farm and the work needing to be done to walk the five miles up the creek to his father's place that morning. James Sr. was surprised to see his son. They talked at length about his son's belief that he needed to be baptized immediately. Finally, James Sr., a deacon in the Primitive Baptist Church, agreed to approach Reverend Henry Hurley who lived a few miles away. Sensing the growing desperation in his son, the father asked James Jr. to wait where he was and not to go home. The worried father hastened away to fetch Henry Hurley, hoping that by fulfilling his son's request, a sense of normalcy would return, but it took some time to travel to where the minister lived.

Reverend Henry Hurley

Several hours later James Sr. returned with the reverend only to find that his son had left. Guessing correctly that James, Jr. had returned home, James Sr. and Hurley traveled the creek to the younger man's home. The dusk was already gathering when they arrived. Too late for them to travel back, the two older men made the fatal decision to spend the night. Retiring for the evening, they went to a separate bedroom from their hosts. The two older men had to use the same bed but quickly fell asleep.

In the middle of the night James Jr. suddenly sat up, awakening his wife. He demanded a light. Martha, not quite awake, told her husband to go back to sleep. This only acted to agitate the younger McCarty more. Somewhere between nightfall and the early hours of morning, James Jr. stepped over the edge beyond sanity. He announced that he needed to locate his gun and get it loaded. While he frantically searched for his weapon, Martha became so alarmed for her own safety that she ran out of the farmhouse. She screamed as she exited, hoping that the sound of her voice would arouse the others in the house. She took off down the road without looking back.

Finding the shotgun, James Jr. loaded it and immediately went to the bedroom where the two older men still slept, unaware their time on earth was fast approaching the end. In rapid succession James Jr. shot each man in the head. Later, James McCarty, Sr. was found on the bed and Reverend Henry Hurley on the floor. The mortal wounds indicated that they died quickly.[3]

Still in the grip of his aberration, James Jr. went to his son Aaron's bedside, waking him up. The seven-year-old boy was told to go sit on the outside doorstep until his father returned. The trusting youngster did as he was told. He watched from the backdoor stoop as his father walked rapidly down to the creek. James, Jr. searched around in the moonlight, finally locating what he was looking for–a large rock. Arriving back at the doorstep, the father commanded his son to lay his head on a nearby block. The boy obeyed, and without hesitation, the farmer brought the rock down hard, taking the life of his son. Picking up Aaron's lifeless body, his father headed down to the creek. Standing by the flowing water for a few minutes, he held the lifeless object of his rage. Finally, James threw his son's body into the water.[4]

Turning his back, James Jr. headed again to the house. Grabbing his two young daughters, Susan and Ella, he started walking toward the road. He stopped long enough to pick up a bucket and filled it with water. He gave no explanation to his daughters. He continued to walk with the two girls until he reached his dead father's farmhouse.

Meanwhile, a weary Martha managed to make it on foot to a neighbor's home unaware of the carnage taking place at her farmhouse. Neighbors were rounded up before she was able to return. Witnessing the devastation was heartrending for the frontier woman. As painful as the sight of the slain older men was, the whereabouts of her husband and children took on an immediacy for Martha.

The group spread out. The searchers soon located Aaron McCarty floating in the water. They feared the worst for the daughters taken from their beds by a dangerous lunatic. The intensive search finally led to the farm of James Sr. where the young farmer and his daughters were found. Fortunately, James Jr., no longer in a violent mode, had not harmed his daughters physically. He did not resist those who restrained him.

The decision was made to take James Jr. to Meridian to be placed in jail there. One reported story related that he was chained to a tree in Meridian, because they feared the dementia would return without warning.

James McCarty, Jr. was examined in Meridian in Bosque County on September 22nd where he admitted in minute detail the killings but insisted that he had been commanded by the spirits to carry out these deeds.[5] Deemed not responsible for his actions, the examining jury sent James McCarty to the Lunatic Asylum located close to Austin without taking him to trial at the district court level for his actions according to one newspaper account. Martha McCarty was left to bury her son, father-in-law, and to pick up the shattered pieces of her life.

The superintendent of the asylum at that time was Dr. Graham. Examining the new patient, he was pleased that McCarty seemed aware of what he had done and even expressed extreme remorse for his actions. Believing progress was being made, the doctor allowed McCarty to read a letter from his wife Martha. The doctor later stated that the letter was loving and supportive. What should have cheered the young man had the opposite effect.

Something in the letter triggered a reaction inside of McCarty. He watched and waited. A few days later an attendant left his own room without securing the door. Seeing his chance, McCarty slipped in, found a razor, and quickly cut his own throat. Shortly afterwards, the attendant and others found McCarty, but it was too late. Only a few minutes passed before the self-inflicted wounds proved fatal. Less than two months since the murders had passed, James McCarty, Jr. was also dead.[6]

Thus ended a tragedy that decimated a Texas frontier family. The actions of someone clearly in the throws of dementia or insanity posed a special problem for the settlers. Sometimes justice could neither be found in the actions of a vigilance committee nor in the courtroom. Sending James, Jr. to the asylum seemed to be the best solution but did not necessarily bring closure for the families hurt by the actions of someone not in control of his faculties.

All the victims of this unfortunate turn of events, including James

Jr., are buried in the Duffau Cemetery.[7] McCarty's widow, Martha, moved with her remaining children to the Oklahoma Territory.

Part Three – The Court Deliberates

A Wrong Move on the Texas Frontier
The Parks Crenshaw Story

Between 1856 and 1871 Erath County sentenced only one person to the Texas State Penitentiary at Huntsville. That person was Parks Crenshaw. For only one person to be convicted to a prison term was telling. Either Erath County was full of law-abiding citizens, or the district court was not the only way citizens sought to administer justice.

Parks Crenshaw ended up in Texas by way of Missouri where he was born. One family story told of Parks at one point having a trunk full of Indian scalps. No one knew how he acquired these "trophies," but the story also related how the trunk was lost during a flood when it floated away, not to be found again.[1]

Instead of enlisting in a Confederate Unit during the Civil War, Crenshaw chose to enlist in the Texas State Troops whose responsibilities included protecting settlers along the frontier of the state where women and children tried to hold on while their menfolk were off fighting for the Southern cause. Generally, the men in these troop units were either too old or too young to serve in a regular Confederate regiment. Conscription laws took men between 18 and 50 years of age prior to February 17, 1864, to serve in the army for the South. So, the Texas State Troops willingly took teenagers and seniors.

Texas wanted the Confederate States of America to fund the Texas State Troops but at the same time not control where the frontier units served. The Texas governor feared that the Southern generals would reroute these troops away from where they were needed along the frontier.

Interestingly, Parks Crenshaw's age on his enlistment was shown as 17 years old, too young for regular Confederate service. He was actually older. So, why did he lie about his age? Did he hope to rebuild his scalp collection while fighting to protect the settlers? Perhaps the real answer lies in the fact that many Texans were willing to fight to protect their state but had little interest in being sent to other Southern states to fight in a war beyond their own state's border. Some men even harbored Union sympathies and joined the Texas State Troops to escape persecution and harassment in their home counties. For whatever reason Parks Crenshaw joined the Texas State Troops on February 1, 1864.

Crenshaw traveled to Erath County to join this protective Cross Timbers unit. His enlisting officer was William Motheral, and Crenshaw was assigned to Company C, Second Frontier District, Erath County. Crenshaw's company officer was Captain William H. Culver and overall commanding officer was Major George B. Erath.[2]

Evidently, the young man's interests ran to other items besides scalps. Parks Crenshaw's enlistment lasted only nineteen days, because he was arrested for theft. What Crenshaw stole or how he was caught has been lost, but what is known is that he was mustered out of the Texas State Troops because of his legal woes June 1, 1864. A conviction before District Judge W. Y. McFarland ensured a prison term of five years. Parks Crenshaw was expelled and his enrollment expunged from the Texas State Troops active records after his felony conviction, effectively dismissing his embarrassing episode from their records.

W. M. Skipper, sheriff of Erath County, transported the newly convicted felon to Huntsville. The Transportation Voucher states that the lawman traveled 460 miles to Huntsville and back to Stephenville. He asked for ten cents a mile for Crenshaw and for round trip mileage for himself and for a guard who traveled with the sheriff to prevent the prisoner from escaping. The total bill submitted November 1864 amounted to $115, a large sum for that time period. The voucher was paid from the State Treasury.

The record of how long Crenshaw may have stayed in the local county jail prior to being sentenced and transported was lost in the fire that burned the county's records in 1866. Although sentenced from Erath County, Parks Crenshaw was documented on the official *Convict Record* at Huntsville as being from Dallas County. He was 20 years old in 1864, 5'9" tall, and weighed 160 pounds when he arrived at the prison's gate. He had a fair complexion with both brown hair and eyes. While he admitted to using tobacco, his record stated he was temperate (a non-drinker). He was not married and arrived with no money at the prison on November 4, 1864.

If Crenshaw had known what he faced as a convict in Texas at that time, he might have had second thoughts about having sticky fingers. Huntsville State Penitentiary opened in 1849. From the start the State Legislature followed the economic philosophy that the prison system should be self-supporting through the use of convict labor. The buildings and workshops for shoemaking, carpentry, and blacksmithing were erected using convict labor. Later, a cotton and wool textile mill was built inside the prison walls.

As the Civil War closed, the ranks of convicts rose significantly. As a result the Texas Legislature devised a plan to lease convict labor out to businesses and plantations in order to control rising costs. Commonly, black convicts were sent to the fields to work while whites and Mexicans were assigned to lumber camps, coal mines, the railroads, or to work inside the prison walls. The terrible conditions and brutal treatment of convicts seem to have been system-wide for all races. Considered non-citizens, convicts had little recourse for complaints and no one to represent them against the intolerable conditions and brutality. Even so, few lawmakers felt compelled to make any changes.

Crenshaw's name does not show up on the prison *Conduct Ledger* which at that time was reserved for those refusing to work, cooperate, or who had attempted

Parks Crenshaw courtesy of Gary Crenshaw

escape. Parks Crenshaw did his time in relative obscurity with no notation of what work he was assigned.

Records do show that Parks Crenshaw served his full five years and was discharged November 10, 1869. He was given $20 and told to sign his discharge voucher by the prison superintendent, T. C. Bell.[3]

After leaving prison, Crenshaw married and started a family. He shifted between Texas and the Oklahoma Territory. Crenshaw raised five children and married a second time. In the later part of his life he lived with his son Tom Crenshaw. Dying in 1922, Parks Crenshaw was buried in Dela Cemetery at Antlers, Oklahoma, in an unmarked grave.[4]

An Overland Stagecoach Overturns
The Dulany Family Story

When Nelson Dulany purchased three tickets on the Sawyer & Company Stage Line going from Navasota to Waco on February 24, 1860, he had every reason to believe that he, his wife Lucinda, and their three children would have an interesting but uneventful trip. They soon found out differently.

Stagecoach lines had been used for government mail contracts in Texas since 1835 but early on doubled as passenger and/or freight transports. With the Texas' railroad system still in its infancy, stage lines quickly became the most reliable public transportation between early population centers and points along the frontier. Stages averaged about 5 miles an hour. Stands were set up in between major stops so the passengers could have a break or get a bite to eat while the horses or mules were fed, watered or changed out.

Henry Shellman provided the first line between San Antonio and El Paso in 1851. One of his most famous drivers was William (Bigfoot) Wallace. One of the more famous routes was the Butterfield Overland Mail that spanned across the West. It crossed much of Texas from Grayson County to El Paso covering hundreds of miles. It took a minimum of six days to cross Texas this way.[1]

Stagecoach travel was not without its problems. Danger from bandits and hostile Indians, especially along the settled edge of the frontier and westward across Texas, was well known. The stagecoach itself was an unwieldy conveyance. The driver had to be careful when loading passengers to make sure the weight inside the cabin and on top was evenly distributed.

Many times passengers were crammed inside the coach together. Those allocated to the center bench inside the cabin had to use each other's back to brace for the trip. On occasion all would be asked to get out and walk in order to get across a muddy patch or around perilous terrain. Other rules of etiquette were expected such as not sleeping on another passenger's shoulder as well as not cursing. Although alcohol was allowed, passengers were expected to share.

Sixteen of thirty-one passenger/mail lines of the State of Texas were owned by Sawyer, Risher, and Hall Stage Lines by 1860. In 1871 the company was divided with Sawyer maintaining control of four of the lines. Sawyer's Stage Lines achieved an excellent reputation if the articles in the newspapers of that day and time are to be believed.[2]

Courtesy Texas State Library & Archives Commission

The *Dallas Herald* in the November 17, 1858 issue published an editorial by an unnamed passenger who stated emphatically that "Messer. Sawyer and Risher have selected sober, gentlemanly, and skillful drivers. They have put upon the route very commodious and comfortable coaches, and their stock is well kept, are in good order and look fine..." Another editorial in the *Houston Telegraph* dated June 27, 1859, stated, "I came up by stage, the line being one of Sawyer, Risher & Hall who are famous for their comfortable stages, good teams and careful drivers..."[3]

Knowing about such newspaper endorsements would lead the Dulany family to believe that their coach trip would have them arriving safely at their destination that February of 1860. W. B. Bates, agent for Sawyer, Risher, and Hall signed the Dulanys' tickets after the $42 fee was paid. It would have been obvious to Mr. Bates that Lucinda Dulany was in an advanced stage of pregnancy, as she was believed to be close to confinement. She was expecting twins.

The first sign that this would be no ordinary trip was that the stationmaster had no qualms about overloading the stage with passengers. With seventeen aboard, the smallest shift in weight or rough terrain could cause the whole coach to turn over. Twelve to fifteen passengers was considered more than a full load.

The driver was a man named John Marshall. When the coach reached the road close to the Brazos River bottom, the passengers were asked to get out and walk. All but Mrs. Dulany complied. During that portion of the trip, passengers later testified that Marshall showed signs of having consumed alcohol and almost overturned the coach with only one person on board.

Passengers the next day noted that Marshall started drinking early on. At Marlin, a stage stand thirty miles from Waco, Marshall procured a bottle of whiskey and two bottles of cherry brandy. At each stop, he showed more and more signs of getting very inebriated. When the coach reached the stop at Hatch, located fourteen miles from Waco, Mrs. Dulany had had enough of the wild and dangerous ride. Through her husband a serious complaint was lodged as well as a plea for a new and sober driver. Mr. Hatch simply told the group that he had no one who could replace Marshall.

With grave misgivings, Mrs. Dulany reboarded the coach. One passenger took the reins and drove for a while. Marshall climbed down on the footboard and kicked the wheel-horses to make them go faster. At the top of the hill Marshall took back over. He went slowly at first but picked up speed as he neared the bottom. While going down a hill, the stage hit a stump, which was protruding 4" to 6" out of the ground, and overturned. Later, passengers stated they believed the stump was avoidable. The stage ended up on its side with passengers from the inside having to exit out the door now located on the upper side.

The last passenger taken out was Lucinda Dulany who was badly injured. The stagecoach continued without Lucinda or her family as she was too badly hurt to reboard. She was carried to a farmhouse while a physician was sought. He did not arrive until the next morning. Her injuries caused Lucinda to go into premature labor six days later. The twins were born in a weakened condition, dying a few hours after birth. Mrs. Dulany remained five weeks longer at the farmhouse before being strong enough to return to Coryell County.[4]

A few months later the Dulanys filed a lawsuit against Sawyer and Risher, claiming damages amounting to $23,542. District Judge Richard Coke presided over the civil trial in McLennan County. The Dulanys cited that drunkenness and gross negligence caused the deaths of their prematurely born twins. They also claimed continued ill health for Mrs. Dulany.

The verdict came back for the plaintiffs, but the jury awarded the lesser amount of $4,125. The motion by the defendants for a new trial was denied. They appealed to the Supreme Court of Texas.

The bill of exception included:
1) The objection to admitting the ticket/receipt signed by Bates without proof of its execution.
2) The objection of the plaintiffs submitting the signed ticket/receipt as a contract.
3) The objection that the jury was not instructed to consider that the Dulanys should never have traveled by coach with Mrs. Dulany in such a "delicate condition," showing the negligence was on their side for taking such a trip.
4) The objection to the district court under Coke's leadership allowing the jury to consider whether the plaintiffs were entitled to compensation for the loss of their children, insisting that common law dictated no compensation is allowed "in a case of injury to infants in the womb of the mother..."[5]

The decision, and its implication, was written up in *American Negligence Cases, A Complete Collection of All Reported Negligence* by Theodore Hamilton and published in 1905. The following is their summation of the case:

> *It was held that where a stage coach is so carelessly driven by a drunken driver that the coach was upset and a female passenger was so injured that a miscarriage resulted, the carrier is liable for all the immediate results of the injury,*

the liability not depending upon the physical ability of passengers but upon the conduct of the carriers."[6]

This case in District Judge Richard Coke's court set a precedent. From then on public conveyances had to be careful that negligence on their part did not create harm for their passengers. The court with this ruling served notice to employers working with the public that their workers as well as the company could be held accountable for the actions of employees while on the job.

Taking the Edge Off
I. W. Lacy Case

Anglos on the Texas frontier had a taste for alcohol—as can be seen in the previous stagecoach story—that encouraged peddlers and local businesses to make room on their shelves for bottles of whiskey. Taking the edge off the rigors of frontier life gave men something to look forward to while they ranched or farmed along the perimeter of Indian country. Regulating the sale of spirits came early from the Texas government. To keep tabs on those purveyors of booze, the government required that retailers obtain a license in the county where they hoped to do business.

The $250 per annum (more if paid in installments) licensing fee for running a tavern was beyond the means of many who migrated to the frontier. While it was fairly easy for the sheriff to keep up with the local saloons, tracking those down who sold "hooch" out of their homes without a license was much more difficult.

Whether it was homemade firewater or bottled spirits, some men were willing to flout the laws in hopes of expanding profits. Selling alcohol without a license was considered a felony. So, indictments

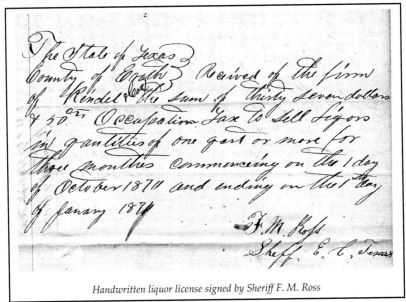

Handwritten liquor license signed by Sheriff F. M. Ross

were issued by grand juries at regular sessions of the district court. Selling without a license, if convicted, could result in a fine up to $1000 and/or three months in jail.

Irvin W. Lacy's main occupation, stated on the 1870 census, was stock raising, though his residence was listed as being within the "village of Stephenville" in Erath County, Texas. Evidently, to make ends meet, Irvin was also selling liquor out of his house. With Texas in the middle of Radical Reconstruction, many participated in activities not considered legal, but it was only a matter of time before someone brought Lacy's side business to the attention of the district court. Marrying Sarah Brumley, the daughter of John Brumley, a former local sheriff, did not prevent Lacy from being arrested for selling alcohol without a license.

I. W. Lacy was convicted during the fall of 1868 before Judge A. B. Norton and assessed a $50 fine. Lacy appealed his conviction through his attorney, S. H. Renick, to the Texas Court of Appeals. The objection was not in the guilt or innocence of Lacy but rather in the definition of what constituted a "dram." The sole witness for the state, Thomas Dickerson, testified that he was served a dram by Lacy but he did not specifically state what was in the dram. Dickerson testified that no words were exchanged after he asked for a dram. He placed a fifty-cent piece on the counter, and Lacy replaced it with a quarter, which Dickerson picked up and then left after consuming his drink. Lacy argued that the State's witness was not clear in his accusation and that a "dram" did not necessarily mean alcohol.[1]

The Texas Court of Appeals ruled against Lacy's appeal, stating that the definition of a "dram" lay in its usage, which was in their opinion only in reference to liquor. Losing his appeal, Lacy still had two other indictments pending related to the sale of liquor without a license. Judge Norton sat on the bench during these trials. He noted in the court records that the jury retired for only a few moments before returning with their verdict of "Not Guilty." The judge's notation indicated his surprise at the outcome, since Lacy had been convicted already on the previous charge.

As an appointed judge who did not live anywhere near Erath County, Norton was aware of the hostility many felt toward him. Did that translate into how juries ruled? The record showed that no one from Erath County was sent to the state penitentiary during Norton's tenure in office.

Irvin W. Lacy left Erath County not long after losing his earlier appeal. He formed a partnership with L. G. Coleman who lived with the Lacys in Stephenville. The two men decided that greener pastures beckoned in New Mexico Territory. Arriving in Colfax County in the early 1870s, the two partners started the L. C. Cattle Company.

Business was good. The two men found they could run cattle into southern Colorado to free grazing land in the canyons of the Ancients National Monument (as it was later designated). Soon, the L. C. Cattle Company rose to prominence and prosperity. The Lacy family grew and L. C. Coleman married the sister of the well-known shootist Clay Allison who worked for the L. C. Cattle Company from time to time.[2]

I. W. Lacy had little involvement in the Lincoln County War in New Mexico where Billy the Kid was involved but did find himself in the middle of the feud between the Coe clan (who migrated north to get away from the Lincoln County War) and the Stocktons. The Coes worked out of Farmington, New Mexico. Frank and George Coe were the main leaders, having ridden previously with Billy the Kid.

Port and Ike Stockton grew up in Johnson County, Texas, around Cleburne before joining the cattle drives heading north. Like Clay Allison, Port Stockton developed a reputation as a shootist, adding notches to his gun as he drifted west into New Mexico. If not for his brother Ike managing to rescue him, Port would have been lynched by a mob in Cimarron, New Mexico. The two brothers moved on to the San Juan area of New Mexico. Conflict erupted between the Stocktons and the Coes. Each accused the other of rustling livestock. Outnumbered, the Stocktons fled to Southern Colorado where Port managed to land a job as marshal for Animas City. The residents soon realized they had made a mistake and stripped Port of his badge. He managed to keep his guns and escaped from the local jail.[3]

While Port was busy in his pursuits, Ike Stockton went to work for I. W. Lacy. They were cousins by marriage. Sarah Lacy's mother, Delilah, was a sister to Ike and Port's mother, Jane.[4] For a time Ike also worked for the Coes in Farmington despite their ire at Port. When a cowboy suspected of working for Port was lynched, Ike retreated, accusing the Coes of making raids on cattle belonging to Colorado ranchers.

The feud between the Coes and Stocktons escalated, forcing local ranchers to take sides. In an effort to wean Lacy away from the Stockton clan, the Coes had friends from various parts of New Mexico send letters to him and his wife Sarah warning that the Stocktons were killing their cattle and stealing their horses. The Coe's strategy failed when Lacy became suspicious at the large number of letters he had received. He sent an employee, Big Dan Howland, to spy on the Stocktons, not knowing that Howland was already in the pay of the Coes. When Lacy figured it out, he fired Big Dan and stayed loyal to the Stocktons.[5]

While the Stocktons were occupied battling Indians who had killed local ranchers and stolen cattle along the Utah/Colorado line, the Coes took the opportunity in late May 1881 to get even. Big Dan Howland showed up in Fort Lewis where I. W. Lacy had gone on business. Big Dan verbally accosted Lacy on the street declaring loudly that Lacy owed him back pay. Lacy refused to pay him anything and turned to leave. Big Dan shot him in the back and managed to escape before he was apprehended for the deed. News of the murder was reported in several leading newspapers including the May 16, 1881 issue of the *San Francisco Bulletin*.

Outraged, Sarah Brumley Lacy offered a reward of $3000 (a princely sum in those days) for the capture of Howland. Sad, but undaunted, the widow sent to Texas for three of her brothers (John, Irvin, and Bill) to help her with the family business. An article in the *New York Times* revealed that the Lacy daughters could ride and shoot a Colt .45 just as good as their brothers, even though they received a genteel education at a Catholic boarding school in Trinidad, Colorado.[6]

The Lacys left Erath when the courts were starting to take control of illegal wrongdoings. Unwilling to accept court interventions, they chose to leave Texas. They found their niche and destiny in the territory of New Mexico.

Charged With Murder
The James Taylor Story

While many of the details have been lost with the disappearance of the trial file, the fact remains that former Virginian, James Taylor, at age thirty-four, took the life of John Simpson, a resident along Armstrong Creek in Erath County, in September 1869. The blue-eyed, brown-haired killer stood 5'3" and weighed 144 lbs.[1]

A letter written to *The Dallas Weekly Herald* and published November 6, 1869, stated –

> *Taylor was at Simpson's house and wished to eat a watermelon. Simpson invited him to go with him into the field, and when in the act of picking up a melon for him, Taylor shot him through the back part of the head killing him instantly. . .*

Fearful of the consequences of his actions, Taylor, whose occupation was listed as plasterer but who was later called a U. S. Army deserter, hastily absented himself from Erath County, hoping to evade the law.[2] Perhaps he was aware that Erath, like so many other frontier counties, had a tendency not to wait for the wheels of justice to turn in regular court. With appointed district judges holding court only twice a year and sometimes missing one of those scheduled visits, locals did not always believe in the judicial system that the Radical Reconstruction government in Austin, led by Governor Edmund Davis, provided.

Vigilantes adhered to the idea that it was their duty to mete out swift justice to keep some sort of order or at least as a way to send a warning to other would-be felons. While livestock thieves, especially those who took horses, were the most prevalent targets of these vigilance committees, many sturdy oak trees served as hasty scaffolds and signals to those thinking about going on the wrong side of the law. By 1869 although six men had been indicted, no one from Erath County had been convicted of murder in the judicial district court.[3]

Information on his capture in Denton County was scarce, but Taylor was found there by the county sheriff, B. E. Greenlee. The following was published in the October 7, 1869 issue of *The San Antonio Express* –

> *A man by the name of Jim Taylor was "jerked up" near town last Friday night by our Sheriff. It is alleged that he murdered a man in Stephensville [sic], Erath County, a year ago – Denton Monitor September 18th.*

Why did James Taylor choose Denton County, a locale still in Texas but only forty miles from the Red River, for his refuge? The answer might be found in a previous month's news article prior to Taylor's arrest. It revealed information about the capture of a wanted man named Randolph Spencer in Denton County and highlighted the assertion that he was a part of a notorious group known as the Taylor gang. Perhaps Denton County was a place where James Taylor thought he would be safe among friends and relatives.[4]

Brought back to Erath County, James Taylor posed a problem for local officials. They did not have a jail safe enough to house men accused of serious crimes. Some may have had concerns that members of the Taylor gang might make an appearance. Between fairly easy escapes and local mobs bent on administering immediate justice, the decision was made to move Taylor to the county accommodations in Waco.

Needing help, Erath Sheriff G. W. Keith deputized local merchant John Frey to help guard the prisoner en route to McLennan County, approximately ninety miles away. Sensing that this might be a dangerous duty, Frey declined to help the sheriff. Angry that Frey refused to do his duty, Sheriff Keith lodged a complaint with District Judge A. B. Norton. While helping the local sheriff was considered a "civic" duty, the judge weighed the anger of the sheriff with the mood of the community. He ruled that indeed Frey should be held accountable. Even so, the judge only fined Frey $1.00 for his refusal to assist the sheriff.[5]

James Taylor's trial did not take place for two years after the murder he committed. Many factors contributed to this. A changing of appointed district judges from A. B. Norton of Dallas County to J. P. Osterhout of Bell County, along with a realignment of counties within districts, led to the spring term of 1870 of the district court in Erath being scrapped. Erath was moved first from the Nineteenth to the Fifth Judicial District and then to the Thirty-Fourth Judicial District.

Although Judge Osterhout ordered that James Taylor be brought down from Waco for the fall term of 1870 of the district court, the case was not brought up but instead was continued to the next term. At the spring term of 1871 the judge was informed that Taylor was without legal representation. William Lowry and E. A. Jones were appointed, and the case was set for the August 1871 term.

The defense attorneys once again applied for a continuance, but Judge Osterhout overruled the request. If it was their hope that the passage of time would help their client, Lowry and Jones came up short when the jury convicted James Taylor of second-degree murder and sentenced him to twenty-five years at Huntsville. Taylor was lucky the jury did not find him guilty of first-degree murder. Perhaps the defense tried to convince the jury that Taylor was not in his right mind at the time of the murder.[6]

As no further appeal was made, Taylor was transported to Huntsville Penitentiary. Not willing to remain in control of the state, James Taylor successfully escaped from his guards while working at Lake Jackson (located south of Houston) on the convict lease program in 1876.

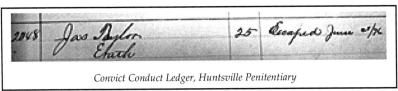
Convict Conduct Ledger, Huntsville Penitentiary

James Taylor was never caught and probably disappeared into the territories of either New Mexico or Oklahoma like so many other wanted desperadoes did when things got a little too "hot" in Texas. Those who managed to get there were seldom tracked down and brought back.

The importance of this conviction lay in the fact that James Taylor was the first to be convicted of murder in Erath County. With one such conviction "under their belts," juries in Erath County seemed more willing to allow the legal wheels of justice to send felons to the state penitentiary on a more regular basis.

Marital Bliss
The Court Steps In

In the eyes of the district court, marriage was viewed as a legal contract in which the husband and wife had certain contractual obligations. Divorce was not so easily procured in the nineteenth century in Texas. Either party had to show just cause which might include adultery, abandonment (a minimum of three years absence), or physical cruelty—requiring a ruling from a jury.

The outcome of divorce proceedings often depended on the community's values or even the female's social standing. Some other acts on the part of the husband or wife that could be brought to the attention of the court include actions of moral turpitude or breaking the law—prostitution, seduction, rape and bigamy—all of which might lead to a criminal indictment if the district attorney were so inclined.[1]

Early divorce laws in Texas showed a definite double standard where personal or sexual behavior was concerned. The following newspaper article from 1872, while sarcastic in tone, was not too far off the mark as to the attitudes of the time. Women were often considered the equivalent of being the personal chattel of a man –

> *A Case of Wife Beating*
> *Pompey Brown (colored) was brought before Justice Johnson this morning upon a charge of beating his wife, Mary Brown. It seems that he had been in the habit of beating her, and she, not being disposed to take a whipping every day, as good, submissive wives should, she separated from him some time ago, and they have lived apart since. But feeling, yesterday, that it was necessary to his peace of mind that he should whip her again, he hunted her up and gave her a sound beating, and she was so unreasonable as to go and have him arrested. It has come to a pretty pass, in free America, when a man cannot whip his own lawful wife! Judge Johnson, being an old fogy about such matters, put him under a pretty heavy bond.*[2]

A husband's violence toward his wife, if shown to be "provoked," was often overlooked by an all male jury. The wife, on the other hand, needed eyewitnesses, preferably males, who could vouch that she did nothing to initiate the violence toward her.

Erath County was not immune to the passions of human behavior. While divorce was considered a blight on a family's social standing, many cases were still put forward in the district court. Even so, some abandoned or ill-treated spouses simply put "a good face on it" and pretended, at least in public, that all was fine on the home front.

The first notation in the *District Minutes of Erath County* referencing illegal personal behavior was the case of Sarah Long and W. N. Dodson, who were charged in 1868 with adultery. Dodson was married. The accused couple quickly disappeared from Erath County rather than face the judicial "music." The district court was informed that they could be found in Hayes County. The sheriff of Hayes was sent a *capias*, which ordered him to take them into custody. The *District Court Minutes* noted that District Judge Norton issued a fine of $100 against the Hayes County sheriff for not serving the *capias* warrant. Unable to prosecute without the defendants in custody, the case was finally dismissed in 1870 by the district attorney, James Boyd.[3]

Abandonment was the most common reason used to obtain a divorce in Texas in the nineteenth century. It happened on both sides but more often than not, the husband was the one to take off—many times not informing his wife of his intentions or else lying about his destination or reason for travel.

A spouse using abandonment as just cause had to wait three years to file. If the wayward spouse came back during that time, the just cause was null and void. Should the spouse leave again, the wait time started over. A wife had to prove that her husband had not supported her during his absence.

Adding insult to injury, Mary Harley planned for some time her abandonment of husband William in 1870. Not only did she run off with another man, William Crocket, but she also loaded up most of the household furniture and food. She managed to stop in Stephenville and run up charges on her husband's account at a local dry goods store before leaving with her lover. The jilted husband had no choice but to pay the bills she left behind before taking flight.[4]

Another Erath account involved John Russell Holloway who married Mary Alice Crane, July 15, 1874. The marriage was stormy from the very beginning. Mary Alice never seemed to be happy as Holloway's mate. She even came to suspect that her husband had feelings for his cousin, Emily Mahan. When he gave Emily a silver ring, Mary became enraged. She berated Russell even in the presence of others, stating on more than one occasion that he was not "worth the powder and lead it would take to kill him." [5]

For Christmas 1875, Mary Alice announced she wanted a new pair of expensive gaiter shoes. Russell did buy her a pair of good serviceable leather shoes. Mary Alice was so angry when she saw the cheap pair of shoes she threw them into the fireplace. Russell tried to placate her, saying he just did not have the money to buy the shoes she wanted. Mary Alice replied she would get the money even if it meant being a prostitute. Instead, in January 1876 Mary Alice ran away with a young man named Bud Goodman. Holloway filed for divorce.[6]

William Gunter thought of all the angles and used this knowledge when he was accused of bigamy in 1882. He did not deny that he had gone through two marriage ceremonies. The fathers and daughters all showed up in court to testify against him. Undaunted, Gunter put forth the defense that neither of the marriages were valid because both girls were under the age of fourteen (the age of consent in 1882) when he "married" them. While the *Stephenville Empire* newspaper raged editorially against Gunter's duplicity, the district court was forced to bring a verdict of "Not Guilty." [7]

Citations had to be published in the local newspaper for several issues if the defendant could not be served the divorce petition. These citations repeated the allegations plus details for all in the community to read. One case that probably raised an eyebrow or two was *John Bagwell v Margaret Bagwell*. Married in Johnson County, the couple took up temporary residence in Tarrant County with relatives. John left Margaret in Fort Worth and traveled to Erath County to improve the land he had obtained, build a cabin, and plant the crops. Margaret was not exactly staying at home (according to the citation printed in the *Stephenville Empire*) while John was working. He averred that she was running around in an unseemly manner. Margaret was seen in the company of a known prostitute, Birdie Parks, who frequented the Red Light Saloon in Fort Worth. John finally retrieved his wife and moved her to Erath County. The quiet life and hard work was too much for Margaret Bagwell. She left her husband and went back to Fort Worth, refusing to return. John filed for a divorce in 1881. He later dropped the case in 1884 but not before the citation was published.[8]

Sarah Burnick found herself abandoned and friendless in Erath County after her husband Frederick made many promises and lured her to join him in Stephenville. The marriage was rocky almost from the beginning after the couple married in Louisiana. She claimed later that he was quarrelsome, abusive, and failed to provide for her. He left, telling her he would send for her when he found work or land for them to live on. He was gone for five years without a word. He finally wrote Sarah from Stephenville, begging her to move there so that they could be reunited. She moved to Texas only to find herself abandoned again eight months later. While Frederick lived with Sarah, he publicly called her "a whore, a damn prostitute, and a bitch." He went so far as to beat her so severely that a doctor had to be called, and Frederick was arrested but later released. After he got out of jail, Frederick Burnick disappeared for good.[9]

Marian DeLave had additional problems when she filed for a divorce from William DeLave. Convicted of felony theft in Johnson County, DeLave was sentenced to fourteen years in the state penitentiary. Legislation was passed in 1876 that allowed a spouse to divorce someone convicted of a felony but a wait time of one year was imposed after the conviction. If the governor pardoned the spouse in prison during that year of wait time, the divorce suit could not go forward. Marian filed for her divorce in May 1880, only to find out that her erstwhile husband had escaped from prison. Her petition had to be published, since it could not be served, and she had to use abandonment as her reason for the divorce.[10]

The laws governing the end of a marriage concerning a spouse's conduct with the opposite sex weighed heavily in the favor of the husband. A wife could be divorced for simply conducting herself in an unseemly manner or in an amorous way around other men. Just one instance of adultery on her part was considered just cause for the husband. On the other hand, the husband could only be divorced if he was actually *living* with another woman, not his wife.

Even though juries could interpret certain aspects of divorce cases according to the laws, bigamy was considered clear grounds for having a marriage annulled. Mattie Mites moved to Erath County from Blount County, Alabama, in early 1896. She lived with her half-brother, A. C. Garrett, before marrying J. D. Bishop. Marital bliss was short-lived when Bishop learned that his bride had never bothered to divorce the husband she had left behind in Alabama.

Shocked, Bishop took his bride back to her relatives and filed for an annulment in Judge Straughan's court. The interrogatories on file in the case show that Mattie married Will Mites in late 1889. A son, Joseph, was soon born to the union, but the marriage lasted less than a year. Mattie's relatives admitted under questioning that no divorce was ever sought or obtained. Mattie averred that she believed that she was divorced because she had lived separate and apart from Will Mites for a long enough time that "the law

Citation as it appeared in the *Stephenville Empire*, October 3, 1891 gave her a divorce." Texas courts did not quite see it that way. The Bishop marriage was annulled. Mattie stayed in Erath County, making a life for herself and her son. She lived with her mother Jane Phillips.[11]

In the 1991 Erath case of *Stephens v Stephens*, the wife not only accused her husband of beating her but also of adultery with a local woman, Mrs. Lizzie Nance. The citation accused him of living with Mrs. Nance in various counties in the state after they fled together. The citation called Mrs. Nance a prostitute and asked the court to allow Mrs. Stephens to use the profits of their farm for her own benefit, since her husband took off with the said prostitute. The court obliged.[12]

Much like vigilantes who disregarded the courts when choosing to string up outlaws without giving them the benefit of the law, some spouses tried to ignore the obligations surrounding marriage by just disappearing or taking up with others. The recourse left to the remaining partner was to turn to the district court for relief. Only there could the bonds of matrimony be officially dissolved.

Part Four – The Court Grows Up

A Woman in a Man's World
The Phebe Haws Story

Phebe Haws, a native of Tennessee, married John A. Gibbs from South Carolina in 1851. Touring through the South, the Gibbs lived in Mississippi, where son John H. was born, and Alabama, where daughter Nancy Jane was born, before succumbing to the lure of Texas. Two more children, Willie (female) and Frank joined the Gibbs family after they settled in Erath County. They managed to acquire several town lots plus farmland. John, age 31, was listed as a "grocer" on the 1860 census with Phebe being listed as a housekeeper though she would soon become an innkeeper.

Their seemingly perfect world fell apart after John Gibbs was arrested and indicted for theft of beef steers in the fall of 1868. On top of this setback, Phebe became embroiled in a controversy concerning the death of Eliza Jane Painter, a local resident. Prominent Stephenville citizen, Dr. W. W. McNeill, made it known that he believed Phebe Gibbs was responsible for Eliza's death, intimating that poison was used. Phebe took exception and instituted a lawsuit against Dr. McNeill for defamation of character. In her complaint Gibbs said that within the hearing of W. S. Armistad and others Dr. McNeill expounded, "That damn woman has murdered my patient Eliza Jane Painter." Also attributed to McNeill was the following statement,

Dr. W. W. McNeil

"Our beloved Sister Painter no longer occupies her seat amongst us. She has been murdered and the bloody murderer is now present." Phebe Gibbs was in the room at the time of this comment.

In his answer to the lawsuit Dr. McNeill denied the allegation but could not resist stating that Phebe did not have a good reputation, name, or respect in the community. He went on to say he did not make the alleged statements in the lawsuit but, if he had, they would have been true.[1]

This was not the only lawsuit over these supposed libelous statements. Phebe also sued Peter Gravis, a Stephenville Methodist minister, and others connected to an editorial in a newspaper, *The Christian Advocate*, published in Galveston, which implied that Phebe was responsible for Ms. Painter's death. This suit was settled out of court with Gravis agreeing to print the following retraction in the newspaper for three successive weeks—

> *Mr. Editor, There appeared in your paper of June 18d 1868 over my signature on authority of Sister Eliza Jane Painter who died in Stephenville Texas on the 29d day of April 1868 in which it was stated that 'I could not say it was a dispensation of divine providence, but that it was the work of the enemy of souls in human form that the crime would stain the reputation of the gallows and darken the reputation of the foulest fiend of the doleful regions of the lost. Five physicians were called in who pronounced it a clear case of strychnine. It was sent to her in some fresh pork from one of her nearest neighbors who from all the circumstances was aiming to avenge herself on some of our best citizens who had detected and arrested her thieving husband. They have robed [sic] her of temporal life but thank God they could not touch her soul.' Now I wish to say in all candor that none of the above was written upon my own knowledge, but from representations made to me by parties prejudiced against those upon whom the statements reflected, and I am now convinced that the statements were premature and am very very sorry indeed that I ever lent an ear to the statements*

> that called me to pen the obituary in the language alluded to, and I most emphatically deny any intention to injure any one especially do I deny any intention of maliciously injuring, Mrs. Gibbs, the party who has taken offence to the innuendo in the obituary...[2]

Phebe Gibbs may have decided she had to do something to stem the tide of gossip she felt was unleashed by McNeill, but did she realize at the time how difficult it would be to win a suit against someone with as high a social standing in the community as Dr. W. W. McNeill had? It is reasonable to believe that she learned quickly that public opinion counted for a lot. Since her chances of success were slim in Erath County, Phebe had her lawyers go before Judge Osterhout to request a change of venue, arguing that Mrs. Gibbs could not receive a fair trial because of all of the publicity. McNeill retaliated by having men sign a petition stating they could be impartial. Judge Osterhout ruled in favor of allowing the change of venue to Ellis County.[3]

In the middle of the defamation lawsuit Phebe Gibbs sued her husband, John A. Gibbs, for a divorce. Her reasons for the divorce were that her husband was often drunk and insulting, exhibiting intolerable cruel behavior. Perhaps her anger at her husband not supporting her in her lawsuit against McNeill was the final straw that ended the union. The original petition against Dr. McNeill had only her name on it. She spoke of her disappointment at length in her divorce papers. Texas law required a jury (of only men) to decide what actions constituted intolerable and/or cruel behavior. Having a spouse traveling on the wrong side of the law did not ensure a wife a divorce. If he subsequently had been gone for three years, she could have had the bands dissolved without a legal proceeding. Phebe opted for the trial.

John Gibbs must have, at least initially, wanted to repair his relationship with his wife. An amendment to the defamation complaint indicated that John had joined Phebe in the defamation lawsuit. Evidently, this was not enough to mend the break. Advised that she might not have a strong enough suit to prevail, Phebe filed another amendment to her suit for divorce, stating that her husband had committed adultery in her home with a Negro servant. The jury found for the plaintiff. A motion for a new trial was filed by A. D. McGinnis and G. S. Shaw for "the community" requesting the verdict be set aside, stating that it was contrary to law. Judge Osterhout overruled the motion.[4]

Not satisfied with prevailing in her suit for divorce, Phebe Gibbs filed an *ex parte* requesting that the court allow her to go back to her maiden last name of Haws.[5] She stated that as a businesswoman it was important that she have a "good" name. Since her husband was still in trouble with the law, having also at that point been charged with murder, Phebe felt she had no other choice. Later, she went to court to change her minor children's names to Haws as well. In a twist, when John Gibbs filed for a bail bond hearing, Dr. McNeill agreed to be one of his sureties. Disappearing shortly afterward, John Gibbs forced Dr. McNeill to lose his bond money. Gibbs was listed in the *Fugitives from Justice* booklet published by the Texas Adjutant General and distributed to the Texas Rangers. Gibbs was never recaptured.

Proving she could be successful in the male-dominated world of the courts, Phebe Haws was also a success at business, running a boarding house/hotel on the west side of the square called the Stephenville House. Made up of two log cabins constructed with "rawhide" lumber from native timber and including a dog trot, the unpretentious hotel was popular with single men and those who flocked to town when district court was in session, along with buffalo hunters who operated out of this frontier town. According to Mrs. Pearl Cage, the establishment was known locally as the Gold Belt Hotel because of the leather belt Innkeeper Haws wore with a gold nugget embossed on it.[6] Interestingly, while a new courthouse was being built in 1876, the Erath County Commissioners leased a store-room next to the hotel belonging to Phebe to use as a grand jury room during sessions of the district court.

W. H. Fooshee, in his remembrances of early Erath, mentioned staying at the Stephenville House. He wrote in 1923—"When I first saw Stephenville in the spring of 1871…The only hotel in the place stood on the corner where the White Drug Co. is now doing business, and was run by Mrs. Phebe Hawes [sic]."[7]

Ms. Haws' court proceedings were far from over. The next time she was on the receiving end. She was sued for nonpayment of a promissory note to her lawyers over the McNeill defamation lawsuit. Another local lawyer, Wilsen Peacock, acquired the note and pushed for payment. Phebe refused to pay it, saying her original attorneys had "dropped" the case after it was transferred to Ellis County. Peacock took her to court but lost when the jury ruled in Phebe's favor.[8]

In all, Phebe Haws turned to Judge Osterhout's district court eight times (not counting her former husband's criminal legal woes) to settle business and personal issues. In another case she had to sue Dr. W. W. McNeill again in order to prove her ownership to the land upon which the Stephenville House was built. The court records burned in 1866 causing original landowners and subsequent buyers to have to reestablish the path of ownership to the land. Dr. McNeill was the administrator of the John M. Stephen estate. When he would not help her, Phebe sued and prevailed.

Relying on males to decide her legal issues, Ms. Haws never lost a case. She moved comfortably in this male-dominated world. She knew all the officers of the court; many had stayed at her place of business. When she moved from Erath, Phebe deeded lots to L. N. Frank, attorney, stating that his advice and help with her children had been invaluable.

Phebe Haws ran her hotel until 1880 at which time she pulled up stakes in Stephenville. Why did Phebe sell a thriving business? It possibly stemmed from more legal woes. A local carpenter, Harry Barrett, publicly shot A. T. Francis inside a saloon on the square. Phebe sought counsel for Barrett and even co-signed a promissory note for payment. The attorneys sued her for payment after Barrett was convicted and sent to prison. In her legal reply Phebe stated that she was forced to co-sign but was verbally promised that she would not have to pay them anything unless they successfully represented Barrett. Unexplained was why these attorneys dropped this lawsuit. Also left was the mystery as to why Phebe chose to try to help Harry Barrett.[9]

The lady innkeeper sold or gave away all of her real estate holdings in Stephenville, and then moved to the newly emerging town of

Cisco in Eastland County. Mrs. George Langston in her 1904 *History of Eastland County Texas* mentioned Phebe twice –

> *In this white town were two or more stores of general merchandise, two or three grocery stores, a number of restaurants, doctors' offices, and Mrs. Haws' hotel, which stood about the middle of Broadway between the Daniels and Broadwell homes…Mrs. Haws began the building of her hotel, which was blown down in a furious gale but immediately replaced before the sale of lots, and managed the same until her death…*

Phebe Haws died in 1891 at the age of 57. She was definitely a feisty frontier woman unafraid to compete and succeed in a world mainly dominated by men, proving the wheels of justice could also work for her. She is buried in Oakwood Cemetery in Cisco. Her daughter, Nancy Dowdy, also ran a hotel in Cisco during the 1890s and was buried beside her mother.

Bigamy Leads To Murder
The W. F. Holland Case

Marriage on the frontier was a time for celebration. John Hayes, a stonemason, took Mary Edwards, the daughter of Dr. William Edwards, as his wife in 1861. A son was born to the union. Dr. Edwards later testified that the celebration was short-lived when information came to him that John Hayes already had a wife in another state. He stated that Hayes was arrested but escaped and disappeared. Since the records of the Erath County Clerk's office burned in 1866, no legal documents dispute Edwards' account.[1]

With Hayes gone and thought to be out of the picture, Mary Edwards married again to William Frank Holland. Eleven years after the departure of Hayes, he returned and demanded that Mary choose between him and Holland. She decided to stay with Holland. Was it possible that Mary Holland was the bigamist? John Hayes filed a complaint at the district court level against Mary, asking for custody of his son. He stated in his filing that the real reason he left Erath County was because he "became impelled and moved by the spirit of patriotism when he saw his country's flag imperiled," so "he promptly entered the naval service of his country continuing in said service until the close of the unfortunate rebellion through which his country has passed..."[2]

Sheriff John Waller signed as Hayes surety in his complaint against his wife. Would a sheriff vouch for a previously arrested bigamist who had reportedly escaped from jail? Later news articles published after Edwards was recaptured dubbed Hayes as a "parson." He may have been a circuit rider or simply a lay minister. Possibly, the newspaper got his occupation wrong.

The Civil War had been over for five years when Hayes returned. Why did Hayes wait so long to return to his family in Erath County? Did he suspect that his in-laws would disown him because he fought for the Union?

For some unknown reason a compromise was worked out, and the case in district court did not go forward. Young Jack went to live with his father, John Hayes. How Mary Holland felt about this was not noted but may have led to the eventual murder of her first husband.

In September 1872 Dr. William Edwards extended an invitation for his grandson Jack to attend a religious camp meeting near Duffau going on under his direction. Hayes reluctantly agreed to let Jack go on Friday but firmly stated that he would be there on Sunday evening to take his son back home. When Hayes arrived Sunday afternoon, he was convinced to stay a few hours longer to participate in the religious activities. As the late afternoon shadows stretched out, Hayes announced he wanted to leave. Frank Holland and Joe Edwards commenced to arguing with Hayes. Heated words were exchanged. Hayes left after angrily stating that they could not keep his son. With only two hours left until sunset, Hayes set out but never made it home. His bullet-riddled body was found by Farmer Harper and his son.

Sheriff Waller, Hayes' landlord, decided to investigate. He later testified that he found the unarmed Hayes shot through the head, as the Harpers had told him. The younger Harper had heard the shots and witnessed a saddled horse running without a rider. He also saw two men on horseback leaving hurriedly. Waller investigated the crime scene carefully and noted the horse tracks. He recognized one set of tracks as being from his own pony that he had loaned Hayes to travel to the camp meeting to get his son. Waller was familiar with the pony's tracks. Following the signs back a ways, Waller could tell that the pony's gait was normal until it ran a short distance off the road to the spot where Hayes' body was found. Two additional sets of horse tracks ran on either side of Waller's pony being ridden by Hayes. One was a large horse with two shod and two unshod hooves. The other horse was unshod. This set of tracks led Waller back to the Edwards' campground.

Waller's filed report led to the arrest of Frank Holland and Joe Edwards the next day. When taken into custody, both men had pistols on them. One showed signs of recently having been discharged. Witnesses from the campground testified at the trial that Holland and Edwards left about a half hour after Hayes did that fateful night. The two men announced they needed to feed livestock. Holland rode a large horse with two shod and two unshod hooves. Edwards rode on a smaller, unshod horse. When the two men returned to the campground, their horses appeared to be tired. The men seemed excited, ate no supper, and sought out Dr. Edwards for private conversation.

In the end Frank Holland was convicted in Judge Osterhout's court on circumstantial evidence that relied heavily on John Waller's testimony. The jury led by A. J. Windham assessed a life sentence in the state penitentiary.[3]

Joe Edwards, also charged with murder, escaped from jail before being tried. He disappeared to the north into Indian Territory, as so many before him had done to escape justice in a courtroom.

Holland appealed his case to the Texas Court of Appeals, citing errors believed to have been made at the district level in Judge Osterhout's court. Through his attorney, Holland complained that key witnesses were not present, that the circumstantial evidence was not strong enough for a conviction, along with several other exceptions. The conviction was affirmed with Justice P. J. Ogden writing the opinion. He noted, "...therefore the law has made the juries the exclusive judges of the facts in all criminal cases..."[4]

So at age 31, W. Frank Holland was taken to the penitentiary by Sheriff Waller who was authorized by the court to take a deputy while transporting Holland to Huntsville. Once delivered, the sheriff submitted a travel voucher so that his expenses were reimbursed by the state.

Huntsville State Penitentiary at this time, however, was no longer controlled by the state. As a cost cutting measure, Texas leased the facilities and prisoners to the Ward Dewey Company of Galveston from 1871 to 1877, which was mostly the time during which Holland was a convict. Holland had few rights as a prisoner and no recourse if subjected to harsh treatment.

W. Frank Holland did not serve out his life sentence. Noted in the prison *Conduct Ledger*, Prisoner No. 3161, W. F. Holland, of Erath

County was pardoned by Governor Roberts, October 30, 1879, six years after arriving at Huntsville. The two reasons given were "good conduct and loss of eyesight." No indication was given as to the circumstances surrounding Holland's sight impairment. Was it accidental that this thirty-seven-year-old man lost his vision, or was it self-inflicted, possibly the result of ill-treatment or a fight? Certainly it indicates that Holland could no longer work and would simply be a burden to the state. So, a life sentence was commuted to a six-year term, and W. Frank Holland was released.[5]

In 1885 Sheriff John Gilbreath managed to capture Joe Edwards, still wanted for Hayes murder, in Indian Territory, bringing him back to Erath County. District Judge Nugent recused himself from Edward's trial, as he had been part of the prosecution team that sent Holland to prison for the same crime. Judge C. K. Bell presided. Edwards was given the same life sentence that Holland received in 1873. He was sent to Rusk, also known as the East Texas Penitentiary.[6]

After serving eleven years, Joe Edwards started the process to receive a pardon from Governor Culberson. Receiving a gubernatorial pardon could be a lengthy endeavor. Even if the assistant superintendent for the penitentiary or the Board of Pardons and Parole recommended a convict's release, governors were reluctant unless a petition of local citizens from the county where the offense took place was also received. Who signed the petition was likewise considered important.

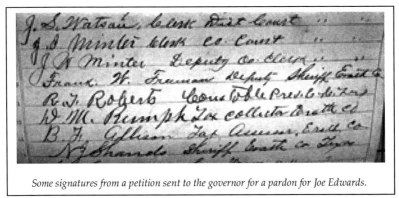

Some signatures from a petition sent to the governor for a pardon for Joe Edwards.

The process for Joe Edwards was started by M. B. Floyd, a Fort Worth banker. He managed to pull together an impressive petition from Erath signed by several judges, jurors, attorneys, sheriffs and other well-regarded citizens. Separate letters from the trial judge, C. K. Bell, and the prison assistant superintendent, James Gibson, were enough for Governor Culberson to issue a pardon and early release for Edwards in 1896.[7] Reunited with his wife Martha, Joe Edwards eventually moved to Ranger in Eastland County.[8]

Attempted Citizens' Arrest Ends in Deadly Force
The Dr. W. M. Barry, S. O. Berry, and John Shelby Story

On August 28, 1875, J. M. Yarbrough headed into Stephenville. The young farmer's purpose, outside of looking for a good time, has been lost. He took with him a pistol, even though he knew he would be breaking the law. While having a firearm on the farm was permissible, city ordinances outlawed the carrying of firearms in public in town.

Once in Stephenville, Yarbrough came in contact with J. W. Wilkes, the city marshal. Noticing Yarbrough was armed, the lawman confronted him with the intention of making an arrest. Instead of yielding quietly, Yarbrough panicked and fled.

Marshal Wilkes called out to bystanders to help him apprehend the fleeing culprit. Dr. W. M. Barry, S. O. Berry (postmaster), and John Shelby (grocer) wasted no time in mounting their horses. They took out after the fugitive. Realizing he had been tracked down, Yarbrough quickly took refuge in a thicket located close to a farmhouse. When the pursuers caught up, no one seemed to know what to do.

S. O. Berry

The posse reported later that Yarbrough was told to surrender and that when he did not they feared for their lives, as the fugitive was armed. Concerned that at any minute they would be shot, Berry, Barry, and Shelby all took turns shooting into the thicket.

Yarbrough called out for them to stop. The members of the posse afterward stated that they ceased shooting at this point. Mrs. E. Dunaway and W. W. Arnold, witnesses, disputed this account later in court. Regardless, Yarbrough was shot, and medical help was sought. Dr. Crow and Dr. Burroughs were brought forward to attend Yarbrough's wounds. Both medical men later testified they thought at the time that the young man had a chance to live, but a short time afterward he died.

Since the shooting took place outside the town of Stephenville, Sheriff H. G. Waller arrested all three members of the citizens' posse. In November 1875 the grand jury indicted them for the murder of J. M. Yarbrough. A habeas corpus hearing took place, and bail was set at $4000 for each defendant. Dr. Barry and S. O. Berry had no trouble securing bail, but John Shelby remained in jail. In no hurry to have the case heard, the attorneys for the defendants managed to postpone the trial several times. This was not an unusual tactic used by lawyers. They felt that time distanced emotions swirling around the accused deeds of their clients. This strategy worked more times than not in early courts.[1]

For John Shelby, waiting in the small cramped jail cell, it must have seemed like an eternity, but on January 8, 1877, he escaped. In the uproar that followed, J. W. Murphy came forward to file an official complaint against the new sheriff, James Mastin, and the jail guard, J. T. McGinnis.[2] He stated that it was his belief that the sheriff helped those who wanted to see the grocer free from the county accommodations.

A warrant was issued for Erath's lawman, Sheriff Mastin, and for McGinnis, charging that they be brought before Justice of the Peace Wood to answer the charges. An examining trial took place. Murphy once again issued his accusations, stating that there was no evidence that the guard (McGinnis) put up any resistance, shot off his pistol, or raised any kind of alarm. Murphy stated that he lived close enough that he would have heard shouts coming from the jail.

During the cross-examination, Murphy stated that it was his job to supply food and water to the inmates. He admitted that the county court had condemned the jail. He also admitted that he did not witness the escape and that Sheriff Mastin frequented the jail at night to make sure all was well. Two prisoners, E. M. and James Monk, who chose not to escape, testified that a man came into the jail about midnight and told Shelby to get his things, as he was leaving. They stated that a few minutes later the guard McGinnis was brought and placed in the jail by a different man. McGinnis remained in the jail with them until early morning. After due consideration the court refused to go forward with the case, and the charges were dropped against the sheriff and his guard. Shelby disappeared and eventually the case was dropped against him, as the court could not go forward without the accused being there.

Dr. William Barry and S. O. Berry still faced a trial. With court only meeting a couple of times a year and with a couple of extensions, two years passed prior to a jury taking on this cause. The local townspeople crowded the court as both defendants were prominent citizens. Strong witnesses for both the prosecution and defense testified. Keeping order and the trial moving along was a challenge for District Judge J. R. Fleming. The jury did not take long to come back with an acquittal verdict for both men.[3]

According to District Clerk William Fooshee the visitors' gallery erupted in loud cheers for the defendants. Seems Stephenville supported these local citizens. Fooshee also related that Judge Fleming was incensed and showed it by levying fines against several celebrating observers.[4] No official record corroborated the events Fooshee related, but certainly the judge had the authority to admonish, even assess fines to rowdy gallery members—and he probably did.

Three Views to a Killing
The John Wesley Hardin Story

Among the most famous shootists from Texas' wild-west days was John Wesley Hardin. Scholarly works have devoted many pages to recreating and analyzing the life of this gunslinger. His first and only high profile trial for murder took place in Comanche, Texas, the scene where the Brown County deputy sheriff, Charles Webb, was gunned down. Sitting on the district court bench when Hardin's trial commenced was the Honorable James Richard Fleming of the Twelfth Judicial District.

For the researcher hoping to piece together what happened that fateful day in May 1874 when Webb died, difficulties arise, not just because of the passage of time, but also because the available information does not match up. What is unique to this story is that the main character, Hardin, chose to put down on paper his view of what happened. Although obviously slanted to his benefit, Hardin's account

John Wesley Hardin

was rare as few defendants accused of murder from that time wrote their thoughts down. Trial testimony from Hardin's appeal offered the state's view of it all, and into the mix came newspaper accounts, usually reported to the papers by "eyewitnesses" along with a bit of moralizing from the paper's editor. Accuracy never seemed to be the primary objective of these frontier newspapers, since misstatements were rarely corrected, leaving the readers with impressions not necessarily connected to what really happened.

The *Weatherford Exponent* in their October 13, 1877 issue reprinted an article that appeared in a British newspaper. Their imaginative, but not very believable, explanation of what happened in Comanche that fateful day stated—

> *Two years ago, Hardin, who was a religious fanatic, went into a saloon and, without the least provocation, shot and killed Sheriff Webber* [sic], *and then commenced an indiscriminate slaughter of men, women and children. This led to a general engagement between the whites and the Indians, which was finally put down by a regiment of Texas cavalry called the Rangers, but not till many lives had been sacrificed. During the battle Hardin escaped and has ever since been a terror to that region.*

Rather than trying to sort through the numerous accounts, three views to Webb's killing can be recounted. The first view encompassed newspaper reports, first to shed light on the "deadly" events that took place in Comanche, Texas. The *Dallas Weekly Herald* reprinted a story from The *Houston Telegraph* based on words of a citizen of Brown County. The reader of the *Herald* could not be sure if this "citizen" was in Comanche or simply telling what he heard from those who were there.

The news account began by calling what happened a cold-blooded murder that had been committed in front of a saloon on the public square of Comanche when Deputy Sheriff Charles M. Webb was killed by John Hardin, Budd Dixon or Dickson, and two others whose names were unknown. The murderers, according to the newspaper, were part of a band of cattle thieves, which had been operating in the area. The shooting was connected to these activities. The newspaper insisted that the deputy sheriff was murdered, because he was responsible for arresting three members of the gang earlier.

The killers rode into Comanche and laid in wait in a saloon for the deputy sheriff. As soon as he entered, the assassins started a quarrel with him. The killers moved into position, two in front of Webb and two to one side. According to the news account, the deputy retreated outside, but the outlaws followed, pairing off again and drawing their six-shooters. Seeing his peril, Webb drew first and fired quickly, but his shot went wild. When the smoke cleared, Webb fell mortally wounded.

The *Herald* stated that when the sheriff arrived on the scene, John Wesley Hardin handed over his pistol saying, "Take that and then take me, if you can." The sheriff left some of his men to guard Hardin, so he could disarm the other shooters who were quick to cooperate. Seeing his chance, Hardin mounted a horse and left under a hail of flying bullets from the gun of Henry Ware.[1]

The deputy sheriff, Charles Webb, was deemed by the newspaper as "a brave and honest man, and the people were not to brook his slaughter in silence and aw [sic]." Numerous newspapers reflected the rage and anger shown through the actions of the local citizens. The *Dallas Weekly Herald* reported, "Vigilance committees were organized, and sent in search of the desperadoes with instructions to shoot all who refused to surrender, and hang all who did submit."[2]

No idle threat, newspapers reported later that eleven members of the gang of thieves had been caught and executed. The *Indianapolis Sentinel* picked up the story and reported that Hardin's brother, Joseph Hardin [who was not present at the death of Webb], along with William and Thomas Dixon were taken by "an aroused populace." The mob waited until Sheriff Carnes was called away to apprehend two of Hardin's cohorts before carrying out the midnight executions—although the newspaper did not state this. Even though under guard with the Texas Rangers close by, the men were removed from the downtown area of Comanche and given scarce time to pray before the nooses were thrown over the limbs of a tree. [3]

Far from decrying vigilance committees' activities, which included the dispatching of any man caught and thought to be an associate of John Wesley Hardin, the newspapers gave tacit approval of the lynchings by printing that this was necessary for "people determined to clear the county of all desperadoes at once."[4] Evidence seems to indicate that no one was indicted for the deaths of the eleven plus men hung in the locals' rush to judgment.

The main object of these vigilante committees, John Wesley Hardin, evaded arrest, although he managed to stay in Comanche County for several days. After the death of his brother and several relatives, Hardin realized that emotions were not going to calm down enough for him to "turn himself in." He finally left the county, and a statewide and national manhunt was declared. The *New Orleans Daily Picayune* stated unequivocally that Hardin was arrested in Shreveport in early September 1874. The final sentence read, "There is no doubt about the identification."[5] It was not Hardin in the Shreveport Jail as he was in New Orleans at the time. No retraction was ever published in the *Picayune*.

Sensationalizing events was endemic for many newspapers, both small and large, in the nineteenth century. Fear of libel suits was not a consideration. Throwing in their "two cents worth" was not ill received by the readers. Moralizing or projecting outcomes was perfectly acceptable in that pre-litigious world. Defaming the character of those accused of crimes was acceptable even if it "tainted" the jury pool when the trials commenced.

The second view of Webb's killing can be gleaned from the court records connected to the trial of John Wesley Hardin, which took place in October 1877 after he was eventually captured in Florida. The trial file has long since disappeared from the district clerk's office. Fortunately, Hardin appealed the guilty verdict in his trial, and summaries of the major witnesses are included with the higher court's opinion confirming the ruling of the lower court.

The prosecution was led by District Attorney Silas Buck from Stephenville, County Attorney N. R. Lindsey and John D. Stephens from Comanche, along with S. P. Burnes from Brownwood. For the defense the lawyers were Judge S. H. Renick of Waco, J. A. Lipscomb from Brenham, Colonel Thomas Nugent of Stephenville, and Honorable W.S.J. Adams of Comanche. The *Weatherford Exponent* in their October 13, 1877 issue had this to say about the defendant—

> *In personal appearance, Hardin does not impress you as a desperado. He is of medium height, rather heavy build, and round shouldered-with a slight rolling swagger in his gait. He appeared in court dressed in a nice blue-gray suit, blue cravat, rings on his fingers, a mustache and goatee, and pomatum on his hair.*

The testimony summaries in the appellate record presented the prosecution's case.[6] The story of the events leading up to Webb's death centered around proving that a conspiracy was hatched at the Waldrup ranch located west of Comanche. According to William Cunningham, who stated under oath that he was there and that eight men, including John Wesley Hardin and his brother Joe, congregated at the ranch to spend the night in the middle of moving a herd of cattle from Brown to Comanche County. Cunningham stated that Mrs. Waldrup complained bitterly about the treatment she received at the hands of Deputy Sheriff Charles Webb when he came to the ranch two weeks previously to arrest her son. The witness went on to say that Joe Hardin assured Mrs. Waldrup that Webb would be "taken care of" when they had him in the right place.[7]

As for the actual events on the day of Webb's death, James Carnes, brother of the sheriff, was used as a witness, because he was in the Wright Saloon when the shooting took place. He stated that when Webb came into view, Hardin remarked, "There comes that d—d Brown County sheriff, now."

According to Carnes, Webb started to pass Hardin to enter the saloon. Hardin asked Webb if he was the sheriff of Brown County to which Webb replied he was the deputy sheriff. Hardin asked if Webb had papers for him. Webb's response was that he did not know to whom he was speaking. Hardin's reply was, "I am that d—d desperado, John Wesley Hardin, as people call me; now you know me." In the appellate opinion, Judge White stated that testimony showed that

Hardin added, "I am considered an outlaw, but I always carry the documents with me that will protect me." Judge White did not say which witnesses stated that they overheard this or if it was a part of the witness summaries given by the lower court.

James Carnes continued his testimony saying that Hardin next asked Webb what he was holding behind his back. Webb said it was a cigar and showed it. Hardin asked Webb if he had been making disparaging remarks about the Comanche sheriff not doing his duty. Webb denied it. Mr. Thurmond called Webb out to the street. Hardin stopped Webb from leaving, saying he was not through speaking to the lawman. When Webb turned toward Thurmond anyway, Hardin caught his arm. Webb backed away and then said, "No, G-d d—n you, I am not afraid of you." [8]

Webb drew his pistol and fired as soon as it was out of the scabbard. Hardin, James Taylor, and Dixon all fired at Webb. Hardin was in front of him, Taylor to the left, and Dixon to the right. Webb fell on the ground. Hardin exclaimed, "Shoot them every d—d one." At this point the witness ran for cover. Put into evidence, according to the appellate report, was that Hardin and Taylor mounted horses and left immediately but nothing was stated as to what happened between the shooting and Hardin's exit.

At 8PM on Saturday September 29, 1877, the jury retired after listening to eight hours of arguments from the counsels for both sides. They were out only two or three hours before returning a verdict of guilty but only for second-degree murder against John Wesley Hardin.[9]

One eyewitness had this to say about the bench—

> *Judge J. R. Fleming presided at the trial with marked ability, impartiality and firmness, and the charge of the court on the law was thorough and exhaustive, embracing some twenty-four sections.*[10]

Some questions beg answers concerning the appellate record. One could be that although two lawmen, Deputy Frank Wilson and Sheriff John Carnes, were present or came up shortly after the shots were fired, their testimony (if indeed they were called as witnesses) was not included in the summaries. Would not the word of lawmen present be deemed important to shed light on the events of that day? At the time of the trial Wilson had succeeded Carnes as sheriff of Comanche County, but John Carnes, the former sheriff, was still living in Comanche County. On the other hand, if the sheriff did not testify, it would not be put into record that Hardin turned his gun over to Carnes after the shooting. Hardin complained later that he was not able to get this bit of information into evidence, which might be an indication as to why Carnes did not testify.

The distinct bias shown toward the defendant in both the appellate record and in Appellate Judge White's written opinion while stating that Charles Webb was "universally known and characterized by the witnesses as a quiet, peaceable man, and a brave and efficient officer" was startling. Applying the law and rules of proper procedure to a lower court's ruling should be devoid of sentiment or at least should be written in a fair and impartial manner. The first line of the second paragraph of the appellate record stated, "Though yet a young man, the appellant, John Wesley Hardin, has succeeded in achieving a remarkable and widespread reputation for sanguinary deeds." It then went on to tell about how he and his gang terrorized communities. None of this had been proven in a court of law nor was apropos to the current case, yet was included in the "Prior History" of the case.[11]

Appellate Judge White called Dixon and Taylor "dastardly and inhuman assassins." He stated that Webb "was taken without provocation, in cold blood, with premeditation, and in pursuance of a diabolical conspiracy."[12] The question one might put to this, if the judge's statement be true, was why did the jury convict Hardin of only second-degree murder and not first-degree murder. Why was he given a prison sentence and not the noose? None of Hardin's confederates were still around to exact any type of post-trial retribution as evidenced by the fact the appellate record showed no defense witnesses, and Hardin stated he had no one to testify on his behalf, as they were all dead, scattered, or too scared to do so. More than one person proclaimed that the state did not prove the conspiracy theory; yet Judge White's remarks seemed to indicate he believed they did.

Did Hardin have enough evidence of reversible error to get his conviction overturned? Appellate Judge White wrote a lengthy opinion to all exceptions presented, citing cases to support his finding and dismissing those used by the defense to support their appeal. The court deflected even the technical errors, such as the fact that the indictment was faulty, as it did not state when or where the deceased died. What makes this especially interesting was that the Texas Court of Appeals had earned a reputation as "turning criminals loose on mere technicalities."[13] Could a man whose capture garnered the greatest reward ever offered of $4000 be allowed to slip through the judicial cracks? Certainly, it did not happen on Judge White's watch. Seemingly, Hardin's reputation and his past had caught up with him.

The third view of the death of Charles Webb came from the man convicted of the deputy's murder–John Wesley Hardin. Somewhere between his release from Huntsville after serving sixteen of the twenty-five years assigned by the jury in Comanche and being shot in the back in El Paso in 1895 by John Selman, Hardin wrote his life story. While some historians were skeptical that the manuscript was really the words of Hardin, because it was too polished and literate, others pointed out that Hardin received a good education through his Methodist minister father and managed to earn a law license shortly after leaving prison.[14]

Hardin had a different story to tell than the one published in the newspapers or the testimonies of the states' witnesses at his trial. May 26, 1874, was his twenty-first birthday, and Hardin made big plans to celebrate. Weeks ahead of time, he arranged to have a day of horse races at a track located a couple of miles from the town of Comanche.

On May 5th while waiting for the big racing event, Hardin joined his brother Joe in going to Brown County to retrieve some cattle. With evening coming before they could get the herd home, the decision was made to spend the night at Mrs. Waldrop's ranch. After supper Hardin heard about Charles Webb for the first time when Mrs. Waldrup told the gathering that the Brown County deputy sheriff had cursed and abused her when he showed up the week before to arrest her son Jim. Bill Cunningham at the trial implied a conspiracy was hatched that night, but Hardin denied it, saying that his brother Joe never made the statement about "getting Webb" at the proper time.

Hardin told about a large crowd attending the races and that all three of his horses won handily. He walked away with $3000 on his birthday. He was ready to celebrate even though several men warned him that Charles Webb had arrived from Brown County with the intention of murdering him and capturing Jim Taylor before the sun went down.

Showing his devil-may-care attitude, Hardin told his informants he hoped Webb would put it off until dark or altogether. Heading for town, Hardin and his companions went from saloon to saloon to celebrate using the outlaw's winnings to buy drinks for his friends. Hardin wrote that his companions started warning that he had been drinking too much and would not be able to protect himself if trouble brewed.

Hardin sent his younger brother Jeff to the stable to get a horse and buggy to go home and then invited everyone to Wright's Saloon for one last drink. Comanche Deputy Sheriff Frank Wilson arrived and asked Hardin to step outside with him. Wilson told Hardin he needed to go home. Hardin stated he was preparing to go. Wilson reminded him that it was a violation to carry a pistol. This statement put Hardin on guard. He told the deputy his pistol was behind the bar and then opened his coat, which did not reveal the pistol Hardin kept hidden under his vest. As they stood there, a stranger to Hardin came into view.

Hardin terminated his conversation with Wilson, saying he needed to settle up his bar bill. He told Jim Taylor he was ready to leave as soon as he got a cigar. As Hardin headed for the bar, he overheard Dave Carnes remark, "Here comes that damned Brown County sheriff." Hardin turned to see the same stranger he had seen earlier coming toward the saloon. He had two six-shooters and walked with his hand behind his back. At about five steps from Hardin, Webb stopped.

Hardin started the conversation by asking if Webb had papers for him. Webb said he did not know him. Hardin replied, "My name is John Wesley Hardin." Webb said he did not have papers. Not satisfied, Hardin kept up the questioning by asking if Webb had been making disparaging remarks about the Comanche County sheriff. Webb denied it and stated he knew of no one else who had.

At this point, according to Hardin's account, Dave Carnes stepped forward and took the time to introduce Hardin to the lawman. Hardin then asked Webb what he had behind his back. Webb showed he was holding a cigar. Hardin invited Webb to join them in a drink or another cigar. Webb accepted.

Hardin wrote that he turned to go through the north door of the saloon when Budd Dixon yelled, "Look out, Jack." Hardin turned back. Seeing Webb pulling his pistol, Hardin jumped to the side, pulled his concealed pistol, and fired. Webb's bullet grazed Hardin in the left side, but Hardin's shot to Webb was fatal, entering through the man's left cheek. Webb managed to get off a second shot as he fell against the wall, but it just went into the air.

Jim Taylor and Budd Dixon also shot at Webb to protect Hardin. Frank Wilson started to draw his pistol. Hardin covered him and warned the lawman to hold up his hands. He did. Hardin was told later that the plan was for several men to rush up after Webb had shot Hardin in order to arrest Taylor. Instead, according to Hardin's account, the crowd realized that Webb was the one shot, and they ran to the square yelling, "Hardin's killed Webb. Let's hang him!"

Sheriff John Carnes arrived with a shotgun asking who had done "this work." Hardin admitted he had and was willing to surrender if Carnes would protect him from the mob. To show his good faith, Hardin handed over his gun.

At least ten men ran around from the corner of a building and fired on Hardin and Taylor. Carnes yelled at them to disperse, but he was overpowered and disarmed. Sizing up the situation, Hardin and Taylor left on horses hitched nearby. Pulling out a knife, Hardin cut the hitching rope and leaped into the saddle almost simultaneously. Hardin's position was that he only left because the law had no control over the milling mob. Some truth can be attributed to Hardin's assessment. Within a few days his brother Joe and ten others believed to be associated with Hardin were summarily hanged without benefit of a trial.

Hardin wrote about being fearful that the Texas Rangers would not be able to protect him from being lynched when he was taken back to Comanche for trial. Knowing what happened to his kin lent credence to that.

Hardin also wrote about Judge J. R. Fleming. He adamantly believed that the district judge should have recused himself from the trial. Hardin wrote that he was told that the judge had given counsel to Frank Wilson prior to the events that led to Webb's death. He also blamed the judge for not shifting the trial to another county on a change of venue.

From Hardin's point of view, he should have been acquitted, since Webb drew his pistol first. Hardin felt the state had failed to prove any conspiracy on his part, because if they had, he would have been convicted of first-degree murder and hung.

Only through the efforts of Hardin's lawyers to break down the testimony of the states' witnesses were they able to save the life of their client. Doubt was thrown on Cunningham's testimony on the conspiracy and more than one witness admitted that Webb drew his gun first.

Hardin presented no witnesses for his defense. He believed the mob had either killed all who might be willing to testify or ran them out of the county. As the rules set out by the state legislature on trial procedure prevented a defendant charged with murder to testify on his own behalf, Hardin was effectively kept silent.[15]

Hardin presented his case well in his autobiography but does not explain everything about the day Webb died. Why did Hardin keep stalling his exit from town? Was he anticipating trouble or was he spoiling for a fight with Webb? Did he pretend to be getting drunk so someone would lead Webb to believe Hardin was incapacitated? It does not seem very believable that Hardin turned his back on someone he had been told was after his blood. Was his conversation with Webb really meant to provoke Webb into attacking first? Was Hardin the victim or did he just want to present himself in that light?

Confirmed by the Texas Court of Appeals, Hardin's verdict sent him to Huntsville for a term of twenty-five years. The *Conduct Ledger* for Huntsville showed that Hardin did not take to the striped life too well. He planned escapes and got several lashings for his trouble, along with stints in the "dark cell."

John Wesley Hardin emerged from prison in 1894 with a full pardon from the governor and a determination to turn his life around. Events and his volatile nature dictated otherwise. He was shot in the back in a saloon in El Paso less than two years after his release. Thus ended the life of a notorious shootist who spent time in prison but probably more for his reputation of past deeds than for the killing that took place in Comanche, Texas. Years later, one of the chief prosecutors in Hardin's trial, N. R. Lindsey, admitted that he did not think Hardin intended to kill Webb that long ago day but simply wanted to scare him.[16]

Bad Luck Horse Thieves
The C. E. Aiken & A. B. James Story

Twenty-year-old Perry Sikes had taken a trip west of Erath County. He was on his way home to southeastern Hood County, August 21, 1879, when his party met up with two men. It was about three miles east of Stephenville, and the men were driving thirteen head of horses. Sikes was simply annoyed at first, because the horses surrounded his wagon, causing him to lose time stopping to let them pass.

Suddenly, something about the herd caught Sike's eye. It was a familiar brand "HAMP" on one of the horses. Then he spied one with "JS" on it. The two cowboys quickly moved the herd, leaving Perry to ponder. He was pretty sure the brands he saw were for horses belonging to his brother-in-law, J. H. Cosper, who had received them as a gift from his father-in-law, John Sikes.

Young Sikes needed to be sure before he did anything. He unhitched one of the horses from his wagon, saddled up and took off in the direction of the retreating wranglers. Sikes circled around to make it appear as if he were traveling east toward the herd of horses driven by the two men he did not know. Sikes greeted the two men and commented on what fine horses they had. He recognized three geldings he was sure belonged to his brother-in-law. Striking up a conversation, Sikes rode along with the men. He asked where they had obtained the horses. The men stated they had received them from James Sharp in northwestern Tarrant County. Sikes made a friendly offer to trade for one of the horses once they reached Stephenville, hoping to get the cowboys to stop there.

Sikes moved on ahead, telling the men he would see them at the courthouse square later. He then headed for the sheriff's office to swear out a complaint against the two suspected horse thieves. Sikes was certain the horses in their care were stolen. Sheriff R. T. Long had already seen the horses milling around the courthouse square when the complaint was filed. With a signed warrant, the sheriff found C. E.

Aiken in a store purchasing bacon while A. B. James was outside with the horses. The sheriff arrested both men. He told a deputy to take the stolen horses to a pasture east of town until everything could be sorted out.

Perry Sikes, satisfied the thieves had been arrested, took off for his father's place to let them know that he had been passed on the road by men who had his brother-in-law's horses in their possession. J. H. Cosper went back to Stephenville with Sikes to positively identify his stolen property. Cosper informed the sheriff that because the horses ranged over a wide territory, he had not seen them for twelve days. He also said that he had never met the men who were arrested for stealing.

District Attorney Silas Buck moved quickly. After obtaining two indictments each against C. E. Aiken and A. B. James, he acted rapidly to expedite the case to go to trial. Judge Nugent was scheduled to hold a session of the district court in Erath County the following week. So a few days after being arrested, C. E. Aiken was tried. His court-appointed attorneys barely had time to pull together a defense, and the only witnesses they brought in were Aiken's brother J. S. and James' brother Newt along with a former hired hand named Moody from their ranch in McCulloch County.

The defense did not try to dispute whether or not the horses were stolen, only that the defendants were not the ones who had taken them. Their story was the same one they had told Sikes when he rode with them—that they had obtained the horses through a trade with James Sharp. They used their witnesses to prove that they owned some horses that could have been used in a trade, but the witness attachments that went out for James Sharp and John Fuller, a supposed witness to the horse trade, were returned without being served. James Sharp never attended court in Erath, since he ended up with his own legal problems in Hood County for stealing cattle.

M. J. Aiken swore under oath that he and his brother C. E. moved from Denton to McCulloch County in 1874. He stated that they moved several horses with them and that C. E. had gone back to Denton in May to work for the summer. Newt James added that when C. E. left Denton he had a least six horses with him.

Being caught with stolen horses held sway with the jury who convicted C. E. Aiken, attaching a five-year sentence for him to serve. Through his lawyers, Aiken immediately filed for a new trial, stating that the court did not allow enough time for defense witnesses to be found. Judge Nugent ordered a new trial for Aiken to be held in December 1879. He ordered James and Aiken to be sent to the Comanche County Jail for safekeeping.[1]

At one point Aiken asked for a continuance, still hoping for testimony from James Sharp, but in his amended motion he stated that there was no bill of sale for the horses as it was an oral deal. This admission was tantamount to a confession as far as the district attorney was concerned. If C. E. Aiken had known what was in store for him, he probably would have taken the five-year sentence. Not only was he convicted a second time, but the new jury also doubled the sentence to ten years instead of five. His appeal to the Texas Court of Appeals warranted only a cursory perusal before the conviction was upheld.[2]

A. B. James received the same treatment when he, too, ended up with a ten-year conviction, also in December 1879. The district attorney went for another conviction for the additional indictments, only to be met with some resistance when juries in December 1879 and April 1880 could not agree, causing mistrials. Finally, the district attorney gave up and retired the charges. By then the first convictions had been upheld by the Court of Appeals.[3]

Bad luck continued to stalk C. E. Aiken when he entered Huntsville State Penitentiary June 17, 1880. Little more than two years later he fell from Row 5, the East Build-

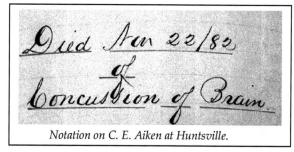
Notation on C. E. Aiken at Huntsville.

ing, suffering a concussion. He died in the prison infirmary November 22, 1882. No notation was made as to whether or not this fall was self-inflicted, an accident, or deliberate on the part of someone wishing him great harm.[4]

A. B. James, on the other hand, had a bit more luck. He entered Huntsville June 6, 1880. He was transferred to Rusk State Penitentiary January 18, 1881. He managed to get away from a guard only ten days later while working on a Texas & Pacific Railroad gang. He was not recaptured.[5]

Stock theft, especially horses, still alarmed and angered the frontier settlers. While vigilante groups occasionally dealt out their own brand of justice, more and more citizens turned to the courts to handle the problem by the 1880s. Strict rules governed the transfer and sale of livestock. Marks and brands had to be written down and filed. Between 1856 and 1875 sixteen defendants were convicted of livestock theft, while fifty men were sent to the penitentiary between 1876 and 1885 in Erath County.

What's Yours Is Mine
The Jasper Reynolds Story

When farmer John Whisenant and his wife left their homestead along Resley Creek in Erath County on a Saturday in October 1879 to visit his father, he did not anticipate that later that evening his home would be invaded. After a full day of visiting and traveling, the Whisenants returned to find thieves had made off with a lot of personal clothing. On Monday Whisenant set out to try to find anyone who might have seen any strangers in the area the previous weekend.

Whisenant's closest neighbor was Noah Whisenhunt. Whisenant had traveled past his neighbor's house on the way to his father's place the previous Saturday. He noticed then that some of Whisenhunt's relatives were visiting again, including Jasper and Annie Reynolds, Jasper's brother William, along with Drew Griffin and his wife Mary. They were mostly camping out close to the main farmhouse.

The Reynolds and Griffins were wandering families who rarely stayed long at any one location. They lived out of their wagons, moving from place to place. They had visited Erath County several times previously, staying from one to four weeks at a time before pushing on to another location. They called Kimble County their home. Even though Jasper's parents lived in Erath, Reynolds preferred to stay with his brother-in-law, Noah Whisenhunt, when visiting the area. John Whisenant spoke briefly to Reynolds as he returned on Saturday.

Whisenant went back on Monday to speak to Whisenhunt but only found Reynolds who was friendly, voicing sorrow over the neighbor's stolen goods. He stated he had no knowledge of what might have happened. After canvassing the neighbors, Whisenant came up empty-handed as no one noticed any unusual activity.

On Tuesday the Reynolds and Griffin families loaded their wagons and headed out of Erath County. They traveled twelve miles east the first day and camped beside the Bosque River the second night. That evening they were joined by George Upshaw (who would have his own troubles with the law in Erath County a year later though his case was dismissed due to the lack of credible evidence) and Marion Garland, neighbors from Kimble County. Drew Griffin left for a period of time that evening. When he came back he was carrying items wrapped in an oilcloth.

Jasper Reynolds was approached by Griffin to carry some of the load from his wagon. Reynolds agreed to the transfer. The next morning they headed into Hood County.

Meanwhile, John Whisenant formed a firm belief that the two men who had just left with their families were involved in the robbery of his place. Concerned they would get away, he traveled to see Justice of the Peace J. D. St. Clair who lived on Green's Creek. Warrant in hand, Whisenant turned to Constable Robert St. Clair to form a posse. The makeup of that posse was mostly John's relatives, including Sam and Joe Whisenant, as well as Felix Massie. The trail of the slow-moving wagons was easy to pick up and follow.

The posse quickly overtook the Reynolds and Griffins at Hemming's Mill in Hood County. They chose to move past the parked wagons and approach them from the east, the direction that the wagons were heading before they stopped. The horses and mules were unhitched but still in place. No women or children were visible. The members of the posse guessed that the women were probably inside the wagons.

Standing by his wagon was Drew Griffin. He made little resistance when the posse rode up. William Reynolds was also taken into custody. Lulled into believing that Griffin was resigned to being arrested, Constable St. Clair and his men turned to finding Jasper Reynolds. Griffin indicated that he was inside the mill. The men entered and ordered the young man to give up. Reynolds sprinted for the back door.

A voice called, "Stop or we'll shoot!"

The chilling words hit home. Jasper halted in mid-stride. Turning, he stared at several shotguns leveled in his direction.

During the excitement of stopping Reynolds from fleeing, the posse did not notice that Drew Griffin slipped away. The posse made a quick search of the area but found no clues as to the direction he took. While several worked on this futile effort, St. Clair turned his attention back to carrying out the warrant he had in his possession.

He told the women and children to vacate the wagons. A quick search in Jasper Reynolds' wagon turned up two stolen coats.

Satisfied they had identified the culprit, the posse discontinued their search for Drew Griffin. The wagons were turned and headed back to Erath County. They made their way to the home of Justice of the Peace St. Clair where a more thorough search was made. Not only were the articles lost by the Whisenants found in the Reynolds' wagon but also some items lost by a neighbor J. B. Walden.[1]

Taken to Stephenville and placed in the Erath County Jail were Jasper Reynolds (age 20), Annie Reynolds, his wife (age 17), William Reynolds (age 15), and Mary Griffin (age 30). Where Mary's three children were housed was not noted in the record.[2]

After interviewing the women and William Reynolds along with other witnesses, the grand jury brought back three indictments against Jasper Reynolds and Drew Griffin (in absentia). While the Sheriff's Docket noted that the women and William were not indicted, it simply meant that the grand jury chose not to take them to trial. They were released from jail on November 5, 1879. While Annie Reynolds went to live with her father-in-law, J. M. Reynolds of Erath County, Mary Griffin did not stick around for long after she testified in Jasper Reynolds' first trial, as she was not called for the second one. Did she know where to find her husband and left to join him? In any case he was never captured.

Wasting no time, District Attorney S. C. Buck moved quickly from indictment in late October to trial in late November. Court-appointed attorneys Kennedy and Young tried to slow down the process, but Judge Nugent, new to the bench, was in no mood to approve any continuances even though major defense witnesses, George Upshaw and Marion Garland, were yet to be served subpoenas.

While the state rested most of its case on finding the missing and stolen items in Jasper Reynold's wagon, the defense tried to throw some doubt by placing witnesses on the stand who implicated the missing Drew Griffin as being the actual thief who duped an unknowing Reynolds into carrying stolen goods. Using Judge Nugent's instructions, the jury was unimpressed with the defense's side. Jasper Reynolds was found guilty of burglary and sentenced to five years of hard labor. The defense filed for a new trial. Turned down, they appealed the case.[3]

The absence of key defense witnesses was not deemed enough to overturn the verdict. The appellate judges took exception to the lower court judge's "Charge of the Court" to the jury. The opinion stated the following—

> *It may often happen that the testimony in defense has been fabricated, and that so inartistically as to bear upon its face an air of improbability or actual untruth; but even then the court is not relieved from the duty of considering it in framing his charge, as it is the right of the defendant to have its truth or falsity determined by the jury and not by the court.*[4]

The opinion went on to state that the defense's testimony supported the case that the burglary was perpetrated by another party and that the lower court failed in its instructions to allow the jury the opportunity to decide if they believed this testimony, which might have rendered an acquittal. The appellate court overturned the verdict and remanded the case back. This meant that the district attorney had to retry the case if he wanted to pursue it.

While waiting for the Court of Appeals to rule on the first case, District Attorney Buck went ahead with the second trial before Judge Nugent against Jasper Reynolds for the theft of additional property found in his wagon. This was the property belonging to the Waldens. The only defense witness used in this trial was Jasper's brother William. The other family members had no credible information about this property or even when it might have been stolen. The jury found Reynolds guilty and upped the punishment to seven years. The appellate court took a different view of this case because of the lack of witnesses to promote the idea that Drew Griffin might have taken this property as well. The verdict of the lower court was upheld.[5]

With this conviction the district attorney chose to dismiss the first case that had been overturned. Jasper Reynolds entered Huntsville June 4, 1880, at the age of twenty-one. He served five years–the length of his first conviction. The *Conduct Ledger* showed that Reynolds was disciplined only one time and was transferred to Rusk Penitentiary in 1883. His job assignment was to work on the Texas Central Railroad. He was discharged September 3, 1884 and was given $11.15 upon his release.[6]

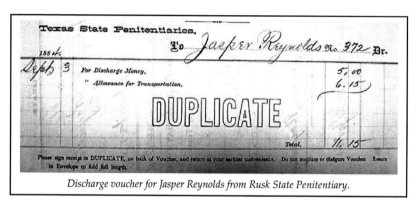
Discharge voucher for Jasper Reynolds from Rusk State Penitentiary.

What is interesting about Jasper's story is that it reflects the prevailing public attitude toward theft. Today some might agree that seven years is a long time to serve in prison for items valued at around $50 even adjusted for inflation.

Reynold's case was more the norm than an anomaly in Erath County. J. R. Bell was given two years for stealing shirt studs and five years for taking a watch in 1873. C. M. Davidson stole $2.00. He was fined $100 and assigned three months in the county jail on top of the time already served while waiting for trial. Pleading guilty only lessened the time to be served a small amount. Marion Perkens and Prior Carnes were caught stealing. Perkens pleaded guilty and earned two years prison time. His partner Carnes went to trial and ended up with three and a half years.[7]

Early settlers in Texas took a dim view of thievery. Taking a horse earned a noose, mostly without the benefit of legal process. Given the opportunity though, juries were tough on those whose sticky fingers took items not their own no matter how small in value.

Revenge
The Morg McInturf Story

At the end of another long day Robert Hamilton, age thirty-six, sank gratefully onto a chair next to the blazing fireplace. As dusk deepened, the farmer pulled off his boots, warming up on that cold December day in 1878. His teenage children, Alice and Jim, heard whistling coming from outside. The dogs started barking, and Alice heard a voice call out "Be gone." When a greeting was heard, Hamilton hastily stood up and went to the door, leaving his shoes behind even though the temperature was showing signs of the sleet and snow that would fall later in the night.

Hamilton looked at his wife, Elizabeth, of over fifteen years. They had been through so much together, as he tried to carve out a good existence in the frontier county of Erath. She was pregnant with their third child. They had settled on their farm a little over a year previously after migrating from Denton County following the Civil War.

Unconcerned with who might be outside, Hamilton did not object when Jim and Alice followed him to the door. Hospitality was an ingrained quality in families living on the frontier. Passing strangers were often offered a meal and even a place to spend the night. Outside, Robert found a lone man astride a pony. He wore a Yankee blue army overcoat, a white hat, and a wool nubia (scarf) around his neck, which partially hid his face. Hamilton walked over toward the visitor. Alice stayed by his side while Jim waited in the doorway closer to the warmth of the fireplace. Though the evening had darkened, the shifting clouds parted occasionally to show a bright moon, enough that Alice recognized the rider as someone who had occasionally worked for them but said nothing about knowing who it was.

"Haloo," called the visitor in a gravelly voice. After a return greeting, he continued, "I suppose you are Mr. Hamilton. Do you know if Mr. Payne's corn has been sold?"

"It has," Hamilton replied.

"I'm needing thirty or forty bushels of corn."

"Mr. Chambliss has that much or more to sell. Why don't you get down and spend the night?"

"No, I need to get on. I'm new in the neighborhood. Been working for Mr. Bass."

The visitor paused. He fumbled a bit nervously inside his coat. "Say, do you know where a man named Thomas or Thompson lives around here?"

Hamilton raised his arm to point down the road. At the same time, the visitor pulled out a pistol from his jacket. Alice spotted the firearm when the moon glinted off the metal. She shouted, "Oh, Pa. Morg will shoot ya!"

The visitor laid the pistol across his left arm, taking aim. Without another word, the man fired. Hamilton clutched his chest, calling out, "Don't shoot me anymore, Morg. I am a dead man." The flash of the ignited powder ever so briefly lit up the man's face, confirming to the Hamilton siblings the identity of the intruder.

"Good day, sir," called the visitor no longer using the gravelly voice. He rode off rapidly. Hamilton staggered back, as his two children rushed to help him back into the house. Shutting the door, Hamilton stayed close as if listening. Then he called out through a crack, "Who-ee, who-ee, who-ee."

Turning, Robert asked his wife to check his wound. After she affirmed that the bullet had exited out his back. He allowed her to ease him down.

"Who did this?" asked Mrs. Hamilton.

"Morg McInturf and them," gasped Hamilton.

"I'm going for help," called Jim as he headed for the door.
Hamilton turned to his wife, "I am a dead man, but thank God I died innocent." He closed his eyes and said no more, dying before his son returned.

The next day Jim Hamilton left his bereaved family to get the law. On the ground he spied a saddle blanket. He recognized it immediately as being one he had seen Morg McInturf use in the past. In fact, he had pulled threads out of it, which was still noticeable. Jim picked up the blanket, knowing it would be important to the case. He did not count on it taking so long to bring Morg in to answer the charge of killing his father.[1]

Five years passed before Morg McInturf was arrested in Van Zandt County by Sheriff W. D. Thompson and then turned over to Erath County Sheriff J. C. Gilbreath on April 14, 1884. The delay came from the fact that the first indictment called for the arrest of Morg "McIntosh" (rather than McInturf) for Hamilton's murder. Once the error was spotted, the warrant was carried out.

McInturf planned a jailbreak almost from the beginning of his stay in the county accommodations (or Gilbreath's Hotel as locals like to call it). McInturf stood by the door to the cage day after day and studied the key used by the guard to unlock the door. Only a few of the prisoners were aware of his plans that included shaping a key from lead, using his memory of the outline of the real key. McInturf used the tin from an oyster can to make a handle for the "key," and tacks out of his boots to rivet the two together.

McInturf's escape was short-lived when he stopped to beg a meal from a farmer who lived north of Stephenville. While the unarmed farmer wanted to try to nab McInturf on his own, his wife warned him off from doing it. As soon as McInturf left, Jack Wells headed over to get Ed Whitacre. Together they overtook McInturf near the Shelby schoolhouse and took him back to Stephenville. Both refused the reward offered.

A bit of a showman, McInturf seemed to relish being in the spotlight as the mastermind of the jailbreak. He even agreed to re-enact how he managed to do it for some local notables, which included showing how he made the key by making a new one. When asked why he did it, Morg replied that he was accustomed to an active life, and it was necessary for him to liberate

> **He Unlocked it With His Little Key.**
>
> In presence of a large number of gentlemen Morg McInturf, last Tuesday, showed how he managed to unlock the jail door. He made a new key without having any model to go by under the supervision of the officers, just to show them that he could make one, and with it unlocked the jail door, in the presence of the undersigned. The key was made of lead and tin, and showed that McInturf was no slouch of a workman.
>
> Article from _the Stephenville Empire_, July 5, 1884

himself. Morg's reward for this bit of entertainment was to find himself taken to the Comanche Jail, a much stronger edifice. He made no attempt to escape from it.[2]

Defendant Morg McInturf hired very able defense lawyers: Kealy & Kealy; Neill & Young; and J. P. Groome. Only Neill & Young were local to Stephenville. One wonders how McInturf managed to hire such able attorneys when he represented himself as a laborer when he first met the Hamilton family a couple of months before the shooting. Perhaps the fact McInturf was also under indictment for stock theft was a clue to his real source of income. The defense strategy was to bring in witnesses who swore that McInturf was seen by them on the evening of the event in a place far distant from the murder scene. All of these witnesses were careful to state that when they saw McInturf he was riding a "flea-bitten mare," indicating that he did not own a pony as described by the Hamilton children.

The defense also tried to introduce the idea that Hamilton was executed by descendants of men murdered during the Civil War by a regiment in Denton led by Colonel James Boling. They wanted to show that Hamilton was a part of this group, even though Hamilton's wife stated that her husband was not a part of Boling's regiment. The defense pointed out through Mrs. Hamilton's testimony that the Hamiltons had to move constantly, at least seven times, after the Civil War was over—an indication of a man on the run. Judge Nugent disallowed any testimony pointing to unknown assassins as no concrete evidence was introduced to point in that direction.

Using the records of the district clerk, the prosecution established a motive for the murder. In early December 1878, Morg Mackintuff [sic] was indicted for theft of a mare in Erath County. During grand jury testimony, M. E. Ringer of Eastland County indicated that Robert Hamilton could give incriminating evidence against McInturf and that Hamilton had confiscated a red bell from one of the stolen mares he had seen in Morg's possession. When Hamilton was called as a witness, he traveled to Stephenville to give testimony against McInturf. When Robert got back home, he shared with his wife his concern that McInturf might go after him for turning State's witness. A few days later Hamilton was dead.

The jury brought back a guilty verdict as to Robert Hamilton's death against Morg McInturf in April 1885, assessing life in prison on a first-degree murder verdict. The defense attorneys filed several "Bills of Exception and Errors." Judge Nugent allowed most of them but refused to allow the defendant to have a new trial.[3]

Interestingly, the defense used only one major point on which to hang their hopes of overturning the verdict of the lower court. The law had been changed recently to allow for a jury to assign a life sentence for first-degree murder. Prior, the punishment assigned would have been death with no other options. The defense argued that since the murder took place before the law was changed, the jury erred in assigning life in prison. That was a major gamble. If the Court of Appeals agreed and remanded the case back, a second guilty verdict would result in execution. The appeals court ruled that since the assignment of life was considered a lesser punishment, it could be used. So they upheld and confirmed the lower court's ruling.[4]

Morg McInturf was taken to Huntsville Penitentiary March 18, 1886, but was later transferred to Rusk some time the same year. When he arrived, McInturf was 31 years old, 5'9" and 125 pounds. On January 21, 1892, he managed to elude his guards long enough to escape, using his small size to disappear into the sewer located in the furnace yard.[5]

Murder Near Rat Row
The Harry Barrett Story

A local carpenter in Stephenville, Harry Barrett stood 5'7" and weighed 135 pounds. He kept to himself but did enjoy a nip or two at the local saloons. The Whitney Saloon was one of his regular hangouts on days he was not employed to build or to help renovate existing businesses or houses in his adopted hometown.

A. L. Francis, 6'4" and 225 pounds, had been in Stephenville only a few months. He hung around downtown looking for odd jobs, and he was a familiar face in and out of the saloons as well.

Both men, Barrett and Francis, had already had their troubles with the law. Barrett had been indicted for assault with the intent to kill Thomas Hayden in Erath County in November 1878. Out on bail, he was still awaiting his trial. Francis was an ex-convict who had twice served time at Huntsville. He was convicted at Fort Griffin (Shackelford County) for theft in 1873 and for assault with the intent to murder, an incident that took place in Bexar County in 1875.

With obvious volatile tempers, the two men became verbally intertwined on the morning of May 1, 1879. Affable and outgoing for the most part, Francis was already in the Whitney Saloon when Harry Barrett arrived. The saloon was located on the northeast corner of the courthouse square and faced south on Washington Street. It had three inset front doors with separate screens located approximately three feet from the doors. One additional opening was located on the side facing Graham Street.

Francis was already drinking with a couple of friends at the bar when Barrett arrived through the side-door and walked over. He ended up standing next to Francis who had his elbow on the counter while talking to another patron.

In a loud voice and with his back to Barrett, Francis asked, "Do you know this miserable carpenter Harry Barrett? He is hell on the charge especially when he gets hold of a poor widow."

Taken aback, since he had just arrived, Barrett reacted angrily to what he believed to be a blatant insult. Realizing this, Francis quickly tried to defuse the situation by telling Barrett that he was only joking. He then apologized and offered to buy Barrett a drink. A few minutes later Francis invited Barrett to throw some dice in a friendly game for drinks. Far from over, this was just the beginning of an entire day of intermittent confrontations between the not entirely sober men.

The bartender later testified that the two seemed to have overcome the earlier tensions. After Francis left, R. L. Whitney, the proprietor, told Barrett to "go on" and not to get into trouble since he had been drinking.

Whitney also stated that he saw Barrett head over to the hotel. He did not name the hotel, but it was probably the Stephenville House, located on the northwest side of the square and owned by Phebe Haws. When Harry Barrett was later indicted for murder, Phebe came forward to help secure legal representation for him. One has to wonder what her interest in this single carpenter might have been.

Harry Barrett arrived back at the Whitney Saloon about an hour later. He was still fuming about Francis' remarks from earlier. He told Whitney that he had not forgiven the insult. Whitney told him to go sleep it off. So, Barrett went over to the Rat Row Saloon—so called after the nickname locals had given to Washington Street after it left the square toward the east.

When Francis left the Whitney Saloon that morning after the incident with Barrett, he had gone down to Benche's Blacksmith Shop. J. H. Woodward was sitting there having a horse shod. He watched Francis retrieve a guitar. Francis told the group gathered in the shop that he was going to play music (a somewhat ironic activity since he had been drinking) for the Baptist Church picnic.

The two men—Barrett and Francis—met up on the street several times during the afternoon. The tension between the two escalated with each verbal exchange. Several of the confrontations took place in front of George Langsdale's butcher shop. At one point Francis talked Barrett into throwing dice again. Barrett won. Taking his winnings, Barrett got up to leave. Francis begged him to continue in order to have a chance to win back the money lost.

The dialogue escalated with both men raising their voices. When Barrett would not guarantee a rematch, Francis started asking what

Barrett had against him. Barrett told Francis to go away. When Francis would not leave, Barrett offered to fight him. In reply Francis stated that he did not want a fuss and besides he was not armed with even a knife. Barrett's reply was for Francis to go away and get armed. Francis kept saying he was not going to do that.

The two men separated, but before long Francis was back insisting on asking Barrett once again what he had against him.

Barrett finally retorted, "I have got this against you. You are a God-damned son-of-a-bitch!"

Francis yelled, "This is more than I can take!" He raised his hands in a threatening manner. He caught Barrett by the arms near his shoulders. Francis forced Barrett, the smaller man, backwards toward the Whitney Saloon with enough force to push the screens open.

J. D. Parnell, owner of a blacksmith shop, was standing nearby. He yelled at both men to quit their fighting. At this point Francis relaxed his hold on Barrett. He threw back his hands and turned to face Parnell, saying, "I will. I will do as you say, Uncle Jim. I have nothing against him and don't want to fight."

Once Barrett had his arms free, he backed away, reaching into his pocket. He pulled out a pistol. Without saying another word, he shot Francis who was not looking at him at the time. Barrett watched as Francis crumpled to the floor; then Harry turned and announced that he had done it in self-defense. Barrett walked over to the bar and asked Whitney if he would hide the gun. The saloonkeeper declined. In short order Harry Barrett was arrested and later indicted for the murder of A. L. Francis by a grand jury in August 1879.[1]

The case was heard in Judge Nugent's district court. Both sides had a lengthy list of witnesses. In the end Barrett was found guilty of murder and given sixty years in December 1879. Barrett's attorneys appealed the case. They appealed mostly on technicalities and whether or not they were allowed to fully explore self-defense as an alternative finding instead of murder. The Court of Appeals affirmed the district court's ruling.[2]

Harry Barrett arrived at Huntsville on June 17, 1880. He was transferred to Rusk Penitentiary on January 7, 1883. He received punishment for carelessness in April of 1884 and for cutting another convict with a knife in November 1885.³

Barrett was not without friends on the outside. E. W. Bush, an attorney from Rusk, Texas, went to work almost immediately to try to obtain a pardon from Governor John Ireland. The first application reached the governor's desk in 1885. He did not act on it except to tell Bush that he needed to hear from the citizens of Erath County in order to consider executive clemency. Undaunted, Bush set about getting a petition circulated and signed. Many prominent citizens came forward. A summation of the case was given with the petition but written in a way to make the deceased Francis appear to be "an overbearing, violent and dangerous man, very quarrelsome and nearly always under the influence of intoxicating liquors" when alive. The presiding judge, T. L. Nugent, signed the petition. Interestingly, one letter supporting Barrett's pardon came from Jesse Dowdy, the son-in-law of Phebe Haws. So why did not Phebe just write the letter? The answer may be found in the fact that females could neither vote nor sit on a jury. Signing a petition would carry no weight in the male-dominated society.⁴

More important to Barrett's fate was the letter from Silas Buck who was the district attorney during Barrett's trial. The former prosecutor's letter was impassioned in his opposition to giving Barrett a pardon.

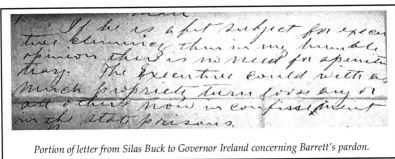

Portion of letter from Silas Buck to Governor Ireland concerning Barrett's pardon.

Buck stated that it was his duty to stand up for law and justice. Buck's letter was effective in slowing down the process. Governor Ireland backed away from giving amnesty.⁵

A full pardon was finally issued to Barrett on September 25, 1889, from Governor L. S. Ross "for reasons on file." It was noted that the pardon was recommended by District Judge C. K. Bell and District Attorney Leno Estes.[6] Did they feel that sixty years was too long for what happened on May 1, 1879?   Perhaps!

A Traveling Murder Case
The David Kemp Story

When F. A. Smith went into Hamilton with W. L. Locklin on Monday, May 2, 1881, the beautiful weather belied the deadly turn of events that neither could have predicted. Smith worked for Locklin They were in town to pick up some supplies needed on the farm. Arriving from the north, they parked the wagon next to Cropper's Hardware Store and commenced to making their rounds to the downtown merchants who surrounded the courthouse square. Finishing up, they started back. Smith announced he would retrieve the wagon, so they could load up the supplies and head home.

As he passed by, Smith paid little attention to Dan Bogan and David Kemp who had their horses tied to the hitchrack in front of Cropper's until he untied the wagon to drive it across the courthouse square. Twenty-nine years old, big and brawny, Smith lived his life with little fear of other men.

As he edged the wagon forward, Smith soon realized that he was blocked from entering the square. Horses were hitched to his right and a post was on his left, which did not leave enough room for the wagon to pass. Obviously, nothing could be done about the post, so Smith called out to no one in particular, "Could someone move those horses?"

Close by, twenty-one-year-old Dan Bogan and nineteen-year-old David Kemp were in the middle of their own drama. Arriving in town that morning, Kemp found himself following Bogan around. The older man seemed bent on the idea of getting knee-walking drunk before mid-day. Later, Kemp found Bogan in front of Cropper's Hardware Store, proclaiming in a loud voice that he could beat up any man in the town of Hamilton.

Kemp, holding the reins and leading Bogan's horse, urged his companion to mount up so that they could leave town. Bogan ignored Kemp and continued to wander up and down the sidewalk between Cropper's and Dr. Perry's Drugstore, challenging the universe with colorful expletives.

When Smith asked that the horses be moved, Bogan decided he had a target on which to focus his inebriated anger. Instead of simply doing what was asked, Dan Bogan stomped over toward Smith yelling, "Go to hell!"

Impatient and caught off guard, Smith yelled back, "You can go there yourself!"

Arriving at the wagon, Bogan replied, "If you'll get off that wagon, I'll whip you, you son-of-a-bitch!"

Bogan's friend, David Kemp, remained on his horse. He made no move at first to interfere. Neither did merchant W. T. Cropper who observed all the interactions. Another business owner, Thomas Emmett, seeing that the confrontation was escalating, walked over to where the two men were shouting profanities at each other.

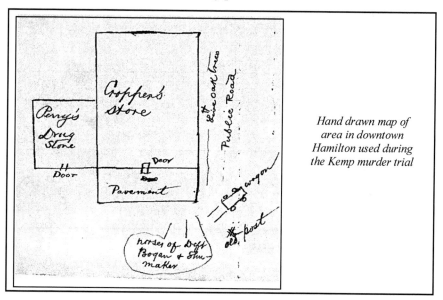

Hand drawn map of area in downtown Hamilton used during the Kemp murder trial

When Smith stayed seated, Bogan walked to the back of the wagon. Reaching in, he grabbed a chair and lifted it out. Waving the wooden chair around like he might use it as a weapon, Dan continued to challenge Smith to fight.

Another witness, E. Shumaker, rode up to Smith and urged him to stay in the wagon, but Smith, no longer in the mood to listen, finally stood up and proclaimed, "I've had enough."

F. A. Smith took off his coat and hat. He then jumped down in front of Dan Bogan who continued a stream of profanity aimed at Smith. When Bogan was faced with Smith eye-to-eye, he retreated a little ways. Much the larger man, Smith advanced. Bogan suddenly lost his swaggering bravado.

"You will curse a man, but when he gets out to fight, you won't fight," thundered Smith.

Bogan nervously put his hand inside the front of his coat. Then he withdrew it.

"Draw your goddamn pistol, and I'll knock you down," challenged Smith.

Incensed, Bogan reached back into his coat. As Bogan withdrew his six-shooter, Smith struck him a blow. By this time, David Kemp had dismounted his horse and walked to the back end of the wagon. Smith had his back to Kemp and did not see him.

The blow to Bogan by Smith caused him to stagger backward a few feet. His hat fell over his eyes. Smith followed, landing a second blow. This time Bogan fell to the ground, still holding his pistol in his right hand. Smith wrenched the pistol away and flung it a few feet from the escalating hostility. He grabbed Bogan, lifting him up, his fist poised to strike again.

David Kemp finally sprang into action. He rushed up behind Smith and struck him on the head with a pistol. The blow caused the gun to discharge, and the weapon glanced off Smith's shoulder. Smith turned to confront his new attacker. He also picked Bogan's pistol off the ground where he had flung it. He held the gun by the cylinder to use it like a club. Kemp's blow did not seem to have affected Smith at all. Glaring at each other, no words passed between the two men.

Kemp turned his pistol, aimed, and pulled the trigger. A malfunction caused the gun to fire a squib (a defective cartridge). Undaunted, Smith advanced on Kemp who was already backing away. The larger man moved forward and used his arm to keep knocking Kemp's pistol arm to the side, while the teenager kept trying to shoot Smith. More squibs were fired.

Bogan gathered himself and arose from the ground. Watching the other two men squared off, he grabbed a large rock, ran up behind

Smith and struck him twice in quick succession. The second blow seemed to paralyze Smith temporarily. He stooped forward, putting his hand up on his head where he had been struck. He still held Bogan's pistol. The distraction gave Kemp the time to reuse his pistol. His last two shots were live and found their mark. With his last strength, Smith threw Bogan's firearm at Kemp. It struck him on the neck, glanced off and landed a considerable distance away.

While some witnesses scurried indoors as the air filled with pistol shots, others stood rooted as the scene unfolded before them. They watched as a wounded Smith walked slowly in a circle, then collapsed. A few minutes later, F. A. Smith lay dead, killed by someone he had not met before that day.

Even though David Kemp rushed to his horse in an attempt to get away, he did not travel far before he was arrested and brought back into town. Lodged in jail, the young man awaited his fate. Too poor to obtain legal counsel, he had no way of knowing what was happening with his case until after the fact.

The absence of representation, even though Kemp was only nineteen and legally a minor, did not seem to be a concern of District Attorney C. K. Bell who was determined to move the case forward rapidly. The grand jury met on May 10, 1881, and listened to the testimony of witnesses, which included Thomas Emmett who was not only a major witness but also served as a grand juror. A true bill was passed, and David Kemp was indicted for murder.

One week later a special venire for sixty men was issued. By this time friends had procured legal counsel for David Kemp. The motion to quash the first venire was sustained. The sheriff went out with orders to secure sixty more men to be possible jurors. They showed up on May 25th. The defense filed another motion to quash the venire. District Judge Nugent sustained the motion again. The sheriff was charged with finding another sixty men as drawn by the district clerk in open court in the judge's presence. The final motion to quash was over-ruled. However, no jurors were selected from this third venire. The judge then ordered one hundred talesmen to appear in three days time—then another one hundred talesmen for June 2nd. Realizing a fair and impartial jury could not be found, Judge Nugent changed the venue of the trial from Hamilton to Coryell County where Gatesville was the county seat. The defendant was also transported to Coryell to await trial.

Judge Thomas Nugent also presided over the district court in Coryell County. He immediately ordered the clerk to issue a venire for sixty men to serve as petit jurors. Defense motions were overruled, and the case went to trial. The verdict was guilty of first-degree murder with a punishment of death by hanging.[1]

Someone reading the "Statement of Facts" from the Coryell County trial or the *District Court Minutes of Hamilton County*, going through the futile effort of trying to secure twelve unbiased men to serve as petit jurors, might find it all a bit curious or a seemingly over-the-top reaction to an affray that turned into a shooting incident. A death sentence also belies the evidence. The answer can be found, perhaps, in the fact that this was not David Kemp's first trial for murder. Only a year before David Kemp and three others—W. A. Kemp, Walker Bush, and James Highsaw—were indicted for the murder of William Snell on January 10, 1880, in Hamilton County.

William Snell, a respected stockman, was ambushed as he left Hamilton at dusk to travel home just a few miles from the town. No witnesses to the murder came forward, although some campers stated they heard the shots and found the man's body the next day. Kemp and the others were indicted when several people came forward to state that a feud had been brewing between them.

Although the district court in Hamilton attempted to try this earlier murder case, the district attorney found it impossible to impanel an impartial jury. The case was sent to Erath County on a change of venue. David Kemp produced witnesses who swore that he was eight miles away from the scene of the murder when it happened. The jury brought back a verdict of "Not Guilty." The district attorney dropped the charges against the other men who had been indicted in the same case. Many felt sure of the guilt of David Kemp, and it may have influenced the severity of the punishment meted out by the jury in the second murder trial over the death of F. A. Smith.[2]

Jeremiah Vardiman and a team of lawyers worked to save the life of their client. Judge Nugent overruled the motion for a new trial, so

Vardiman gave notice of filing an appeal. The sheriff of Coryell took David Kemp to McLennan County for safekeeping in late June 1881. The local jail was not safe for extended-stay convicted inmates.

Although the defense team filed several errors in their appeal, only one sufficiently held the attention of the appellate judges. The verdict of the district court was overturned and remanded back due to a lack of evidence or testimony to show express malice on the part of Kemp, which was necessary for finding someone guilty of murder in the first degree. Also noted by the appellate court was the fact the prosecuting attorney had not shown that a requisite cooling-off period had taken place between the start of the altercation and the death of F. A. Smith.[3]

David Kemp finally earned the right to bail, as he awaited a new trial. Judge Nugent set it at $10,000, a pretty steep sum for that time. The second trial for David Kemp in Coryell began in June 1882 with a call for a venire of sixty citizens. The district court had the same difficulty as Hamilton did. An impartial jury was not to be had. Judge Nugent transferred the case to Erath County.

Did this seem like déjà vu for David Kemp? He made a second trip to Erath County to defend himself. Whatever his hopes were for a second acquittal, the Erath jury was in no mood to accept his defense that he acted out of fear for his own life and for his companion Dan Bogan. The verdict was guilty of second-degree murder with a prison term set at twenty-five years.[4]

Once again District Judge Nugent sent David Kemp to Waco for safekeeping, writing the following into the District Court minutes—

> *Whereas it satisfactorily appears to the Court that an effort will be made to release the prisoner David Kemp who is now confined in the jail of Erath County and who has been at the present term of this Court convicted of murder of the second degree and whereas there is great danger that such effort may prove successful if said Kemp should remain in the jail, and whereas it appears that the jail of McLennan County is the nearest jail in which the def't can be safely kept, it is ordered that the sheriff take Kemp there.*[5]

The appeal to the higher court this time rested solely on the judge's charge to the jury. Since Judge Nugent's charge was substantially the same as in Kemp's previous trial in Gatesville, and because the defense had not objected to the charge in the previous appeal, the appellate court ruled—"In our judgment the evidence is amply sufficient to sustain the verdict, and to justify the penalty assessed."[6]

David Kemp arrived at Rusk Penitentiary on June 6, 1883. He faced twenty-five years of hard labor starting at the age of twenty-one. His conduct ledger showed an unsuccessful escape attempt on September 7, 1885, where Kemp managed to obtain some civilian clothes. He was caught and placed in solitary confinement for two days.

Three years into his term at Rusk, one of Kemp's attorneys started the process for a gubernatorial pardon. Governor Ireland was convinced that the facts of the case warranted a pardon but only a conditional one. So, with only three and a half years spent on a twenty-five year sentence, David Kemp was freed on January 17, 1887. His freedom would only last if he stayed out of trouble. This was an early type of parole, a program not officially initiated until 1905. Kemp was given his travel money and shown the gates to the prison.

Hamilton was Kemp's first stop, but he did not linger there for long. Accepting work for a family in Nolan County, he moved on. Eventually, the ex-convict moved to Eddy, New Mexico, located close to Carlsbad where he managed to steer clear of law enforcement.

Infanticide
The Anna Williamson Story

What really happened that mid-September day in 1881 when Anna Williamson went into labor? The sixteen-year old faced the ordeal alone and unmarried. Normally, a young Negro girl, laboring to bring a child into the world, attracted little to no attention, but something went terribly wrong. Was it a coldly calculated murder or a horrific accident when Anna's baby died during or shortly after his birth? Opinions differed among Stephenville's diverse population.

When news of the newborn baby's suspicious death reached authorities, the commissioners' court ordered and paid for the inquest into the death of the Williamson baby.[1] The result showed that Anna was arrested and booked into the county jail by J. H. Boyd on September 16, 1881. There she waited for her fate to play out.

The indictment for murder was brought by the grand jury on October 14, 1881. Isaac F. Cowan was the foreman. In the indictment Anna Williamson was accused of strangling her newborn son with a string around his neck and by also stuffing a rag down the baby's throat—or by some other means unknown to the jury. Witnesses for the State included J. L. May, Sallie Motheral, Charlotte Keith, Sallie Westbrook, Jane Harris and others (mostly women).

A special venire was called to appear at the courthouse on October 24th, just ten days after the indictment was passed. Not clear was when Williamson was able to obtain legal representation, whether through her own efforts or through counsel being appointed by the court, but it had to have been prior to the convening of the venire. Her attorneys were twenty-eight-year-old Lee Young and J. E. Drysdale.

The first effort of the defense attorneys was to try to quash the indictment by saying that it did not specifically state that the alleged murder took place in Erath County. Judge Nugent overruled the motion to quash, and the trial moved rapidly forward. Scrambling, the defense submitted the following as witnesses for Williamson: F. R.

Young D. R. Burroughs; Titus Turner; J. R. Randle; A. M. Borders; Sallie Motheral; Martha Whitney (Anna's sister); Dr. J. M. Williamson; and a Dr. Allen.

Selection of a jury plus the trial took only two days. None of the actual testimony still exists, but Judge Nugent's charge to the jury gave the reader an idea of how the defense approached the establishment of the innocence of their client. They introduced the possibility that the child died accidentally during the actual birth and was dead before being ejected from Williamson's body. They asserted that death was from bleeding around the naval cord. If indeed the baby died before being completely born, it was not murder, according to the statutes in place at that time. Young and Drysdale had to file a motion with Judge Nugent to get this added to the jury charge.

The judge was very clear in his written statement that the evidence in this case was circumstantial. The jury led by W. E. Cody found Anna Williamson guilty of second-degree murder, sentencing her to six years in prison.

The defense attorneys immediately filed a motion for a new trial. This type of motion was rarely granted, but in this case, their assertion of faulty evidence and jury irregularities got the judge's attention. The motion indicated that some type of confession was made by Williamson prior to the trial, but Young asserted that the confession was done involuntarily, thus not admissible. The alleged jury misconduct was blatant and forced the judge to seriously consider granting a new trial.

The motion for a retrial also argued that juror John Zimmerman expressed his opinion to townspeople of the defendant's guilt prior to the trial starting. Even worse was the conduct of juror Thomas Murphy who decided to visit Hyatt and Watts' Saloon without a court officer and after he and the rest of the jurors had been sequestered for the night. While there, he drank whiskey and talked to other patrons about the trial.

Adding fuel to the motion for a new trial, the defense attorneys averred that several jurors "held conversation with other persons who were not jurors from the windows of the courthouse" during the trial. Anna Williamson signed these motions with an "X," indicating her inability to write, although the 1880 census stated that she had received some education.

Judge Nugent quickly convened a hearing, interviewing several of the jurors. Anna Williamson was granted a new trial while Thomas Murphy was fined $100 for misconduct. Not wasting any time, the retrial was almost immediately held. No thought was given to allowing the high emotion and excitement to die down before commencing the second trial.

The same State's witnesses were called while Williamson's lawyers added yet another physician, Dr. Ritchie, to their list. Their purpose seemed to have been to strengthen the view that whatever Anna may have done was the result of her having been delirious and not in control of her faculties during the birth of her son.

All of the efforts of Young and Drysdale were to no avail. The testimony of the town's matrons trumped that of the defense's doctors who supported Williamson's story. The new jury led by J. L. Walker came back with a guilty verdict of second-degree murder and with the same amount of time assigned to prison–six years.[2]

Despite their best efforts, the defense lawyers were not able to get yet again a new trial. Although an appeal was sent to Galveston for the Texas Supreme Court to consider, the outcome of the case was affirmed. Williamson was sent to the state penitentiary March 5, 1882. The *Conduct Ledger* for the prison reveals that she was leased out to do farm work. She served five of the six years assigned.[3]

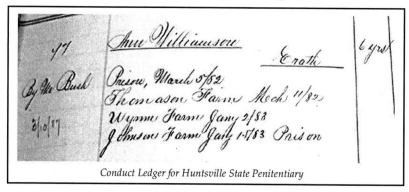

Conduct Ledger for Huntsville State Penitentiary

No records exist that gave a hint as to Williamson's fate once she served her time. She was twenty-one years old when released. What happened to her was lost in the mists of time.

Anna Williamson's story is important. She was the first female convicted of murder in Erath County.

Road Work
The John Henning Story

A respected citizen of Erath County, John Henning, owned a farm close to the Stephenville/Eastland Road in the 1880s. Henning had a wife and three children along with other relatives in the county. When he first exhibited erratic behavior and feelings of persecution was not known. What was for sure was that Henning resented the work every male citizen was required to do to keep the public roads in good condition.

The concept of landowners and citizens maintaining public roads goes all the way back to the ancient Egyptians who required all of its citizens to work a certain number of days a year on public projects such as roads. The State Constitution of 1876 for Texas lays out the specific expectations for men living within each county.[1]

Entry in the Erath County Commissioners' Court Road Minutes for 1881

The maintenance of county roads fell to the commissioners of each precinct to organize. The provisions of the state constitution state that in January of each new year, commissioners were responsible for selecting or appointing an overseer for each road in their precinct plus a listing of any "hand or hands liable to work on roads." Falling to the overseer was the job of assigning a schedule for the ten days of required road work for those men living along his part of the public road and reporting those who refused to participate.[2] The road overseer for Henning's section was listed as J. E. McCleskey, but the person who went to inform John Henning he had not completed his required road labor was J. B. Lewis, a neighbor. Henning told others that he was being harassed about doing this required roadwork and standing on his doorstep on the morning of January 31, 1882, was a neighbor with whom he had quarreled. Something snapped inside. Henning grabbed his gun and without warning pumped bullets into Lewis who died from his wounds.

As word spread and Sheriff W. B. Slaughter arrived to investigate, Henning gathered a few belongings, kissed his family goodbye and set out to avoid arrest. A warrant for him was sent throughout Texas and the territories of New Mexico and Oklahoma. A break came in late October when Sheriff Slaughter received a telegram from Springer, New Mexico, located in the northern part of the territory, that John Henning had been taken into custody.[3]

The sheriff immediately sent a telegram to Austin to obtain the necessary requisition from Governor Oran Roberts, so he could transport Henning back to Texas. Leaving Stephenville, Sheriff Slaughter stopped in Dublin to pick up Deputy Phil Chilton to go with him. Arriving in New Mexico, the sheriff learned that Henning had managed to hide so long because he worked as a laborer for the Atchison, Topeka & Santa Fe Railroad. The Texas sheriff had to cool his heels for a few days waiting for the Texas governor to send the necessary papers, but he was finally able to return with his captive who gave little trouble on the trip back to face a trial for murder.

John Henning, lodged in the Erath County Jail, awaited trial. He was denied bail, so waited it out until the spring docket of 1883. Henning's trial was highly anticipated, and many arrived early at the courthouse, hoping for one of the coveted spots in the visitors' gallery next to the jury box in District Judge Nugent's courtroom.

A special venire of sixty was issued at the beginning of the spring court session of 1883 but yielded only three accepted jurors for Henning's trial. So another venire was drawn, this time for one hundred men. Most of the names drawn were for newcomers in the southern portion of the county, so a jury was completed. It took longer to select the jury than it did to try the case.

The main strategy of the defense was to show that John Henning was insane on the day he took J. B. Lewis' life. To do so, they brought in several local doctors—M. S. Crow, J. M. Williamson, J. L. May, W. W. McNeill, and J. T. Foster—along with former Sheriff R. M. Whiteside to testify on the defendant's behalf.

The prosecution counterbalanced by placing witnesses on the stand who could present John Henning as a vindictive man quick to exact vengeance from an insult or an effort to do him wrong. A large man, Henning had a fine broad forehead, but his height at 6'4" was intimidating.[4]

During the trial proceedings, a reporter for the *Stephenville Empire* was surprised at the number of observers who expressed a desire to see Henning swinging on a gallows but did find a few with more moderate opinions. None stated they thought Henning should be turned loose.[5]

A reading of District Judge Nugent's charge to the jury showed very specific instructions about insanity as an excuse for taking the life of another. He wrote that—

> ...at the time of committing the act, the party was laboring under such defect of reason, from disease of the mind, as not to know the nature or quality of the act he was doing....that is that he did not know the difference between the right and wrong as to the particular act charged against him. The insanity must have existed at the very commission of the offense...[6]

After a fairly short period of deliberation, the jury found John Henning guilty of murder in the first degree. Eschewing execution, the jury awarded life in prison as his punishment. At that time "life in prison" meant just that. The reporter writing about the trial indicated he felt a great deal of prejudice existed against John Henning and thought this may have played a role in the jury's decision. No appeal was made on the verdict.

While Henning awaited transportation to Huntsville, a near jailbreak took place at the county accommodations by Winfield Baker, in for horse thievery. Fun loving and full of jokes, Baker decided to show how easy it would be to break jail. He managed to pull the jail cell door slightly so that when the bar was pushed through during lock-down, it slid to the wrong side of the door. Baker delighted in pointing out the mistake to the jailor Bill Chaney who pulled his pistol, not amused.

Interviewed later, Henning stated that if he had known the cell was unlocked, he would have tried to make a break for it. As it was, the prison contractor arrived to take Henning and five others to the state prison. Sheriff J. C. Gilbreath, who had replaced Slaughter, cautioned the contractor that Henning was a dangerous man.

The contractor replied, "You can't tell me anything about men. I have been handling men for years."

The convicts were taken to the nearest railroad for transportation. The station was located in Alexander. The men were lined up in front of the hotel to receive a meal. When Henning was handed a plate full of food, he threw it as far as he could. The plate hit another prisoner in the head, and the food landed in the street. The unfortunate assaulted prisoner had to have stitches before boarding the train.

The contractor stated, "That man is dangerous."

Sheriff Gilbreath quipped back, "No, he's not dangerous. I have been handling men for years. You can't tell me that man is dangerous."[7]

The contractor managed to get Henning and the others to Huntsville on May 22, 1883. To harness the big man's aggressive behavior, John Henning was put to carrying bed railings up a three-story building to the top floor. He started with carrying just one then added more and more until he was transporting fifteen to twenty at a time. His large frame and weight was a plus in doing heavy work.

John Henning lived for fifteen years in the state penitentiary. He died having never left the institution. During the last portion of his life, Henning's grip on reality slipped beyond his control. Little provisions were made for the criminally insane prior to 1900. Rusk Penitentiary's way of dealing with insane inmates who were disruptive was to separate them from the general population.

The following was written into Henning's page of the *Conduct Ledger—*

> *Died April 13, 1898 of the debility of insanity complicated with Diarrhora* [sic]. *The above convict* [Henning] *had been confined in Solitary Confinement for many years on account of his insanity.*[8]

Murder After Dark
The Monroe Coldiron and Brink Favors Story

Like many settlers on the Texas frontier, the citizens of Erath County looked forward to the Christmas season. With crops safely harvested, stored or sold, and spring planting a future endeavor, they relaxed and spent time with friends, neighbors, and relatives who came calling. During this time, wives had a little more indulgent attitude if their husbands took a nip or two from the whiskey jug. Seeing folks roaming the roads was not unusual.

When Frank Trout dropped by to see J. Pink Floyd on Sunday afternoon, December 30, 1883, nothing seemed unusual about it. Floyd had been working in his corncrib and happy to have a reason to take a break. Frank was his neighbor, living south one mile just across the Comanche County line. Whistling as he arrived, Trout was seemingly in a great mood.

Frank Trout was not the first visitor of the afternoon. Monroe Coldiron and Brink Favors had stopped by earlier. Coldiron, a frequent visitor since Floyd was taking care of his eight-year-old motherless daughter, Missouri, rode an unshod pony while his companion, Favors, sat on a large dark iron-gray horse.

Floyd was glad the two sets of visitors did not arrive at the same time, because bad blood had been brewing at least on Coldiron's side. Whispers of gossip had been swirling among some of the local men about Trout. John Highly, another neighbor, had been surprised on Christmas Eve when several men stopped by. They were drunk, and one told Highly they might go after Frank Trout, because he had molested Coldiron's daughter. When asked for proof, none was produced. After some hollering and shooting off guns, the crowd dissipated.

Floyd certainly did not want a confrontation that holiday season. Coldiron told Floyd earlier that he intended to give Trout a whipping. Floyd calmed him down until Coldiron finally stated he would drop it. Still, it was better the two men stayed apart as far as Floyd was concerned.

When Frank Trout arrived, he inquired if Floyd was going to

church. When the farmer responded negatively, Trout decided to stay and visit. Two hours later, he announced his departure. Floyd bid Trout farewell and went inside his home.

Ten minutes later, Floyd was startled by the sound of gunshots. He went out on the stoop and peered into the darkness. He heard Trout calling for help. Floyd's wife, Alice, did not want him to go out. He quickly reassured her and hurried toward the voice calling, "Oh, Lordy."

Trout was already moving toward Floyd's house but soon stopped, too weak to continue. Jack Ward, a neighbor who had been home reading the Bible to his wife when he heard shots, appeared to help Floyd get Trout back to the house. The men laid Frank on the floor. Weak but willing to talk, Trout told them that when he got to the crossroads from Floyd's home, he stopped when he saw something at the base of a tree. He walked over to investigate.

Two men jumped up and mounted horses. A voice called out to identify himself. Trout, unaware of his danger, answered. One of the men then informed him that they were going to kill him. Trout stated that on hearing the metallic click of arms, he started backing away, but not fast enough. When the first bullet hit him, Trout turned to run. The attackers followed, continuing to fire. Hit more than once, the wounded man turned back crying, "Don't shoot again, I'm already dead."

Weakening, Trout paused before continuing his travails. He stated that one of the attackers rode up close to him, looked down, then turned and galloped off. When the men asked, Trout responded that he did not know who attacked him. He added that he only knew of two men who had a grudge—his brothers-in-law, Broadfoot and Jim Warren. Listening, Floyd knew of someone else but stayed silent about it. Obviously, Trout was dying and did not need any more grief.

Although a doctor arrived later, little could be done, except make the wounded man as comfortable as possible. From the moment he was shot in the chest, Frank Trout knew his life was down to hours and minutes. He died at daylight the next morning, not knowing for sure who had plotted his demise.

Excitement over the murder electrified the close-knit community located close to the border with Eastland County. Early the next day, men gathered to try to piece together the puzzle of what happened. These early settlers had their own abilities as sleuths. Courts then were not nearly as concerned with what might be deemed as tampering with the evidence at a crime scene as they are today.

The men who gathered at Pink Floyd's place were eager to figure out who committed the Trout murder. M. C. Turnbough and his brother, Deputy Sheriff J. W. Turnbough, studied carefully the tracks close to the murder scene. By measuring, they determined that the two assassins rode a large fully shod horse and an unshod pony.

The investigators divided up and followed the trail of the two horses, which showed that both shooters arrived at the crossroads and left it together. Each group noted something peculiar about the sets of hoof prints. One of the large horse's hind hooves had a little twist in the track as he walked, while the pony track seemed to dig out the dirt from under his foot as he walked. With these distinctive traits, the tracks were not hard to follow, especially since they headed down the furrows of a plowed field.

Another group of men studied the death scene closely. Blood, visibly soaked into the ground, bore witness to the violence done. E. P. Purvis found a ball from a .44 with a powder burn on one end. It was a cartridge ball recently shot. Instead of hitting its intended victim, it had instead hit the ground. Purvis also noticed paper scattered about the ground. Picking it up, he knew this was wadding used in a shotgun. He realized that two different guns were used the night before, a .44 and a shotgun.

As Floyd's neighbors compared notes, both on the evidence they found and the events over the previous week, two names emerged as the prime suspects, Monroe Coldiron and Brink Favors. Several had seen Coldiron together with Favors the day of the murder. J. C. Elliott volunteered the information that he saw them north of his place. Then one-half hour before sundown, he saw Favors on a large dark iron-gray horse and Coldiron on a pony heading in the direction of Floyd's place. Several remembered the brouhaha the week previous over Coldiron's little daughter. All signs pointed to two specific men.

Mondroe Coldiron, age 30, and Brink Favors, age 19, were arrested on Monday, January 7, 1884, by Deputy Sheriff Turnbough for the murder of B. Frank Trout. An examining trial was held in early February by Justice of the Peace Sligar. The circumstantial evidence strongly implicated the two men. They were remanded back to jail to await the district court proceedings.

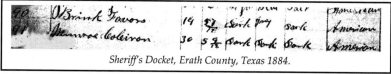

Sheriff's Docket, Erath County, Texas 1884.

Just prior to the habeas corpus trial, Pink Floyd had the scare of his life. Between midnight and dawn a person shook the handle of his front door repeatedly, then violently. The tracks of one man were found the next day. Floyd, spooked by this, moved his family to Gonzales County and had to be sent a subpoena to force him to return to Stephenville to testify.

District Judge T. L. Nugent appointed W. H. Devine to defend the two indicted murder suspects, because they were without the means to hire a defense team. Devine promptly filed for a habeas corpus (bail) hearing. Considering both men as flight risks, Judge Nugent ruled against setting bail but was overruled by the Texas Court of Appeals. Bail was set at $5000 each.

Devine provided an able defense, using time-tested methods of getting continuances. He first objected to the venire, stating that the sheriff did not make a good faith effort to contact all sixty persons named on the list. He then stated they could not safely go to trial because some of the defense witnesses had not been served their subpoenas or at least not in time to attend court. He finally filed for a change of venue, stating that prejudice in Erath was too great against his clients. Judge Nugent overruled all these defense motions, which meant the trials took place in late April 1884.

Most of the same witnesses from the examining trial were brought back by the district attorney with the addition of some testimony by Sheriff Gilbreath and Deputy Sheriff Turnbough. Trying to bolster the circumstantial evidence, the prosecution used the lawmen to testify that they went out to the Favors' place to look at the horse, believed to be the one used by Brink Favors on December 30th. They stated that the horse appeared to be the same but that the two hind shoes had been pulled off which changed the print pattern. They also stated that in their judgment the shoes had been pulled off recently, because the edges of the hooves were smooth—not rough. Another new witness, Frank Craig, established that Coldiron borrowed a British Bulldog pistol from him a couple of weeks prior to the shooting.

Interesting was the fact that the prosecution did not use witnesses to establish motive, even though at least one spoke of the rumored inappropriate action of Frank Trout toward Coldiron's daughter at the examining trial. While establishing a motive was important in trials relying primarily on circumstantial evidence, it may have been more important that the jury did not "nullify" the case by deciding that Trout had it coming—a time honored and successful tactic often used in Texas courts in the nineteenth century.

The defense took a fairly simple route. Brink Favors' older brother, William, provided an alibi by stating that Brink and Monroe came home a little after dark and stayed there the entire evening. William went on to state that the hind shoes on the large horse had been pulled off before December 30th, not afterward. Mrs. Sally Favors, the brothers' mother, was too sick to attend court to support the alibi.

The prosecution countered in their cross-examination by having witness J. C. Elliott state that when he saw Brink Favors on December 30th, he also saw that Favors' horse was shod on all four hooves. He noticed that the two hind horseshoes were also corked.

The court tried Brink Favors first, then Monroe Coldiron next, in early May 1884. The jury came back with the same verdict for both—guilty of murder in the first degree with a sentence of life in the penitentiary. Both men were remanded back to jail.[1]

The two men found that a definite pecking order prevailed at the Stephenville Jail where they were taken after conviction until transportation could be arranged to send them to Huntsville State Penitentiary. The one in control was a man also accused of murder. While acting as a model prisoner and even sending a statement to the newspaper of what a fair sheriff Gilbreath was, Morg McInturf ruled the iron cage where men were kept at the public's expense. His rules, enforced by the other inmates, included a kangaroo court complete with imposed fines.

Neither Coldiron nor Favors liked this hierarchy of power until they caught a hint that a jailbreak might happen soon. Unwilling to wait on the ruling of the Court of Appeals, the two men agreed to take part. Favors, sick with rheumatism, had the privilege of staying outside of the cage during the day. Morg McInturf fashioned a key using lead, a tin can lid, and tacks out of his shoes. On the day of the jailbreak, Favors let him out using the "key." Morg hid above the cage until after the evening lock-in when he freed all the prisoners. On the outside the men scattered.[2]

Looking around, Coldiron and Favors spied one of the sheriff's horses. Grabbing the mount, the two men rode out of town together. While Sheriff Gilbreath divided up a posse to chase after the others, he took on the job of trailing Coldiron and Favors. He correctly guessed they headed to the Favors' farm. Mrs. Favors admitted that her son had been there and had taken a pony with him.

Sheriff Gilbreath and his posse found the sheriff's horse ten miles away at Bill Stone's place. The clues left indicated that Favors' rheumatism was bothering him as a bucket of turpentine used to bathe his leg was left at the site, showing Favors had tried to medicate himself. The imprint of gunstocks warned the posse that the men they sought were armed.

Darkness prevented the posse from continuing. The next day they again followed the tracks that led to the Leon River. Across the swollen river and forty yards above, the banks showed where the fugitives emerged from the currents. The sheriff divided the posse, taking a group across to scour the countryside there.

The dense thicket called the Devil's Truck Patch in Comanche County prevented further progress. Gilbreath found a piece of paper that turned out to be a bill of sale signed by W. P. Favors, Brink's brother. No other clues were found, but the sheriff believed that the two men they trailed were actually the Favors' brothers, while Coldiron struck out on his own somewhere along the way. With the trail lost, the posse turned back, heading to Stephenville where they admitted their failure to apprehend the most wanted of the fugitives.[3]

With their choice made to escape, the convicted murderers gave up their right to an appeal. If caught, the men would have been taken to Huntsville to serve their life terms. Perhaps desperation added fuel to their hasty exit from the county accommodations. Coldiron and Favors were never apprehended.

Family records and stories revealed that Monroe Coldiron after his escape was taken to West Texas where he changed his name. His brother George reportedly visited once a year not telling anyone his destination. Brink Favors, according to his daughter Audrey Favor Rankin, made it to Florida where he lived until Brights Disease took his life in 1899.[4]

Part Five – The Court Takes Control

Moral of the Murder
The Tom Putty Story

The newspaper as a platform to moralize to the public was used often in the late nineteenth century. Passing judgment and stating preferred outcomes on trials was not confined to the editorial pages. Few editors worried about lawsuits for defamation as they might in later times.

The following was added at the end of a news article printed about the Tom Putty murder case—

> *From theft to murder is an easy grade, and trains pull out of 'Murder Station' every 30 minutes in the United States. Parents ye who wear fine clothes, sit in the amen corner, and call the pastor, 'Bro' – do you have family talks with your little boys, and impress on them the importance of living honorable lives? Do you teach them that it is a great sin to loaf about town wasting the golden hours? Verily no; not the one in five realize the importance that 'Character' formation begins with the suckling babe. When he passes six years it is late to begin to try [to] retrive [sic] lost opportunities.*[1]

The events that led to the newspaper waxing eloquent about teaching the young morals concerned Tom Putty, a resident of Lingleville in Erath County, who ended up being charged with murder. The newspaper thought they had it all figured out, but did they?

On the day of the events the newspaper wrote about—November 24, 1891—Ben Anderson and three other men were hauling lumber along the Dublin road to Lingleville. These teamsters had combined their trip to town with a visit to some local saloons. By the time Tom Putty and his younger brother met them, Ben and the others were well on their way to getting drunk.

Tom Putty and his brother were headed over to a neighbor's house to pick cotton. Tom was the oldest of three brothers and married. They were orphans and trying to get by on the generosity of neighbors and by working at whatever jobs they could find.

As the two young men moved to pass the oncoming wagon, Ben Anderson suddenly reached out and grabbed the reins to Tom's horse, while also verbally accosting the young man and questioning his integrity. Tom informed the man he had never met before that day that he was mistaken as to his identity as Tom did not know him.

Anderson insisted he was not mistaken and that he and Tom had had a bruhaha over a horse race a few days earlier. While Tom had an interest in horseracing, he could not convince Anderson that he had the wrong person. Later, Tom realized it was his older brother who had raced his horse against Ben previously. For some reason Ben was still angry over the incident.

Unaccustomed to backing away from a confrontation, Tom Putty was not about to back down from this one, even though he was recovering from a recent illness. Being considered a coward was not something Tom was willing to go through in order to avoid the fight he felt he had not started. He got off his horse but realized immediately that two things were going to work against him. His opponent was a much larger man and was holding a big rock in his hand. Still not willing to run away, Tom reached in his pocket and pulled out his pocketknife. He swiftly stabbed Ben Anderson twice before the larger man could attack and take back the advantage.

Realizing he may have inflicted a mortal wound, Tom Putty quickly remounted his horse and took off with his younger brother, leaving Ben's companions to tend the wounds of their fallen comrade. Ben Anderson lived about a week but finally succumbed to his wounds.

In a panic Tom Putty made the decision to vacate Erath County, hoping to evade arrest. Word was sent out to surrounding areas to be on the lookout for Putty. Word came on December 9th that the Eastland County sheriff had found Putty down in the corner of the county close to Brown County. An official warrant, signed by Justice of the Peace Terrell Bryan, was handed to Sheriff Nath J. Shands who picked up Putty on December 13th. He was brought back to Erath and booked into the county jail. His paperwork showed that he stood 5'8" with black hair, dark eyes and a dark complexion. Putty managed to get out of jail on a bail bond of $2000 on January 21, 1892.

> **MURDERER ARRESTED.**
> Tom Putty, who killed B. F. Anderson near Moccasin Rock several weeks ago, was captured near the corner of Eastland and Brown counties on the 9th inst. by Eastland county officers, and lodged in Eastland jail. He was transferred to Stephenville on the 13th and is still held without the privilege of bail. O. B. Carter was released from jail on the 9th inst.

Stephenville Empire, December 19, 1891

Putty's trial started on May 16, 1892, in Judge C. K. Bell's district court. The jury had little trouble convicting Tom of second-degree murder, awarding an eight-year stint in the state penitentiary. His fate sealed, Putty reportedly confessed to District Attorney George that he had been in trouble before in another Texas county. He revealed that he had stolen a chicken and a turkey there. Fearing he might be indicted for the theft at the time, he told George he left Texas for Indian Territory. Once he thought no one was looking for him, Putty moved to Erath County with his brothers. Unfortunately, his life then took a definite turn for the worse.

Tom Putty did not appeal his conviction. At age twenty-two, he was taken to Huntsville, May 28, 1892, but he was not without friends.[2]

A petition for a pardon was sent to Governor C. A. Culberson on October 1, 1895. Signing this petition and lending weight to it were District Attorney J. Collin George, County Judge Thomas B. King, County Attorney W. J. Oxford and Special Judge N. R. Lindsey from Comanche who adjudicated the case. The twelve jurors who tried Putty also affixed their names.[3]

Judge Thomas King wrote a personal letter to the governor, laying out the details of the events that led to Putty's conviction. He stated that the only witness for the defense was Putty's brother. The judge felt this hurt Tom's case even though the testimony of the sibling was reasonable and accurate as far as the judge was concerned.[4]

The Board of Pardons approved the application but noted that Tom Putty needed to serve at least five years of his sentence before he would be eligible for release. Governor Culberson pardoned Tom on May 6, 1897. [5]

Tom Putty then moved close to Desdemona in Eastland County with his wife, raising five sons and a daughter. Putty renewed his interest in racehorses and made a living doing it.

A Hate Crime
The Tom Lauderdale Story

When Julian Rodriguez moved his family from Comanche to Dublin, he was looking for work. With just a smattering of English, he was able to find income as a day laborer. His wife made tamales, and his fourteen-year-old son, Victor, sold the hot tamales to the community even though he could speak very little English. The Rodriguez family lived in what the *Dublin Progress* called "a wooden shanty with a cloth cover situated in the open lot between the Rio Grande Railroad and the Baptist Church."[1]

On the night of March 6, 1891, the lives of the Rodriguez family changed forever. It started that morning when two Mexican families from Cisco stopped to visit with Julian and his family. They had planned to stay for a while. Mayor R. H. McCain heard about the new arrivals and quickly made a decision. He went over to their home, accompanied by several officers, and advised the Mexican visitors that they would have to leave on the next train. As best he could, the mayor explained that rumors were rampant in the community that the Mexicans either had or were exposed to small pox in Cisco. The mayor told the Rodriguez family that they could stay as they had been in Dublin for several months. McCain kept it to himself that he had sent a telegram inquiring into the rumor and that the mayor of Cisco had replied in the negative. McCain may have decided that the circulating rumors were more powerful than the truth. In any event the two visiting families boarded the train that evening and left.

The Rodriguez family went to bed by 10PM after the other Mexican families left. Much later the snort of horses woke Julian up, but he did not get out of bed. A harsh voice rang out, "Rodriguez, you have until daylight to get out of Dublin. If you don't, you will be dead by morning."[2]

The chilling words nearly froze Rodriguez into inaction. He knew he was in trouble. Staying in bed, he yelled that he understood and was willing to leave if they would give him time. He could hear the men outside whispering, then finally leaving.

A half-hour later several men returned to the Rodriguez home. They again demanded that Julian and his family abandon their quarters. They shouted from outside rather than knocked on the door. Epitaphs and strong language accompanied the orders. Julian called out once again that he was willing to leave if given time. Julian heard one of the men say to the others, "Let's just hang 'em and get it over with." The other men voiced agreement. Julian did not move from the bed, afraid of what would happen next. He did not have long to wait. He heard the sounds of an axe hitting the side of his home. Then abruptly the men apparently left.[3]

Rodriguez hoped that the worst was over. He stayed in bed but was wide-awake and began planning the trip out of Dublin. The peace was shattered once again fifteen minutes later. He heard men outside and the sound of liquid being sloshed onto the walls of his ill-constructed house. Julian peeked through a crack in the wall. He saw two men and could smell coal oil. One of the men started striking matches, but the night breeze blew them out before he could light the flammable liquid.

In a panic Rodriguez called out, begging the men to allow him time to get his family out. The two men outside ignored Rodriguez. They got a box and broke it up to make kindling. While the men were engaged in doing that, Rodriguez rushed his wife out the door with instructions to run to Mr. Keith's house. From behind her home Mrs. Rodriguez turned back in time to see flames starting to catch hold of the walls. Rodriguez and Victor managed to escape the burning abode but were unable to save anything except the clothes on their backs. Later, Rodriguez told authorities that he lost $250 cash that he could not retrieve from a trunk before having to leave to save his own life.

The Dublin Volunteer Fire Brigade was mobilized. W. J. Wassen, C. C. Andrews, and others pulled the hose cart out of City Hall after hearing the fire bell being repeatedly rung at 2AM by Green Patterson, later to be under suspicion for participating in setting the very fire for which he was ringing the bell. The citizens of Dublin were shocked at the news that the fire had been deliberately started. Many contributed to a reward, which eventually reached $500 for the arrest and conviction of those involved.

In 1891 W. J. Oxford was county attorney for Erath and responsible for investigating crimes that could eventually be sent before the grand jury. With several counties to service, the district attorney not only did not have enough time to investigate, but he also had to follow the district judge around to hold court in various counties, leaving much of the grunt work to the local sheriff and county attorney to do.[4]

Oxford headed for Dublin to find out, if possible, who was involved in torching the home of Julian Rodriguez. After some initial inquiries, Oxford was surprised at what Bob Wade had to tell him. Wade stated that he was prepared to turn State's witness but that he wanted to allow Tom Lauderdale to do it, because he had a large family who would experience great hardship if Tom were sent to jail.

In the meantime Tom Wright, another suspect, stopped W. J. Oxford on the street. The young man offered himself up to be a State's witness. It was obvious to the county attorney that Wright was trying to get himself off the hook. Since Oxford was pretty sure that Wright had a principal role in the arson, he had little interest in using him.

Oxford, Wade, Dublin City Marshal Bishop, and W. J. Davies went to see Tom Lauderdale at his home. Oxford did the talking and broached the topic. Lauderdale looked over the gathering of men and hedged by stating he did not want "to get tangled." Sensing a hesitation, Oxford pressed by telling Lauderdale that if he were willing to turn State's witness through the trials, that he would not be personally prosecuted. This assurance was enough for the reluctant witness to agree to testify at the examining trial being held at the Dublin City Hall.

The next morning the witnesses gathered to give their version of the events of the evening when arson was committed. Several, including Bird Shofner, pointed their testimony toward seven men who had spent the evening drinking, mostly at the Dublin Saloon owned by C. O. Wright and where Tom Lauderdale worked as a bartender. Those men besides Lauderdale included Tom Wright, Bob Wade, Sam Hunt, Frank Craig, T. Crowder Farris, and Green Patterson.

The one witness W. J. Oxford needed to show up for the examining trial was Tom Lauderdale. Nervously watching the door, Oxford was relieved when Lauderdale finally walked in. Going over, the attorney again assured his star witness that he would be protected if he testified to all that happened. Oxford was quite certain he was clear with Lauderdale about what was expected of him to receive immunity. Tom did answer the questions put to him at the examining trial, and he implicated all six men who had been mentioned earlier before he arrived. He stated under oath that Frank Craig, owner of the Coney Island Saloon, provided the coal oil used and went with Bob Wade to set the fire. Crowder Farris and Tom Wright followed them out to the home of Julian Rodriguez. A short time later several shots were heard. This information led to the indictment of all the men, *including* Tom Lauderdale.[5]

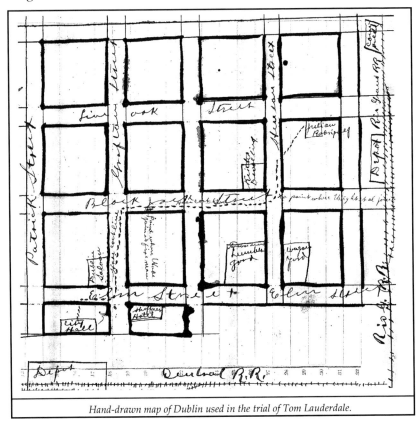

Hand-drawn map of Dublin used in the trial of Tom Lauderdale.

The men were arrested except for Frank Craig who had left Dublin. Rumors were that he was headed for Sherman. Telegrams were quickly sent, and Craig was arrested in Fort Worth by Deputy Marshal Pless Barkley and brought back to Stephenville by train.

After he gave bond, Tom Lauderdale headed for W. J. Oxford's office. He complained about being indicted. The county attorney assured him that it was a mere formality. Oxford went on to tell Lauderdale that if he testified at the trials, Tom would not go to the penitentiary or he, Oxford, would run "necked" through the streets for him.

Evidently, Lauderdale followed the advice of his lawyer, or others got to him, because when it came time for him to testify at the trials, he refused for the reason that his statements would be self-incriminating. W. J. Oxford was furious. Without Lauderdale's testimony, Green Patterson and Crowder Farris managed to get not guilty verdicts, as there were no eyewitnesses to place them at the fire. The district attorney, J. Collin George, dropped his case against Sam Hunt and Frank Craig, but he did manage to get a guilty verdict against Tom Wright and Bob Wade in Judge Bell's court. Then George went after and got a guilty verdict against Tom Lauderdale by reading his written testimony into the record from the examining trial. Lauderdale's attorneys objected.

Lauderdale's conviction was appealed to the Texas Court of Criminal Appeals on the basis that the lower court erred in reading Lauderdale's signed testimony, which amounted to a confession, into the record of his trial over his objections. The admissibility of a confession in a felony case made under an agreement to testify against co-defendants must follow certain strict guidelines. *Texas Criminal Statute* Article 750 states that—

> *If the defendant has been threatened into making, or persuaded into making it, in the hope that he will be permitted to turn State's evidence, and thereby gain immunity from punishment, in no event can such confession be used against him, if he subsequently repudiates the agreement, and refuses to testify as a witness for the State.*

Even though Lauderdale's confession was admissible under common law, it was not under Texas law. The evidence showed that Lauderdale was definitely persuaded by several men, including County Attorney Oxford to testify. The ruling of the lower court was reversed and remanded back to the lower court.[6] District Attorney George chose to dismiss the case, and Tom Lauderdale's freedom was given back to him. Bob Wade and Tom Wright were later pardoned by Governor Hogg.[7]

The Rodriguez family chose to leave Dublin. They moved to Lampasas. Their home was gone and so was their hope of making a life in Erath County.

A Knifing in the Side Room
The Tom Wood Story

Danger came with being a publican, especially along the frontier of the American West. Tom Wood had seen his share of drunks, ruffians, and nere-do-wells. At 5'10" Wood developed a tough exterior demeanor, which caused some to accuse him of being a bully. Others simply testified that being tough on rowdy customers was necessary to prevent these men from getting out of hand. Wood had served as a deputy sheriff of Hamilton County before moving to Dublin, Texas.

Sometimes a saloonkeeper could not anticipate what his patrons might do next. Case in point is what happened in Hico, Texas, when Wood had a saloon there in the late 1880s. On cold days in the wintertime men enjoyed the heat from the stove located at the rear end of the drinking establishment.

On February 4, 1889, Tom Wood sat at the stove with J. D. Reed and James Richardson. The conversation was amiable at the time Wood was called away to serve a customer who had bellied up to the bar. A few minutes later the bartender heard the report of a pistol-shot, coming from the back. Reed sprinted past the saloonkeeper and disappeared into the night. Rushing to the back, Wood found Richardson shot through the head, taking his last breaths. Reed stayed on the dodge for three years before being arrested in Sweetwater for carrying a pistol. For whatever reason, Reed confessed to the sheriff that he was wanted in Hamilton County on a murder charge.[1]

Tom Wood moved on to establish a saloon on Elm Street in Dublin, taking a partner—Bird Shofner. As Hico was not that far away, Wood had some of the same customers. Dublin was a bustling town with a growing population because of the railroad passing through. Business was good.

Whatever dreams of prosperity Tom Wood had in his new locale came to an end on Thursday, October 29, 1891, when Frank Craig entered the saloon in a somewhat inebriated condition. Wood testified that he allowed Craig only one drink before refusing to serve another, telling him to go home to sleep it off.

Undeterred, Craig continued to demand another drink. He slammed his fist down on the counter proclaiming, "God damn you, Tom Wood. You have got the reputation of being a bully, but you have got no edge over me."

Wood told Craig that he wanted no difficulty with him. Having recently been very ill with a slow fever that had lasted for several weeks, Wood was in no condition to take on a drunk. M. M. Hughes stepped up to the bar and induced Craig to go into the side room at the saloon and just take a nap. George Boucher was already occupying the side room but willingly vacated.

When asked, Wood admitted that Frank Craig had been upset with him for some time. Craig and L. O. Franklin had asked Wood to act as an arbitrator in a business disagreement between the two men. It may have been in reference to the Coney Island Saloon Craig had owned at one time. Afterward, Craig angrily proclaimed that Wood had robbed him of the settlement owed him by Franklin.

Believing Craig had been taken care of and hearing the whistle of the eastbound passenger train pulling into the station, Wood went back to the bar only to be interrupted by yelling and hearing the door to the side room being repeatedly kicked about thirty minutes later. Exasperated, Wood headed for the side room after retrieving some money from the ground where Craig had thrown it out the window. He testified later that he entered the room and sat on the cot. Craig started cursing him and then pushed Wood to the floor. The inebriated man grabbed a beer bottle and attempted to hit Wood on the head. The bartender ducked—then dug out his pocketknife.

The two entangled men rolled on the floor. Craig was a much larger man than his adversary and could easily push Wood, weakened by illness, to the floor. Craig had not reckoned with Wood's ability to get his knife opened and in use. Wood stabbed Craig in the neck just below the ear, penetrating down. Even with a terrible wound to Craig, the fight continued.

Hearing the ruckus, Joe DeHon, owner of the Crescent Restaurant, headed for the side room. He found Frank Craig lying on his side with his leg partly over the lower part of Wood's body. DeHon grabbed the knife Wood still held and informed Wood he was taking the weapon. Wood replied, "I know that, but you are too late. Craig is done for."

Several men picked up the mortally wounded man and conveyed him to the Southern Hotel on Grafton Street. Drs. S. L. Herring, R. A. Miller, and J. J. McLemore arrived but soon found the wounded man beyond help. Craig died at 6AM without making a statement. At thirty years old he left a wife and three children behind.

Convinced that he acted in self-defense, Tom Wood set out to turn himself in to the law. He found Dublin's Deputy Marshal Dick Moore who then rode with Wood into Stephenville to turn himself over to Erath County Sheriff N. J. Shands. If Tom Wood believed he could put this incident easily behind him, he was quickly disappointed when the Erath grand jury indicted him for murder.

Craig's brother James hired County Attorney W. J. Oxford to help with the prosecution of Wood. He convinced Oxford that the killing was not only premeditated but was a part of a conspiracy to murder his brother. Oxford convinced District Attorney J. Collin George of this, and they spent a great deal of time trying to find witnesses to prove the conspiracy. The search did not yield the desired results, although Craig's brother promised he could find witnesses and evidence.

W. J. Oxford

A year passed before Tom Wood was brought to trial. Lawyers Nugent, Goodson, Young & Martin had managed to get continuances based on defense witnesses needed to testify on Wood's behalf not being available. In November 1892 District Judge C. K. Bell handed the jury the court's charge. The jury split and was unable to come to a unanimous decision.

The case was held over to the spring docket of 1893. A new district judge sat on the bench—J. S. Straughan. Attorneys on both sides looked over the Order for the Special Venire of sixty men selected as possible jurors for the Wood case. Some men were removed from the list, as they had moved out of Erath County. A couple by mutual consent of the attorneys were taken off the list, as they could neither read nor write. Only forty-nine of the sixty showed up for voir dire.

County Judge W. J. Oxford was given the opportunity to deliver the State's closing remarks. After Oxford led the jury back through the case, he took the defense to task for not bringing up the defendant's character, even though they did bring forth witnesses who had sworn that Frank Craig, though seemingly peaceful, was in essence dangerous when drunk. He was also one of seven men tried for burning down Julian Rodriguez's house earlier in the year. Oxford informed the jury that the State could not bring up the defendant's character unless the defense had first done so. He noted to the jury that the State had been ready and very able to talk about Wood's character but had not been given the chance.[2]

Whether it was the State's witnesses or Oxford's impassioned closing remarks, the jury brought back a guilty verdict. They agreed on second-degree murder and assessed five years in prison. Wood's attorneys immediately filed for a new trial. They stated two errors—one being that W. J. Oxford erred in bringing up character in his closing remarks when Wood's character was not introduced during the trial.

The second proposed error was more complicated. The motion accused one of the case's jurors—J. P. Silar—of being prejudiced against the defendant prior to being selected as a juror for the trial. Defense submitted sworn affidavits by two men who stated that Silar had discussed the case in their presence. One even said that Silar told him that Wood ought to have his "damned neck broke."

District Attorney George moved quickly, filing his own answer to the motion for a new trial. He ignored the proposed error concerning the State's closing remarks but did interview all the jurors including Silar. He then had them each (including Silar) sign a separate affidavit, all of which essentially said that several of the jurors wanted to give Wood twenty-five years as they had not been convinced that the saloonkeeper had acted in self-defense. Silar had sided with those who refused to be that harsh in their deliberations. District Judge

Straughan ruled against the motion for a new trial May 20, 1893.³

Wood's attorneys gave notice they would be filing an appeal on the case but came back a few days later to withdraw the filing. With that, Wood headed for Rusk Penitentiary. His conduct was so exemplary, Wood was made a "trusty" which was a convict the guards relied on enough to give special responsibilities. In exchange the inmate usually received better food and more privileges than the general convict population.

Efforts to procure a pardon for Tom Wood began the year after he was sent to Rusk. He left a wife and seven children behind with little means of support. The community had rallied to help the woman, which may have promoted many to join in the effort to obtain clemency. The first petition was signed by numerous citizens from Erath and Hamilton counties, Judge Straughan and District Attorney George.

Objecting to the early release was W. J. Oxford, still the legal counsel to the Craig family. He provided the signed, written testimony presented to the grand jury. Oxford expressed reservation in releasing Wood early. His letter slowed the process down, requiring those in favor of clemency to provide more information. A key witness, C. F. Cohron, typed out his testimony and sent it to support Wood's story of self-defense. It was enough for Governor Culberson to take action. Wood was pardoned on January 23, 1896.⁴

When Adultery Leads to Perjury
The John Hull Story

Forty-year-old John Hull had been through a very tough two years. Accused of adultery in late 1896, he barely escaped conviction when his case was tried before Erath County Judge Thomas B. King. Considered a lesser crime, those accused of adultery in Texas were tried in county courts in the late nineteenth century. Conviction generated a fine of $100 to $1000, but much worse, at least in small communities, was the scorn heaped upon those accused, which usually led to being ostracized from polite society.

Judge Thomas B. King

Adultery as an offense was not often brought to trial even though many were indicted. Two things worked against the prosecutor. First was the sympathetic all-male jury. Second, even though there might be credible witnesses, many did not want to come forward. Prosecutors tended to allow these cases to languish until dismissed for "lack of credible evidence."

John Hull was one of the unlucky few indicted for adultery in Erath County. He was accused of having carnal knowledge of his wife Annie's sister, Florence (Nona) Edwards. Gossip buzzed around the case, especially when many believed that the parents of the sisters involved had left Erath County to return to Illinois in late 1896, taking Nona in tow. Many believed they left in an effort to separate their daughter from the advances of their son-in-law. If the story being passed around were true, the Edwards were initially successful as Nona did leave with them but only traveled as far as Indian Territory (Oklahoma). They stopped there to visit with relatives, including S. N. Murphy near Springtown.

At this point Nona Edwards made the decision to return to Erath

County to live once again with her sister and brother-in-law. Why she did this is shrouded in mystery. Later under oath Edwards, age 21, declared that she returned because her parents were too poor to support her. One might ask why she packed a heavy trunk and left with her parents in the first place. Why did she decide in the middle of the move that they were too poor? Where did she get the money for the train trip back to Stephenville? Could it be an irresistible attraction to her brother-in-law? On the other hand, if the stories were true about the illicit union between her and John, why would her sister Annie allow her "competition" to return?

The facts were that Nona Edwards did return to Stephenville and was picked up at the station by John Hull who was alone when he fetched her from the train depot. While this was never in dispute, the exact date she arrived became a central issue in both the adultery case brought against Hull and his later perjury case.

The testimony of Hull's neighbor Thad E. Davis was the centerpiece of the prosecution's case led by County Attorney J. W. Jarrott against John Hull. Mr. Davis spoke to the jury, telling how his farmhouse was located five miles north of Stephenville and about 600 yards from the Hull home. He stated under oath that on Saturday morning, November 28, 1896, he was working outside his barn when Hull passed by in his wagon, heading down the road toward Stephenville. That evening Davis was once again outside near the horse lot, feeding his mules, when John Hull passed back by the Davis place. In the back of the wagon was a trunk on the flat bed. The occupants were seated close together with a blanket thrown across their laps.

Davis recognized Nona Edwards as the second occupant with John Hull. Being suspicious and having seen the two together before, Davis decided to follow the couple on foot. He heard the wagon slow down and finally stop. Staying as much out-of-sight as he could, Davis crept up to the "brushy, thickety spot" where the wagon was located. No one was seated on the wagon. Hearing rustling and other human sounds in the brush, Davis slipped over and saw the couple on the ground. They were in the throws of passion with Hull on top of his female companion. Davis was adamant under oath that this companion was Nona Edwards and not John's wife, Annie Hull.

Under cross-examination Davis admitted that the two sisters had some physical similarities, but the defense did not shake him from being positive in his identification. To support his testimony, Davis stated this was not the first time he had seen Hull and Nona Edwards together alone. One time, he saw them when he was walking across the field between the two farms. He stated that Hull was standing up, buttoning his pants and brushing off his clothes while Nona was nearby. Davis also stated that he was sure he had seen the couple over three hundred times driving about together, just the two of them, and that their activities were common knowledge in the neighborhood.

Under pressure, Thad Davis admitted he did not like John Hull and seldom spoke to him and that he shot a cow that had wandered into his field, thinking it belonged to Hull. He also believed Hull participated in helping prosecute Davis for killing the cow even though the owner turned out to be someone else.

Corroborating Davis' testimony was R. S. Sterling who saw Hull pass by that November morning alone on his way to Stephenville. Arthur Giger and Will Baker stated that they passed John Hull when he was heading home that day. They identified his female companion as being Nona Edwards, not Annie Hull.

When the defense, ably led by W. J. Oxford took up their side, two powerful witnesses came to Hull's aid—his wife, Annie, and Nona Edwards. These two women wove a different tale that involved a challenge to Davis' testimony. Annie Hull was first, stating that the woman with her husband on Saturday, November 28th was none other than herself and not her sister. She stated that she could not go to town when her husband left that morning. She had some chores that had to be finished first. After doing so, she went down the road and hitched a ride into town with Hull's twenty-eight-year-old brother, Elijah (who curiously was never available to testify).

Annie Hull went on to state that she and Hull picked up Nona's trunk at the train depot but that Nona did not arrive back for a few more days. At the end of the trip that Saturday she was the one who returned to the farmstead with her husband and her sister's trunk in tow.

Next was Nona Edwards who testified that she arrived back in Stephenville from Indian Territory on Wednesday, December 3rd, not Saturday, November 28th. She stated that she sent her trunk on ahead, thinking she would be on the next train but that her cousins begged her to stay a few more days in Springtown.

Two witnesses were brought forward to say that they were on the train with Nona Edwards on December 3rd. Feeling pretty comfortable with how the case was going, the defense decided to put John Hull on the stand. He stated much the same information as his wife and sister-in-law but added under questioning that he did have relations with his wife in the thicket that day.

The defense was very careful not to call Thad Davis or any other prosecution witness "liars" but that they were all simply mistaken as to who was with John Hull on the wagon (and in the bushes) that Saturday. Were the jurors at least a bit incredulous that a man would have a romp in the outdoors with his wife on a cold November evening when their home was only three hundred yards away? Regardless, the returned verdict was "Not Guilty."[1]

County Attorney Jarrott's reaction to the verdict can best be seen in the fact he did not accept it. Double jeopardy prevented him from trying Hull again for adultery using the circumstances presented in this case, so Jarrott upped the stakes by going before the grand jury of Erath County and obtaining an indictment against John Hull for the felony crime of *perjury* based on his testimony in the adultery case. This time John Hull was faced with a trial at the district court level. Conviction brought with it a two to five year stint in the state penitentiary.

Even though the crime of perjury was treated as a felony, it was difficult to prosecute. Proving someone was lying instead of simply being mistaken proved to be fairly difficult. In Erath County between 1867 and 1898 only two out of thirty-one indictments for perjury resulted in convictions, and one of those was a defendant who was convinced to plead guilty to avoid a longer prison sentence. What made Jarrott want to face this uphill battle, knowing the odds were not favorable? John Hull's defense team probably assured their client that he had little to worry about as far as this case was concerned. History was definitely on their side.

Erath County District Attorney Lee Riddle led the prosecution. County Attorney Jarrott assisted in the prosecution and doubled as a witness even though he had been involved in the trial against Hull for adultery. Today the defense could object to Jarrott's "double duty" but not in the 1890s where such conflict of interest was not seen to exist or at least interfere in the defendant receiving a fair trial. Jarrott's testimony was needed to set the stage for the alleged perjury. Riddle centered it exclusively around the trip into town and back home on Saturday, November 28, 1896.

The defense filed a motion for a continuance, stating that important witnesses for the defense were not available and that some had not even been served subpoenas—yet the trial had started. District Judge J. S. Straughan overruled the motion, and the case continued. The defense did scramble enough to get a couple more witnesses to swear that they saw Mrs. Hull with her husband in town and along the road home that Saturday.

One of those new witnesses was James Turnbow who ran a livery business in Stephenville. He testified that he met the train every day as he ran a "bus" service for arriving passengers needing transportation. Turnbow added that on November 28th he saw John Hull at the depot platform wrestling with a trunk and pulling it onto his wagon and that Mrs. Hull was there with him. He said that he spoke to her.

On cross-examination Turnbow stated he had no sympathy for those who committed adultery, fornication, or incest. Did the prosecuting attorney have to stifle a smirk? Pressed, Turnbow admitted that he kept company with "Old Kate" Morse, a known local prostitute. He was forced to say that he drove her around many times without charging her and that he had even sold her a home east of the Bosque River in April 1895, which she turned into a "whorehouse." Business must have been pretty good as she paid off the note in four years. The census for 1900 showed that Turnbow and Kate were neighbors. She was known to still be in "business" at that time.

The trial looked like a stalemate with the tie going to the defense when Annie Hull was once again on the stand reciting her account. When the prosecution got the opportunity, they asked her a question not posed at the previous trial. She explained that when her husband stopped the wagon three hundred yards from home, she was the only one who got down and proceeded into the thicket. The defense immediately objected to this testimony, stating that a wife could not be made to witness against her husband. Did she realize at that moment the mistake she had made? Regardless, Judge Straughan overruled the objection as the defense had been the ones who placed Mrs. Hull on the stand.

Once the defense rested, County Attorney Jarrott was brought back to read into the record the testimony of John Hull who had testified that on that Saturday in question he had gone into the brush and had intimate relations with his wife. This was enough of a crack in the defense's carefully crafted strategy for the prosecution to convince the jury that John Hull had indeed lied under oath in order to prevent a conviction in his previous trial. A guilty verdict was returned with a sentence of two and a half years in prison for the blacksmith-turned-farmer.[2]

The defense was down but still had some tricks up their sleeves. After going through the usual procedure of filing exceptions to the verdict, a motion for a new trial, and submitting trial errors, notice of appeal was filed for the Texas Criminal Court of Appeals. The brief they filed was lengthy and did not rely on only one central issue or alleged error by the lower court. Though thoughtful and well-crafted in legalese, the case yielded only one error the higher court seriously considered relating to the defense's original motion for a continuance at the beginning of the trial. On this alone the verdict was overturned and remanded back to the lower court.[3]

Often seen as the end of litigation, an overturned verdict usually led to a case being dismissed, especially one not involving major theft or murder. Whatever elation John Hull and his defense team may have felt at having his conviction overturned was short-lived when they were informed that the district attorney intended to take the case to trial once again. One has to wonder at the dogged prosecution of John Hull when so many others in the past had been "let off the hook."

Indeed, the case went back to trial. The defense once again asked for a continuance. Being cautious, the court allowed this continuance but warned there would not be any others. The case went to trial in the spring of 1899.

Testimony from the second perjury trial no longer exists, but it can be safely assumed that it followed much the same tract as the previous trial. Even though a new jury was impaneled, the outcome was the same. John Hull was found guilty of perjury. This jury added six more months to his sentence from the previous trial, which meant three years in prison. The defense did file for a new trial but ended their efforts when that motion was overruled. John Hull finally accepted his fate. He was probably out of money and feeling that even if he received a new trial under Judge Straughan, the next jury might pile on even more time.[4]

John Hull arrived at Rusk Penitentiary in East Texas, June 4, 1899, but was transferred to Huntsville in October 1900. He served only two of the three years and was pardoned by Texas Governor Sayers on May 4, 1901.[5] Interestingly, John's wife and sister-in-law continued to live together on the Hull farm while he was away.

Laws are still on the books that make adultery illegal in Texas. Few are prosecuted today, but John Hull found out just how serious a public prosecutor can be when on a mission.

Sable King
The Frank Lewis Story

The Negro community in Erath County lived in a separate portion of the town of Stephenville in the nineteenth century. Generally, lawmen left the Negro community alone unless their actions became too violent or spilled over into the Anglo community.

Nineteen-year-old Negro Frank Lewis married Arizona Harris (age 16) in May 1879. Less than a year later he was charged with theft of a cow belonging to Dr. M. S. Crow. The jury found Lewis to be not guilty.

Lewis's legal woes were not over as he was also charged with the theft of two bushels of wheat. While he waited for his trial to work its way through the district court, Frank's son Walter was born in 1880. Found guilty in April of 1881, Frank Lewis was faced with a $10 fine and 24 hours in jail.

Another year passed and Lewis was once again in jail—this time for aggravated assault. His fine and court costs amounted to $49.10 in April 1882. In Texas in the 1880s and 1890s persons who could not pay their court fines were eligible to be "leased" out to work for private citizens. Most counties kept records of "Convict Labor." Unable to pay his fines, Lewis remained in custody. The county contracted Convict Lewis out to I. N. Roberts for ninety-eight days of labor where he earned $26.50 toward his fee. He served out the rest of his time in jail, getting out August 10, 1883.[1]

A couple of years later Frank Lewis was caught with someone else's pistol. He was found guilty in March 1886. Once again he faced a fine he could not pay. This time he was contracted out to work for J. D. Lewis from March 3 through June 2, 1886.[2]

The marriage that started with such promise disintegrated into almost constant quarreling as Arizona Lewis tried to get her errant husband to straighten up. What happened next made it to the local newspaper in August 1891—

> *Hit With a Spade*
> *Frank Lewis, not content with everyday life as it is, tried to vary its monotony on Tuesday, August 6, by turning his help mate back to dust from whence she sprang. He had a quarrel with his wife, while under the influence of whisky, and hit her over the head with a spade, cutting a gash as long as one's finger. There was considerable squalling after the assault was made and quite a crowd was attracted. . . .*[3]

Frank Lewis got out on bond to await his trial. In late September the *Stephenville Empire* chronicled a night of revelry in the lower part of the town, south of Dr. Crow's residence. Lewis, dubbed the "Sable King" by the paper, held "high carnival" late into the night. He was full of alcohol and offered to fight anyone who was willing.

City Marshal Fooshee watched Lewis as he cursed anyone who came near him. The lawman finally decided it was time to haul Frank into the calaboose. He noticed that Lewis was armed with an opened pocketknife. Fooshee hesitated, knowing how dangerous Lewis could be when drunk. He placed his hand close to his pistol in anticipation of encountering some resistance, but before he could do anything, someone from the back of the crowd threw a large rock that hit Frank in the face. He went down like a felled tree and lay very still. Some women became frightened and pandemonium threatened the gathering. The marshal managed to break up the tense atmosphere while several men gathered up the inert Lewis and took him to sleep it off.[4]

Frank Lewis had barely recovered from his late night attack when his assault case was taken up by the district court. He later told a reporter that his conviction resulted from the fact that District Attorney George dramatically waved a spade over the heads of the jury while delivering his closing remarks. Lewis, found guilty, was given three years in the state penitentiary. He told the same reporter, "You white people don't understand us niggers, case wese always fightin' and scotchin' around, but we don't mean no harm. We hit de nigger on de head and it don't hurt him, case his head is hard. Therefore de white man don't understand us."[5]

At age thirty-one, Frank Lewis entered Huntsville on December 7,

1891. He served two and a half years mostly as a leased convict on a plantation. Arizona Lewis filed for a divorce on March 16, 1893, citing cruelty and physical abuse. The district attorney, J. Collin George, helped her. The citation was served to Frank Lewis at the Sugarland Plantation in Fort Bend County.[6]

Arriving back in Stephenville the summer of 1894, Frank Lewis was a free man and single. By the next spring he had remarried, this time to Annie Smith. He returned to his old ways of drinking and carousing, unconcerned about getting in trouble with the law. He was arrested two more times prior to 1900, once for assault and again for disturbing the peace. He worked off his fines both times.

Except for his savage attack on his first wife, Lewis was not considered much more than a petty nuisance to local law enforcement. He was well known by all, and he could be found drinking whiskey most weekends, but Frank kept to the segregated parts of town. He was smart enough to keep his carousing within the Negro community where he was both loved and feared at times, especially when he was drunk.

J. Collin George

John Lucas, also a Negro, was well liked on both sides of the tracks. He worked at a local livery stable owned by Eugene Bruington. Lucas was widely known in the Cross Timbers area because he at one time had driven a stagecoach before settling down to a full-time job in Stephenville. Lucas, his wife Harriet, and their children lived fairly quiet lives. He stayed away from trouble, but his niece Sallie married Jenks Wallace, a volatile young man who spent a lot of time with Frank Lewis.

On Friday evening April 27, 1900, Jenks and Sallie Wallace were visiting at Frank and Annie Lewis' place. Others were there as well. A disagreement turned into a physical row between the men and the women. Jenks told his wife to go home. When she refused, he pulled her hair and threatened to kill her. Badly frightened, Frank Lewis' niece Janie Higgins went to get help. She returned with Deputy Harve Keith who broke up the fight, sending Jenks Wallace and Crockett Dunn to the jail. Jenks returned later in the evening.

Having heard about the altercation, John Lucas arrived around midnight to check on his niece. As he stood there watching, Jenks once again pulled his wife's hair. Lucas tried to intervene by telling Jenks he should not treat his wife that way. An argument commenced between the two men.

Walking up from behind, Frank Lewis struck John Lucas in the back of the head with an iron wagon wrench. As he stumbled forward, Lucas was once again hit, this time by Jenks Wallace with another piece of iron about eighteen inches long. With this blow, Lucas went flying out the door. He was knocked out.

After some discussion, Wallace, Lewis, and another man picked up Lucas and left with him. Janie Higgins watched as they walked toward Belle Hopson's place where Mose Burdick joined the trio. The men then slid down the banks of the Bosque River, which was swollen from recent rains. They heaved the unconscious man into the water and left. An inquiry was made when they returned to which Lewis replied that they "threw the black son-of-a-bitch into the creek."

Lewis picked up a Jews harp and commenced to play. Crockett Dunn arrived and started singing. The music lasted late into the night. The next morning Harriet Lucas arrived, looking for her husband. She testified later that Frank told her that she would never see John anymore because he was seen drunk and heading down East Washington Street and probably fell off the bluff into the creek.[7]

Harriet Lucas headed for the sheriff's office, fearing the worst. The creek was searched, and John's lifeless body was found. Following the inquest several men were arrested—including Frank Lewis, Jenks Wallace, Charley Marthel, Mose Burdick, and Crockett Dunn. With several witnesses willing to talk about the events that led up to the death of John Lucas, the case was pretty airtight for the district attorney. The defendants hired a very capable attorney—Clarence Nugent—who tried to insist that the district court should quash the indictments as they had not been brought about by a grand jury composed at least partially of Negroes.

When Special Judge Lee Young (sitting in for Judge Straughan) refused to quash the indictments, Nugent then petitioned that the petit jury should be composed of his clients' peers – persons of Negro descent. Again the district judge declined to intervene into the process, and no men of color were called for possible jury duty.

Named as a principal in the murder of Lucas, Frank Lewis was put on trial first and convicted of second-degree murder. He was assessed thirty years in prison for his punishment.[8]

Clarence Nugent appealed the Lewis case to the Texas Court of Criminal Appeals. He did not try to dispute any of the testimony given in the case. Instead, he appealed the case on the basis of there being no grand or petit jurors of Negro descent. Frank Lewis believed that since he was a Negro, he had a right to have a Negro grand jury and petit jury. To prove this point, Nugent presented information on how "the strong racial prejudice exiting between the white and black races in the county [Erath] in the State of Texas, influenced the action of the grand jury in finding this bill of indictment against defendant."[9]

While Stephenville was not used as an example, Alexander and Dublin were specifically mentioned. Both had had incidents that were reported in the newspapers. In Alexander several masked men terrorized some Negroes brought in by A. B. Sherman and Major Baldwin to work in the flourmill in the year 1882. In Dublin an armed body of men rode into the residential area where the Negroes lived in 1892. These men warned the Negroes to leave within three days. County Attorney W. J. Oxford went to Dublin and remained twenty-four hours past the deadline. He was called back again later in the week before the excitement died down.[10]

Clarence Nugent hoped that by showing what he considered a pattern of discrimination, the appellate court would act on Lewis' case and reverse the verdict. To bolster the point, the appeal stated that Erath County had about 5000 voters and that between 400 to 500 were persons of Negro descent who were qualified as jurors, yet none of these men were selected to sit on Lewis' case.

Texas Appellate Judge Henderson pointed out that while Lewis was claiming discrimination based on federal law, specifically the fourteenth amendment, he failed to show that the lack of Negroes serving as jurors on his case was intentionally done by the officers of the court at the time of the drawing of the venire or by the sheriff when he was serving the jurors their notice to appear for district court. Without such evidence, the issue was not actionable. Lewis' conviction was upheld.[11]

Besides Lewis, Jenks Wallace and Mose Burdick were convicted in the killing of John Lucas. Wallace was already serving his sentence when Lewis arrived in early 1901. Burdick arrived six months later. Only Lewis started serving such a lengthy sentence. Although there were no notations on Lewis' conduct ledger of violations, it stated that Lewis was an ex-convict.

In January 1904 Frank Lewis was moved to Rusk Penitentiary. He was assigned to Camp Wright in December 1907. Less than a year later, Lewis was released and pardoned by Governor Campbell. What was interesting was that Lewis was incarcerated only seven of the thirty years he was given by the all white jury before being set free.

"They Have My Boy in That Damned Hell Hole"
The T. J. Wilson Story

T. J. (Scrap) Wilson had reached the end of his endurance where his son Charley was concerned. An only son, Charley had grown up shadowing his dad who owned a saloon and an attached grocery store in downtown Stephenville. Business had been so good in late 1886 that Wilson branched out and bought a dry goods business in Dallas County. When that business failed, the economic impact was so dire that Wilson was forced to sell his saloon and grocery to his brother Jake Wilson.

> He is having an immense trade. Who? Why, T. J. Wilson of course, and all because he keeps first-class goods and sells at reasonable prices. The quality of his goods are unsurpassed and no one in Stephenville carries a better line of liquors, cigars and groceries. Make his store headquarters.

Advertising by Wilson in Stephenville Empire.

T. J. soon regretted his decision and became obsessed about the deal, believing that his brother robbed him. Then Jake brought in William (Billie) Kay, their nephew, as his partner. T. J. aimed his anger at Billie as well.

The worst was yet to come and would prey on T. J.'s mind. When Charley hit his mid-teen years, he started working for his uncle in the meat market that had been converted from T. J.'s grocery business. Charley drifted between the market and the saloon where he came to admire his older cousin Billie. T. J. worried about the amount of time his son was spending with Billie, and because of his disapproval T. J. quarreled with Charley about his activities and associations. At one point the atmosphere between father and son became so tense that Charley left Stephenville to work in Thurber.

Missing his old haunts, Charley returned to Stephenville, but the tension with his father did not ease. Charley found a sympathetic audience among friends his own age and returned to his job with Cousin Billie. He managed to get into minor scrapes and run-ins with the law. In despair, T. J. turned more and more to frequenting the other saloons in Stephenville.

Charley moved out of his father's home once again. He strained relations even further by moving into the back of his uncle's saloon. He shared quarters with Billie. He joined his friends in mocking his own father and participated in a joke with an official looking notice the young men wrote up, informing saloon men that they were not to serve alcohol to Scrap Wilson. Billie composed it, and Charley made copies and circulated the notice.

Fighting a losing battle, T. J. devised a plan to shock his son back to reality. He went before the grand jury of Erath County and swore out a complaint against his son for selling whiskey on a Sunday. John Oxford, city marshal, stepped over to the Wilson & Kay Saloon while the grand jury was deliberating. Billie Kay had seen T. J. go into the courthouse. He told Oxford that he would beat T. J. to death if he testified against Billie. Instead, Charley was true billed for selling alcohol to William Gilbreath on a Sunday.

The final showdown happened on another Sunday. T. J. Wilson knew that his attempt to get his son back home had not worked. He woke up on December 15, 1895, with a new determination to bring his boy home. After dinner he had a few whiskeys to fortify himself. Then he headed for downtown where he knew he would find Charley.

T. J. found his son in front of Crow's Opera House on Washington Street. When Charley balked at leaving with his father, T. J. did the only thing he could think to do. He grabbed hold of Charley by his coat and started pulling him along Belknap Street northerly toward Sara Harrison's hotel. A crowd quickly formed and started following them.

While this parental confrontation unfolded, Billie Kay arrived downtown. He had borrowed a horse and buggy from E. W. Tabor of Dublin who sold musical instruments. Billie spent the afternoon taking a young lady for a ride. He tied the buggy to the hitchrack and walked down to the back door of the saloon.

Hearing the ruckus, Billie walked over to Belknap Street and watched T. J. pulling his son along. The crowd was jeering and laughing, but T. J. was oblivious in his determination to succeed. Charley's hat blew off. While T. J. bent over to pick it up, Charley pulled a rolled cigarette out of his pocket and lit it. T. J. angrily knocked the cigarette out of his son's hand.

Charley, sensing this was his best chance, broke loose from his father's grip and took off running. The crowd cheered him on as he ran a zigzag route around the courthouse square. His father pursued, but the younger man soon outdistanced his dad. Charley finally sprinted across the square and ran into the meat market, locking the door behind him.

When T. J. finally arrived, he could not get inside the market. So, he started pacing outside, going east several paces and then going several paces west of the entrance. As he walked, T. J. became increasingly agitated. He proclaimed to anyone who would listen that "they have my boy in that damned hell hole" over there, and he could not get him out. He spoke of how his son was not very smart and could easily be led by others. T. J. also stated that he had been robbed but did not say by whom.

The crowd stood around watching T. J. who continued to pace and mutter loudly. Billie Kay ignored the ruckus and gathered his bed linen, which had been drying on a clothesline out behind the saloon. As he was doing this, Walter Penninger found him to relate what was happening. Billie asked to borrow Penninger's knife. He ignored the question when asked what he intended to do with it.

Outside, T. J. continued to walk back and forth, stopping long enough to take a knife out of his coat. He opened it and placed the knife back in his pocket. Soon, Billie Kay came out of the saloon and locked it. He dropped the key into his pocket and walked over to the door of the meat market. Stopping, he put one foot on the doorstep and turned to look at T. J.

With his back to Billie, T. J. did not act like he had even seen the saloonkeeper come from his bar. Then he loudly repeated again his accusations against his brother and nephew concerning his son. Kay stepped toward him and asked him to repeat what he had just said. T. J., looking then at his nephew, obliged.

Billie asserted, "That's a damn lie!"

T. J. shot back, "You're another damn liar!"

The two men rushed toward the other. Billie was much younger, stouter, and used to being active. T. J. was small both in size and weight. Billie threw the first punch, but T. J. came up with an upward jab. The two men tangled, and onlookers could not see exactly who was getting the upper hand in the altercation.

Both men fell to the sidewalk, Billie on top of T. J. When the younger man got up, his opponent remained down. Billie grabbed hold of a post and began stomping T. J. about his head and face, getting in several forceful blows before Sam Roberson pulled Billie away. Suddenly, Billie collapsed to the ground. He lived only a few minutes longer, because T. J. had somehow managed to stab him four times, one of which penetrated his heart. The outcome of the affray caused shock among the onlookers.

T. J. was so badly beaten he had to be carried to the county jail where Dr. J. M. Williamson arrived to examine him. The doctor's report stated that T. J. had a bruised and blackened eye, several bruises around his head on top of much swelling. By morning T. J. was battling a high fever but did eventually recover.

County Attorney J. W. Jarrott signed the complaint against T. J. Wilson and led the gathering of evidence at the examining trial. T. J. Wilson was indicted in April 1896 for the murder of William Kay, but the trial was delayed until the October 1897 docket. A large number of witnesses on both sides testified in Judge Straughan's court. The jury left the courtroom late Saturday afternoon to deliberate. They brought back a verdict Sunday afternoon that found T. J. Wilson guilty of second-degree murder with punishment set at ten years in prison.[1]

Wilson's attorneys filed an appeal based on alleged errors of the lower court, including not allowing a continuance for important material witnesses and not allowing the testimony of J. P. Silar for the defense. Of the six bills of exception only one caused the appellate court to reverse the verdict and remand the case back to the lower court. The prosecution impeached Walter Penninger's collateral testimony over the objection of the defense. The ruling stated that this might have caused the jury not to consider any of that witness's statements about Billie Kay borrowing a knife from Penninger. Because of this, the ruling of the lower court was reversed and the case remanded in January 1897.[2]

The district attorney placed the retrial on the spring 1897 docket. The jury in this trial found T. J. Wilson not guilty. Not everyone got off unscathed. Sheriff Frank Freeman was fined $100 and cited for contempt of court for not sufficiently guarding the jurors and keeping them together. The offending juror was J. B. Jenkins who was fined $50 for separating from the other jurors during the trial.

T. J. Wilson's legal woes may have been over but not his concern for his son Charley who continued to run with the downtown crowd of young men. He was hauled into district court on two separate indictments. One was an assault with intent to murder. The jury found him guilty only of an aggravated assault and assessed a $30 fine.[3] Potentially more serious was his indictment for rape. Luckily for him, the main witness refused to testify, forcing the district attorney to drop the case.[4] So, Charley Wilson dodged a potential "bullet" of a lengthy prison tenure.

'Promise Me That You Will Let Liquor Alone'
The Tom Wright & Frank Leslie Story

"Promise me that you will let liquor alone"—those seemingly hypocritical words were uttered by Tom Wright as he stood on the temporary scaffold erected under the direction of Sheriff Tutt Hume for the first legal execution in Erath County history. The hanging, which took place in Stephenville on November 10, 1899, was the culmination of events set in motion many years before between two opposing forces bent on holding sway in the small town of Dublin, which had had larger but ultimately unrealized aspirations of becoming the county seat of Erath in the early 1890s.

Concerned about the large number of saloons, several important people in Dublin turned their attention to bringing more law and order to their town after losing the county seat vote in 1891.[1] The downtown saloons seemed to draw a certain undesirable lawless element to them. Men, especially of the younger generation, loafed around these bars most evenings. The town's upright citizens decided it was time to take action.

Those who deplored the use of alcohol organized—then took advantage of a provision passed by the Texas Legislature allowing precincts and towns within a wet county to vote on outlawing the sale of alcohol. This provision was called "Local Option." Many of the businessmen were in favor of the local option, believing an alcohol-free town would draw folks immigrating to Texas. Growing Dublin's population would be good for business.

First though, the criminal element needed to be gone or at least neutralized. Local option was a viable way to work toward that goal. The first vote was held in late 1893. The prohibitionists won, effectively shutting down the saloons in Precinct 2, which covered most of Dublin.[2] The temperance movement won a great victory but not the war that continued between the two factions. Bitterness grew between the "pros" (for prohibition) and the "antes."

The late-night lights along Black Jack and Patrick Streets no longer were shining to entice the male population to stop in for a nip or two. As with what happened in the 1920s across America during nationwide prohibition, the strong desire for intoxicating beverages acted as a catalyst for those willing to flout the law for an economic enterprise.

In 1894 County Attorney W. J. Oxford was called over to Dublin to rule on the sale of malt tonic and whether it was intoxicating and, therefore, illegal to sell. This product had been introduced into markets where alcohol was no longer legal. Made from much the same process as beer, malt tonic was advertised as non-intoxicating. Oxford arrived in Dublin and spent two days there.[3] The teetotaling attorney was unable to prove that malt tonic had alcohol content. One might wonder how he conducted the investigation. His ruling did not satisfy the prohibitionists who believed the beverage was nothing more than beer under another name.

By petition another vote on the issue of local option for Dublin and Precinct No. 2 was set for 1895. The topic was a heated one, drawing hot tempers on both sides of the issue. Vocal in his condemnation of demon rum was John C. Adams who delivered many lectures on the topic. At one he went a little overboard when making personal remarks about some prominent citizens. He was confronted by one of those men when C. B. Long went to see him. A fisticuff was narrowly avoided but not the lawsuit filed the next day against Adams who employed W. J. Oxford as his attorney.[4] This zealous attitude by Adams helped him to be elected constable of Dublin. He had served as constable of Stephenville for a number of years previously. He brought a certain vigor and doggedness to his goal of rooting out those who flouted the local option law, which once again passed by a majority of 107 votes.

Several citizens of Dublin decided to get a little more serious about enforcing the law after the second option election. Acting on a complaint, Benjamin Palmer, deputy county attorney, granted a temporary injunction restraining Buck Parker, M. C. and E. B. Gillette, Sam and Jim Prim, and Joe Harrell from running hopfenwels (hop-in-weise) and malt tonic stands.[5]

The sale of alcohol went underground. Some sales were out of private homes where customers were carefully screened. Others kept a jug or two under the counter of a legitimate business. The customers came in, went behind the counter, got a glass or small bottle full, and then left some money on the counter before leaving. No dialogue had to take place. Participants knew the routine.

The efforts to enforce the option law were not nearly as successful as some had hoped. The *Dallas Morning News* carried a story in 1895, stating that the freight receipts of liquor and beer shipped to Dublin the seventeen months prior to the passage of local option, and since it took effect showed a difference of only seven barrels. Because the figures did not include liquor by express, the number was actually fifteen barrels more for the seventeen months since prohibition had been sent to Dublin than before.[6]

Those who had engineered a vote to prohibit alcohol in Dublin were frustrated that many men continued to sell alcohol in defiance of the result of the local option election. This frustration led to further actions by men who were against those who set up "blind tigers" which were illegal bars.

Born in Gonzales County, Tom Wright moved to Erath from Bell County where the stockman set up close to Dublin sometime around 1880. He quickly fell in with other young men who frequented the then legal downtown saloons on a regular basis. At 5'6" the blue-eyed, fair-skinned native Texan brought a certain swagger to his dealings that belied his short stature. Being married did not slow Wright down. He loved the late night-lights.

Wright's first major run-in with the law came in October 1882 at age 25 when he was indicted for assault with the intent to murder T. J. Robinson.[7] For reasons not noted officially, the district attorney had the case dismissed in October 1883. Wright managed to steer clear of the district court until March 6, 1891, when he was one of five men indicted for burning down the home of Julian Rodriquez. It happened after a long evening of drinking and grousing that the Mexicans had brought small pox into the community. Afterward, Wright waylaid County Attorney W. J. Oxford who was investigating the crime and offered to give him some information on the arson. Oxford believed that Wright was one of the principals who set the fire and was not willing to deal with him if he could get Tom Lauderdale who played a lesser role in the event to turn State's witness. So, Oxford ignored Wright's offer. Wright maintained to his death that he did not participate in the arson. Without necessary funds, Wright turned to the court to help him by providing counsel. With little time to prepare, the case was tried. Wright was convicted and sent to Huntsville on May 30, 1891, where he served 2½ years of the five-year term.

The clemency file on the arson conviction for Wright indicated that James Gibson, Assistant Superintendent for Rusk Penitentiary, took an active role in seeking a gubernatorial pardon for Wright, stating in his letter to Governor Hogg that Wright was friendless with a suffering and destitute wife at home who really needed him. On an ironic note John C. Adams signed two different petitions for Wright's pardon, which he received from Governor Hogg on November 5, 1893.[8]

Tom Wright returned to Dublin and his old stomping grounds but found a much different place. The first local option election had passed just three days before his pardon was signed. With the saloon lights permanently out, Tom was unable to return to his previous freewheeling lifestyle. Court records show that Tom joined the element in town who resisted the implementation of prohibition. Some evidence indicated that he ran a "blind tiger" or at least partnered in one for a while. He was hauled before the justice of the peace and county court numerous times for petty crimes, mostly relating to bootlegging. Tom's reputation as a local lawbreaker grew.

John Adams, now an elected constable for Dublin, was urged to be vigilant in his duty, and he had little use for Tom Wright and his brethren. While the pros urged Adams on to greater efforts in enforcing the local option in Dublin, not everyone was enamored with the methods Adams used. He managed to get crossways with County Judge Thomas B. King who opposed Adams' heavy-handed tactics.

Several men in Dublin also became annoyed at Adams. They felt his methods and self-righteous attitude were a bit too much, and those who still sought to profit from the underground sale of alcohol started grumbling among themselves that things would get a bit easier if Adams were not always nosing around.

The tense and volatile atmosphere was ripe for an explosion.

Throwing gasoline on the flying sparks, Gus Blasingame, who was known to run a "blind tiger," went to the justice of the peace and signed an affidavit that Tom Wright had approached him about killing John Adams in order to get him out of the way. Blasingame stated that this was not the first time he had been approached by Wright on this matter. He said that he threw Wright out of his business establishment and told him he would not be a party to any assassination. John Adams was brought in and made aware of the affidavit. Later, Tom Wright wove a tale about how Blasingame wanted to get the heat off himself and his side business. So, he chose to finger Tom to do so.

Infuriated, John Adams set in motion events that led to his death at the hands of Tom Wright. Instead of allowing the law to look into the accusation, Adams decided to confront Wright himself, leading to the deadly conclusion.

On the morning of December 16, 1897, Wright went to the Dublin railroad depot to catch the train into Stephenville. He had to attend court for a perjury charge hanging over his head in a case concerning the sale of whiskey by a mulatto named Hawk out of Jim Tyree's house. Constable Adams arrived at the depot at about the same time as Tom. Seeing Wright, the constable walked over and pulled his pistol. Waving it at Tom, Adams called out, "There's that damn son-of-a-bitch now."[9]

Mayor Richard McCain arrived just in time to step in between the two men, bringing the tense confrontation to an end. On the train into Stephenville McCain asked Wright what precipitated the tense meeting. Unaware of the affidavit, Tom replied that he was not sure what was going on. He admitted that the two of them had a long history of bad blood but that Adams had never been this blatantly aggressive. In town Tom found out from Buck Parker about the affidavit Blasingame had signed.

Frightened, Wright went to see Walter Lowe, a Dublin resident, who confirmed that Adams had been told about Blasingame's affidavit. Back at home Wright told his wife that trouble was brewing, and he was not sure just what to do about it. In an effort to ameliorate the situation Wright went to see his friend Green Harrison who admitted he knew about the affidavit. Green agreed to approach Adams to see if the matter could be settled without trouble. Adams told Green that the only thing he wanted was for Tom Wright to be gone from the county or he intended to kill Wright.

The next day Wright ventured into town. He went to another Dublin resident—Jack Hurt—and asked him to mediate. Hurt declined, telling Tom he best find someone else. Finally, Charley Oats, a friend, volunteered. Adams reacted by saying he wanted no more emissaries, just for Wright to be gone. Not giving up, Wright convinced another Dublin resident—H. H. Andrews—to intercede. His temper exploding, Adams replied, "Where is that God damn son-of-a-bitch?"[10]

Andrews told him that Wright was in the wagon yard, but by the time Adams arrived, Wright was gone. Tom tried one last time to work something out through Bob Utterback, another Dublin resident, but to no avail. Sending all these men to see Adams may have caused him to believe that Tom was weak, but the constable failed to see that once someone is pushed far enough, it is hard to predict what that person might do.

Too nervous to stay at home, Wright went back to Dublin that evening. He found some men congregating at Frank Bratton's ten-pin bowling alley. He stopped in even though he and Bratton had been at odds with one another in the past over Tom's efforts to set up a cockfight in the building next to Bratton. The businessman became so annoyed he turned Wright in to Adams who put an end to that enterprise. Bratton and Wright let their differences fade over time.

As Wright sat and visited with several of the men, Adams came through the door. All talking ceased, and eyes turned toward the town's constable. Spying Tom, Adams wasted no time. He drew his pistol and pointed it at Wright's face, saying, "Tom, are you ready?"

"No, John. I have not got anything and nothing to get ready for," Wright replied.

Adams shot back, "God damn you! You have been trying to hire somebody to kill me. This is the third time I've heard it, and now I have it in black and white."

"John, this is all a lie. If you will give me a chance I will prove it to you. I have had all the trouble I want, and I will get on my knees and kiss you if you want me to, for what you heard is a lie, and I don't want to have any more trouble."

Sensing the confrontation might end in bloodshed, Frank Bratton told the two men, "You fellas can't have a racket in here."[11]

Constable Adams looked at Bratton—then back to Wright before replying, "Tom, you go fix yourself. I don't want to shoot you unarmed; you arm yourself, for the next time we meet I intend to kill you, armed or unarmed. The town is too small and the streets too narrow for both of us to walk on and live, and you have got to leave this town, by god. The next time we meet this has got to be settled."

Bratton asked Adams to leave which he did but still with his pistol drawn. Bratton then told Wright to go out the back door. Wright was reluctant to leave, as he believed Adams would ambush him once he got outside. Crowder Farris and George Thompson agreed to leave with Tom. Adams waited for them at the corner and followed for a while before turning off at Easley's Blacksmith Shop.

Wright went to Green Harrison's place and asked for his six-shooter, but Green told him that his gun was broken. Tom took it anyway. Green suggested that Tom place Adams under a peace bond. Tom was skeptical. He asked Green and Thompson to go to town and get him some shells loaded with buckshot. They both refused.

Thompson told Wright that talk was running rampant through the community about the trouble between him and John Adams. He said some were even taking bets on whether or not Tom would show up for a showdown or would quit Dublin instead. Wright asked Green to go to Adams one more time, hoping that the constable had cooled off and would listen to a plea for a peaceful resolution. Green returned, stating he could not do anything with Adams, because he was very angry. Adams' message back was that Tom knew what to depend on, that he had told Tom himself, and he did not want to hear any more words from him.

The one person who might have given Tom Wright solid advice was Dublin mayor, Richard McCain. Tom headed for McCain's home, arriving after dusk. McCain had not come home from Stephenville yet, so Tom waited, not knowing what else to do. He visited with

Mrs. McCain until the mayor arrived. Going over the events with the mayor, Tom saw his situation as being hopeless. McCain asked if there were witnesses at the bowling alley confrontation. Tom replied that Frank Bratton, Henry Beaver, Jack Leslie, Ed Moore, Tom Bays, Crowder Farris, George Thompson, Walter McCain, Tom Lafferty and others were there.

Remembering Green's suggestion, Wright asked about getting a peace bond. McCain agreed that it could be done but would not likely do any good. Tom asked McCain for a gun for his own protection, saying he was very afraid of Adams. McCain refused to loan the gun and knowing Tom's history, admonished him, "Don't you get into any more trouble. You have had trouble enough."[12]

Traveling home, Wright was surprised when his wife practically jerked him into the house when he arrived at the front door. It was about midnight. She related that while Tom was gone, she heard two men slipping around outside. She recognized John Adams' voice.

With this intrusion Wright felt a sense of defeat. He was out of ideas on what to do, and his wife was thoroughly scared. After much discussion the couple made the decision to leave. With no money Tom needed to sell his land and extra feed. He decided to stay in Dublin long enough to do that.

The next morning—December 18th—Wright went over to Green Harrison's house to take back the broken pistol and to see if Green would purchase Tom's property. Green said he did not have the money. Tom approached several other possible buyers including Joe Bishop and Tom Lafferty but had no luck. With each rejection Tom became more frustrated and tense. He went home to eat dinner.

Frank Leslie stopped by. A hanger-on who barely stayed out of legal trouble, Leslie was excited about the trouble between his friend Tom Wright and John Adams. He had told others that he thought a showdown would take place. This prediction would get him into serious trouble later, as it looked like he was in on the planning with Tom to kill Adams.

Wright told Leslie that he desperately needed a gun, as he had to go to town to get provisions for his family. He did not dare go unarmed. Leslie said he could find a gun but later came back without one. Tom suggested that Leslie try Bob Sneed. Leslie came back with a shotgun. He told Sneed that he needed it to hunt squirrels. Armed, Tom and Frank left for town.

A cold day, the two men traveled down Black Jack Street until they got to the stairway leading up to Richard McCain's office. They climbed the outside stairs, entering the building to get warm. As soon as he saw the shotgun, McCain ordered the two men out of his office. Leslie led the way down the stairway. Tom and Frank waited in front of Sanders Barber Shop.

Looking out toward the crossroads, Wright saw the transfer bus driven by J. W. Collin come to a halt. Then he saw Adams walk up to the rear of the bus and open the door to let little Jesse Maloney out the back. Constable Adams was engaged in completing this request and was not paying any attention to what was going on around him.

Whether Wright planned it as the prosecution would later state or was driven by anxiety and fear of the constable, what he did next is not in dispute. Seeing his adversary and knowing he had the advantage, Wright ran toward Adams. A by-stander, J. B. Tubberville, seeing the turn of events quickly called out to Adams to watch out. Adams turned slightly toward Wright while lifting his arm up, but it was too late.

Wright aimed the shotgun and fired. The charge struck Adams in the right temple and exited out the left. Adams fell face forward into the mud. Wright rushed up to the prostrate man and shot again into Adams' right cheek. The constable was already dead from the first shot. Flushed with excitement and adrenalin, Tom called out to no one in particular, "That's the last of John Adams."

Wright walked over to the sidewalk in front of the Dublin Drug Company and waited. Several men went over to Adams' body and proceeded to move him to the sidewalk on the opposite side of the street from Tom who just watched. Soon, City Marshal Jesse Phillips arrived and arrested Tom who gave himself up without a struggle. Phillips got Tom out of sight before sentiment could cause a mob to form to exact vengeance. Phillips placed a heavy guard around Wright and then sent a telegram to Stephenville, summoning Sheriff Freeman to come to Dublin to get Tom.

In the meantime Justice of the Peace Lowe took Adams' body to Higginbotham Brothers for Barry Trammel, their embalmer, to start preparing for burial. The sheriff arrived and took Wright to Stephenville under the cover of darkness. The inquest was started the next day in Dublin. With fifty-five witnesses, the proceedings lasted for three days with a pause on Monday for the funeral of John Adams. He was buried in the Old Dublin Cemetery. As a result of the inquest, Frank Leslie was arrested as an accomplice in the murder of John Adams.[13]

Sentiment was running high when the Dublin Law and Order Club had their next meeting. This organization had its first meeting shortly after the election in the fall of 1897 that reaffirmed local option for Dublin. These businessmen, lawyers, and well-to-do farmers had originally formed their group due to the frustration of trying to enforce prohibition on a town used to having saloons around. Even though local option had passed in 1893, those wanting to flout the law were able to carry on with little interference. Breaking the law meant little more than a slap on the hand and a fine.

Some of Dublin's most prominent citizens joined the Law and Order Club, contributing money to help prosecute those who broke the local option law. W. J. Clay was elected chairman. On the executive committee were J. H. Latham, R. W. Higginbotham, W. R. Young, R. B. Spencer, and M. C. Witcher. These men testified later that the money collected was put into a fund to pay lawyers willing to help in the prosecution of option breakers.

When the meeting was called shortly after the death of Constable John Adams, it was not to talk about local option violators. Tempers and emotions ran high against Tom Wright. Days of vigilantes and organizing a lynching party were over. Besides, Wright was safely ensconced in the county jail located in Stephenville. If they could not get at Wright one way, they certainly would another.

Because district attorneys traveled so much, it was a common occurrence for the county attorney to do preliminary research on cases. Also common was for private attorneys to assist the district attorney in an important prosecution, either due to an avid interest, a chance for raising one's legal standing in a high profile case or because those with a vested interest in a guilty verdict were willing to pay the best trial attorneys to assist the district attorney.

The Law and Order Club decided to devote $300 to hiring the most competent lawyers available to see that Tom Wright's prosecution brought about the desired result. An application was made to the state for an additional $200 more but was rejected. The club made up the difference, plus adding another $200. The law offices of Martin & George, McMillan & Oxford plus N. W. Palmer were hired out of this fund. The Law and Order Club meant business, and that business was the successful prosecution of Tom Wright.[14]

Grand jury who indicted Tom Wright and Frank Leslie for murder.

With few friends and even less money or resources, Tom Wright was in the worst fix of his life. He had lived on the edge of the wrong side of the law but never anything this serious. Whatever relief he may have felt at besting Adams probably evaporated with each mile he traveled from Dublin to Stephenville. Why Richard McCain and William Daniels agreed to be Wright's lawyers was not known for certain. Did McCain feel some responsibility toward Wright for not helping him earlier? Certainly these Dublin attorneys had a lot to lose by defending someone the most prominent men in town had contributed money to bring down. Ultimately, the stress may have proved too much and possibly contributed to McCain's early death in July 1899 after being ill for several months.

While Wright's attorneys had good intentions, they had little trial experience of a felony this serious. They were up against some of the county's finest and most experienced trial lawyers who were now assisting in the prosecution. This legal team managed to block attempts to get bail for Tom Wright or Frank Leslie. McCain filed an appeal to the Court of Criminal Appeals but did not appear at the hearing to argue the merits of the case, while Martin and George for the prosecution traveled to Austin to assist Assistant Attorney General Mann-Trice, thwarting the defense's efforts.

The Erath County grand jury returned indictments against both Tom Wright and Frank Leslie for murder in the first degree. Trial was set for April 1898. The defense filed for a change of venue, using a signed affidavit by R. V. Spruill and Tom Bays, citing that the case was too well known and much talked about. McCain not only brought in witnesses, including County Judge Thomas B. King, who stated they did not believe Wright could receive a fair trial in Erath but also put many of the members of the Law and Order Club on the stand to admit they had contributed money toward Wright's prosecution.

A counter affidavit stating Wright could get a fair trial was signed by S. S. Davis, H. W. Northcutt and W. M. Northcutt. Two of the three were slated to be State's witnesses at the trial. With the help of his team, the district attorney brought in people from all parts of the county to state they thought Wright could get a fair trial. District Judge J. S. Straughan ruled against the change of venue request.

The trial for Tom Wright went forward and chosen to be on the petit jury were F. M. Bowers, T. J. Chenault, A. A. Kerr, A. J. Blankenship, W. N. Perkins, W. C. Williams, Bob Holt, John Hitower, Sam King, A. J. Wells, Ely Center, and I. A. Griffith who became the jury foreman.

McCain filed two special charges to be added to the judge's charge to the jury. Judge Straughan denied both. The jury returned a verdict of guilty and assessed the death penalty for Tom Wright.

As he was preparing his motion for a new trial for Wright,

McCain was made aware that sitting on the jury was a man who had previously sat on the jury that had sent Tom Wright to prison years before for arson. It was reported that this juror had also made statements prior to voir dire to people indicating he thought Tom Wright should be hung. Worse still was that this same juror, Mr. I. A. Griffith, served as the jury foreman for Wright's murder trial.

Filing for a mistrial due to these allegations, McCain moved for a new trial. Judge Straughan held a hearing on the matter. Testifying against Griffith were J. T. Daniel and Truss Patton, both saying Griffith talked about the trial prior to being picked to serve on it. Brought on to defend himself, Griffith admitted he had been a juror in the previous trial but that it did not prejudice him against Wright and he did not think to mention it at voir dire. He stated he never talked to Daniel about the facts of the case and that Truss Patton simply misunderstood what Griffith had said. That was good enough for Judge Straughan who overruled the motion for a new trial.[15]

In the meantime Frank Leslie, in a separate trial, was also found guilty of first-degree murder. In an unforgiving mood, even though Leslie was not the gunman, the jury assessed Leslie the death penalty as well.

Richard McCain moved to file for an appeal in Wright's case. His inexperience and ill health caused him to fail to file within ten days of the adjournment of court the "Statement of Facts" concerning the Motion for a Change of Venue and that Griffith was not qualified to act as a juror in Wright's murder trial. So, because of a failure to file in a timely manner and the fact none of Wright's lawyers appeared to argue the case before the appellate court, the State's attorney general was able to get the Court of Criminal Appeals to refuse to rule on these two items, which were probably Tom's best chance for the verdict to the overturned. The lower court's ruling was affirmed.[16] His last hope was for people to petition the governor for clemency.

On October 4, 1899, Tom Wright was taken into court for Judge Straughan to pass the death sentence. The judge set the date for execution to be November 10th.[17] Tom Wright had run out of options. He had not set foot outside of the Erath County Jail since December 1897 except for going to the courthouse. He would only have one last trip to make.

With District Judge Straughan setting the date, the citizens had to deal with the reality that Erath County was about to have their first legal execution. A petition that encompassed a plea for the sentence to be commuted to life imprisonment was quickly circulated and signed by hundreds of people in Erath and Comanche counties. The Texas Board of Pardons along with the Attorney General of Texas unanimously supported the petition. Even so, attorney Ben Palmer sent a heavily worded letter to Governor Sayers October 25, 1899, giving reasons not to stay the execution. He wrote that Wright was "backed and aided by a gang of cut throats which kept this section of the country in a constant turmoil for a long time."[18] Governor Sayers sent an order for the execution to move forward.

On November 4th another petition was composed and signed by members of the Erath County Bar. It said in part—

> *As members of the Erath County bar, we beg to express to Your Excellency the dispassionate opinion that the ends of justice will be fully met by a commutation of the sentence of Tom Wright. . . .Many of us are solemnly impressed that the condemned man was very lamely represented. . . . we know that much prejudice, deep seated and wide spread, existed against the condemned at the time of his trial, and that he fought single handed a large and most influential class of our citizens. . . . Hope for a favorable reply we remain, with the highest respect, your obedient servants.*[19]

Sixteen signatures were attached including Thomas B. King, J. W. Jarrott, and J. B. Keith. Also attached was a short note from J. W. Parker, who had been the district attorney during Wright's trial. He endorsed the petition. Mrs. Katie Wright, Tom's wife, carried the plea to Austin in hopes the governor would rethink his position. He did not.

One final attempt was made when George Tyler of Belton and George Pendleton and W. D. Cochran of Temple took up the cause and managed to get an audience with the governor. The meeting ended with the governor agreeing to take the matter under advisement. Two desperate telegrams from outside of Erath were sent at 8:58AM and 9:03AM on November 9th, exhorting Governor Sayers to put off the execution at least a week.[20]

True to his reputation as a law and order public official, Governor Sayers sent this telegram: "Austin, 11:02AM, Nov. 9, 1899. R. T. Hume, Sheriff, Stephenville, Texas. Sir – I decline to interfere with execution of Tom Wright tomorrow. J. D. Sayers, Governor."[21]

Stung by public criticism, the governor sent a letter of explanation to the press defending his decision. He cited the ruling of the Court of Criminal Appeals in Wright's case but went on to say that Tom Wright had been sent to prison once before and that his time was commuted. The governor noted that Wright, instead of learning from his mistakes, went back to his old ways on the wrong side of the law. Sayers firmly believed Wright was guilty of first-degree murder, and the only way to suppress crime was to execute the law.[22]

Sheriff Tutt Hume had the responsibility to prepare for the hanging. It was illegal to have a public execution. So, Hume built a temporary two-story high scaffold with sides all the way to the top. The backside of the jail served as one of the walls of the scaffold. He cut out two windows to let in light and for the last speeches.

The morning of the execution, Wright was allowed to visit with his wife and daughter for a couple of hours. Close to noon she left so that final preparations could be made. With time running out, Deputies Harve Keith and Mack Cresswell unlocked the death cell where Wright was being kept and let him out into the run-around to get dressed and finish his toilette. He was allowed one last meeting with his family and Reverend C. E. Brown who had spent a lot of time with Wright over a period of months leading up to the execution. The preacher gave Wright and his wife a consoling talk and led in the singing of "Show Pity, O Lord Forgive."

Wright did not break down until he was allowed one last embrace with his wife and daughter. Pulling himself back together, Wright gave his wife the Bible he had kept with him during the long months of incarceration. He stated —

> *I am not guilty of this for which I am to die but the law has said that I must pay the death penalty and I expect to try to do it like a man. I forgive all who have deprived me of my life and hope God will do so.*[23]

Wright's family left so that the final preliminaries of the law could be carried out with Sheriff Hume reading the death warrant to the prisoner. Tom called a final farewell inside the jail to Frank Leslie who was awaiting his own appeal. Sheriff Hume led Tom Wright out.

A huge crowd had gathered outside, irresistibly drawn to the spectacle of a legal execution. Although a wooden fence surrounded the jail grounds where the scaffold stood, people sat along the top of the fence. Beyond that, groups of people stood or sat on wagons and buggies quietly murmuring, waiting in anticipation. Some managed to climb up on roofs or to peer out of second story buildings close by.

Sheriff Hume followed protocol. He led Wright up the stairs to the platform, which was filled with several official witnesses, including sheriffs from Comanche, Brown and Hamilton counties along with physicians whose duty would be to check for vital signs after the hanging. Once all were in place, Hume stepped to one of the open windows and addressed the crowd, briefly explaining that hangings by law had to be private and that after the speeches the windows would be closed for the execution to take place. Then at Wright's behest Reverend Brown also spoke to the crowd.

For his final words Wright started by taking up Frank Leslie's cause and asking that only one innocent man be executed for the death of John Adams. He also stated that those who believed Richard McCain or John McCarty had anything to do with Adams' death were wrong. He warned the audience against alcohol and asked the young boys to "promise me you will let liquor alone." He talked a bit about the events that led to his current state, proclaimed his innocence, and then forgave all and hoped they would return the favor.

Wright told the crowd that he had given a last statement to the press about what really happened. Some newspapers printed this statement and some did not, saying that laws of libel prevented them from doing so. Both the *Stephenville Empire* and *Dublin Progress* printed Wright's last statement.

Wright turned back to the group on the scaffold and shook hands with everyone and bade them goodbye. When he finished, he announced he was ready. A silk handkerchief was placed over his eyes; his legs were tied, and his hands were bound behind his back with heavy buckskin string. A black cap was placed over his head as he stood on the gallows. Finally, the noose was placed around his neck.

Wright continued to talk throughout the preparations for the hanging. He gave instructions concerning his burial and belongings. He finally cautioned the sheriff to tighten the noose so that it would not slip and give him a hard death. Many commented later about how calm, cool, and deliberate Wright was during his last minutes.

The hanging of Tom Wright on November 9, 1899 in Stephenville, Texas.

At a little before 2PM Sheriff Hume asked, "Are you ready?" The prompt reply was, "Ready." Releasing the trap spring, the sheriff watched Wright fall ten feet to his death, paying the ultimate penalty. Although Wright's neck was broken with the ten-foot fall, his heart continued to beat for sixteen minutes at which time the physicians pronounced him dead.[24]

Wright's body was placed in a coffin. From her kitchen stairway

Miss Kate Hume, the sheriff's daughter, handed down a bouquet of white roses, which were placed inside the coffin with the body. The sheriff escorted Wright's remains to the train depot. David Deaton, Wright's cousin, took charge of taking Tom back to Dublin for burial in the Old Cemetery. Deaton later became sheriff of Erath County in 1910. In 1930 Wright's coffin was moved to the New Cemetery in Dublin. The rope used to hang Tom Wright is now on display at the Stephenville Museum.

A week after the execution the *Dublin Progress* printed two interesting items. One was a letter from Wright's wife thanking the sheriff and his guards for their many kindnesses and to all who had extended their sympathies to her family. The other was a reprint of one that had appeared in the *Temple Times* concerning the efforts expended to try to save Wright's life. The last paragraph stated what many had come to believe—

> *The doomed man is a nephew of Uncle Tom Wright, of this city, in behalf of whom some of the best people of our county have been induced to look into the merits of the case, and they have no hesitancy in declaring the sentence out of all reason and uncalled for by the facts. . . . Certainly there must have been some grounds of doubt or this powerful array of signatures to the petition of a man who had no friends, would not spring up. There is an awful responsibility resting on someone.*[25]

A defendant's right to competent counsel as related to the Sixth Amendment of the Bill of Rights to the U. S. Constitution as applied to states through the Fourteenth Amendment was ruled on by the United States Supreme Court in 1970 in *McMann v Richardson*. The opinion stated, "defendants . . . are entitled to the effective assistance of competent counsel."[26] The outcome of this case might have helped Tom Wright if it had happened much earlier in time.

Perhaps Tom Wright did leave a legacy worth remembering. One of his comments to the crowd at his execution was a lament that his attorney Richard McCain became ill, leaving Tom without competent counsel during a crucial time in the appeal process. Tom stated that he sent $50 to retired Appellate Judge James M. Hurt to represent him. Judge Hurt failed to do so. Tom's wish was that the judge would help Frank Leslie, as it was too late for Tom's case.

That was exactly what happened. When Frank Leslie's case came up before the Court of Criminal Appeals, Judge Hurt argued the merits of Leslie's case. He honed in on the errors contained in District Judge Straughan's charge to the jury in not separating Leslie's intent from Tom Wright's as far as the death of Adams was concerned. Because of this and other errors, the verdict of the lower court was overturned, and the case was remanded back to the district court of Erath.[27]

Although Frank Leslie was retried, this time the verdict, although guilty, was for second-degree murder. The sentence given was for five years, a far cry from death by execution. Leslie served his time at Huntsville, arriving in 1900. He was leased out a couple of times and escaped from the B. D. Wilson Work Force on May 11, 1902. He remained free for almost a year before voluntarily surrendering in February 1903. He was released in December 1905, having finished serving his sentence.[28]

Justice in Erath had come full circle. Illegal lynchings had been replaced with a government-sanctioned one. Though the irony of this is not lost, neither is the difference. "Judge Lynch" was always a poor substitute for "Judge Blackstone." While vigilante justice may have seemed necessary during its time as a way of taking back control from outlaws, people still lived with a certain fear that such actions could get out of hand. Most knew that law and order were best left in the hands of the sheriffs and the courts. For Erath County, this was achieved by 1900.

Part Six – District Court Judges

The Texas **Nineteenth Judicial District** between the years of 1858 and 1867 was composed of the counties of Erath, Buchanan, Palo Pinto, Comanche, Hamilton, Bosque, Coryell, McLennan, and Bell.

Nicholas William Battle
Nineteenth Judicial District Court Judge
1858-1863

Of English heritage Nicholas Battle's ancestors arrived in America prior to the American Revolution and settled in Virginia. His Methodist minister father migrated to Georgia where Nicholas William Battle was born January 1, 1820, in Warren County. After a traditional Southern upbringing, he attended William & Mary College in Virginia where he earned a degree in law. Settling in Monroe County after returning from college in 1842, the future judge completed his legal studies in earnest under the tutelage of the Honorable A. M. Spear, an eminent Georgia jurist.

Two years after being admitted to the bar in 1844 in the town of Macon, Nicholas Battle married Mary Ann Cabaniss, the daughter of Elbridge Cabaniss, another Georgian lawyer. Battle joined the Baptist Church and practiced law in Forsythe, Georgia, for a few years before the new State of Texas beckoned. The young ambitious lawyer and Mary Ann emigrated in 1850, settling in the Waco area.[1]

Nicholas Battle showed his interest in civic duty in 1852 by leading a group of businessmen who were intent on getting the first railroad to Waco. He also agreed to chair a committee to plan and build the Waco Masonic Institute, which included both a male high school and a female academy. Seeking to enhance his legal career, Battle sought and won the position of district attorney for the Third Judicial District Court in 1854. Early in 1858 he was elected district judge of the newly created Nineteenth Judicial District.

Judge Battle brought to the bench the same principles of hard work and being prepared by which he practiced law. In 1859 the *Texas Pioneer* newspaper contained a description about the judge—

> *We are pleased with the promptness and decision with which Judge Battle presides. Whilst enforcing good order and quiet, he has nothing dictatorial or harsh in his manner...His charges are given with ease and a plainness which mark the able lawyer and the jurist who understands his profession.*[2]

A letter from Stephenville, Texas, dated October 23, 1858, to *The Standard*, Clarksville's newspaper, showed the esteem in which the Erath County residents held Judge Battle. It stated—

> *Our Judge, Battle, presided with all the dignity and impartiality, suited to the occasion...he has discharged the duties of his station....for which he has our most sincere regards.*

Judge Battle resigned from the Nineteenth Judicial District in order to serve the Confederacy, first in the Indian Territory and then as Inspector General to Brigadier General Samuel Maxey. He entered the war as a lieutenant colonel in Colonel Edward Jeremiah Gurley's Thirtieth Regiment of the Texas Cavalry and served throughout the war with distinction.[3]

With the defeat of the Southern forces, Nicholas Battle returned to his home in Waco to resume the practice of law. While many Southerners looked for ways to continue their control and domination over the newly freed slaves, Judge Battle showed his backing for the new Freedmen through his support for one of his former slaves, Shedrick Willis, who after the war owned a boardinghouse and worked as a blacksmith.

Mr. Willis decided to enter public service. With Judge Battle's backing, Governor Edmund Davis appointed Shedrick Willis as an alderman (city councilman) of Waco for two terms. During this time, the city council appointed Judge Battle as the city attorney. The *Houston Daily Union,* August 7, 1870, applauded both appointments.

Shedrick Willis' legacy was immediate but also far-reaching. His great-great-great-grandson, Wallace Jefferson, not only became a lawyer in San Antonio but was also appointed to the Texas Supreme Court in 2001, the first African-American to achieve this status. In 2004 he was appointed Chief Justice of the Texas Supreme Court. [4]

In 1874 Democrat Richard Coke managed to oust the unpopular Edmund Davis from the governor's mansion in Austin. As evidence that Judge Battle had friends on both sides of the political aisle, the new governor appointed the judge to the bench of the Criminal District Court of Waco, Marlin, and Calvert. He held this position for only two years. His stint on the judicial bench ended when Texas adopted a new constitution April 16, 1876, which abolished his judicial district.[5]

Judge Battle moved to Seattle, Washington, in 1888 to the area where his sons had migrated. The judge never returned to Waco but did leave a legacy of legal opinions and judgments in Texas along with the community of Battle in McLennan County. Judge Battle died August 22, 1905, at the age of 85 and was buried in Seattle, Washington.

Wilson Yandell McFarland
Nineteenth Judicial District Court Judge
1863 - 1865

Erath County's second official district judge was W. Y. McFarland from Bell County (Belton). McFarland was born February 28, 1809, in Smith County, Tennessee. Studying law, he also worked as Deputy Clerk to the Sumner County Court in the town of Gallatin, Tennessee.

Sometime between 1833 and 1838 McFarland moved from Tennessee to Texas, like so many who saw the adventure and endless possibilities that Texas had to offer. He was in his twenties. He served the new Republic of Texas as a patriot, soldier, and delegate to the state constitutional convention.[1]

McFarland's first county of residence in Texas was Washington. Early on, Wilson McFarland practiced law. Several of his cases made their way through to the appellate level, showing a high rate of success for the young attorney. At one time McFarland also served as the county attorney. At age 45 he married a young lady named Mary Summers from Virginia. In the mid-1850s, he moved his family to Bell County where he was listed on both the 1860 and 1870 census. By 1860 the McFarlands had three daughters (Emily, Anna, Mary) and one son (Wilson Yandell).

W. Y. McFarland was listed among the men who served in a company of Texas Rangers under the direction of Captain George B. Erath in 1838. The Texas Rangers protected Erath while he surveyed land for settlement by emigrants pouring into Texas. Erath was working in Coryell County when he named a survey after McFarland.

W. Y. McFarland made contributions to his community of Belton, supporting the founding of Rutersville College for men and women. He was also appointed to the board of examiners for competency for teacher certificates and was a charter member of the Bell County Agricultural Club. McFarland was also a member of the local Masonic lodge.

After the McFarlands purchased extensive acreage in the western part of Belton, they built their home along Killeen Road, on high ground. It became known as the McFarland Addition.

W. Y. McFarland was a states' rights Democrat but did not serve in the military in the Civil War.[2] He was over 50 years old at the beginning of the war. Instead, he served as district judge of the Nineteenth Judicial District in 1863 after N. W. Battle stepped down to fight in the war. Sources differ on whether McFarland was elected or appointed to this position. McFarland served as district judge from 1863 to 1865 when he was replaced by Richard Coke, appointed by Governor Hamilton who removed Judge McFarland as "an impediment to reconstruction." Judge McFarland ran for office in 1866 after Richard Coke was appointed to the higher judicial position. McFarland lost the election.[3]

Mary McFarland died in 1861. Judge Wilson McFarland died February 21, 1872, at age 62. He and his wife were buried in the South Belton Cemetery.

Richard Coke
Nineteenth Judicial District Court Judge
1865-1866

Future Texas Governor Richard Coke was born March 13, 1829, to a prominent family in Williamsburg, Virginia. Richard and his six brothers enlivened the Coke household. All became either doctors or lawyers. Richard chose the latter, attending William and Mary College to acquire his early legal education.

In 1848 Richard Coke visited Congress where his uncle and namesake was serving. Senator Sam Houston inspired the young attorney (age 21) to emigrate to the new State of Texas. Coke arrived in Texas in 1850 where Governor James Pinckney Henderson advised the young man to settle in McLennan County. Admitted to the Texas Bar in 1851, Richard Coke also took a bride, Mary Evans Horne, age fifteen, and started a cotton plantation along the Brazos River, eventually comprising 2700 acres. He farmed with the use of fifteen slaves.

Towering over others, Coke was 6'3" and weighed about 240

pounds. He used his commanding presence to enter politics, securing a role in the removal of Indians from Texas in 1859. Governor Hardin Runnels appointed him to the Texas Peace Commission. This committee's recommendation to remove the Indians was met with a lot of approval from the local settlers, including those in Erath County.

Coke also attended the Texas Secession Convention in early 1861 to represent McLennan and Bosque counties. The delegates voted to repeal Texas' annexation to the Union. Coke served in the Confederate Army and was wounded in 1863 at Bayou Bourbeau (Muddy Creek) in Louisiana. He managed to return to the war until his service ended in May 1865.

The future governor's private law practice did not last long. On September 1, 1865, Provisional Governor A. J. Hamilton appointed Coke, despite their political differences, to the bench as district judge for the Nineteenth Judicial District. More importantly, Hamilton valued Coke's integrity.[1]

Judge Coke quickly learned that holding district court along the frontier was no easy matter to accomplish. He set out in October 1865 to complete the judicial circuit only to find that Palo Pinto and Hamilton counties had yet to reorganize following the Civil War. Coryell and Comanche counties could not hold court due to Indian threats. Only Erath, Bosque, and McLennan were prepared to hold court.[2]

Coke's tenure lasted only a year before he was elected to the Texas Supreme Court. He lost his appellate judgeship, along with the rest of the appellate judges, once the Radical Reconstruction program was put into effect in mid-1867 with military commander Philip Henry Sheridan taking control of Texas.

Richard Coke returned to Waco to practice law while watching the political events unfold in Austin. Edmund Davis was appointed Reconstruction Governor for the State of Texas. With Davis' policies alienating a good portion of the state's populace, Coke saw his chance and decided to run for governor as a Democrat in 1873. He won by a wide margin. Not ready to give up his position, Davis appealed to Washington for support but found little, even though his own appointed justices of the Texas Supreme Court ruled in his favor. Backed by the Democratically controlled state legislature, Governor Coke was finally sworn into office January 13, 1874.

An effective governor, Coke instituted educational and tax reforms and opened Texas A&M University in 1876. He also provided more protection along the border from marauding Mexican bandits and enlisted federal support for troops in areas where Indians continued to raid. Leaving the governor's chair, Richard Coke did not abandon politics. He subsequently served in the U. S. Senate 1877 – 1895.[3]

Back in Waco, Richard Coke returned to his Brazos valley farm. He suffered from exposure in the early spring of 1897 and never fully recovered. Governor Coke died at home, May 14, 1897. He was buried in Oakwood Cemetery, Waco.

Thomas Harrison
Nineteenth Judicial District Court Judge
1866

Thomas Harrison, like so many jurists in early Texas, was born outside of the state. Judge Harrison started life in Jefferson County, Alabama May 1, 1823, but his family soon moved. He grew up in Monroe County, Mississippi. Harrison was a direct descendant of Benjamin Harrison, a president and signer of the Declaration of Independence.

Harrison's first trip to Texas in 1843 allowed him to study law with his brother-in-law, William Jack, in Brazoria County. The new lawyer returned briefly to Mississippi before returning to Texas to volunteer for the Mexican War. Afterward, Harrison settled in Houston in 1847. He was elected to the state legislature in 1850 but resigned before finishing the term.

In 1855 he moved to Waco where he set up his law practice.

In 1857 Harrison ran for district judge but lost to incumbent Judge R.E.B. Baylor. Harrison married Sarah Ellis McDonald in 1858 while continuing his law practice in McLennan County. They had five children, three boys and two girls. Eventually, Harrison became a trustee for Baylor University.[1]

An anecdotal story about Thomas Harrison took place in the mid-1850s. He was traveling by horseback along a prairie road in Hill County, Texas, when he met a man on foot who stopped Harrison supposedly to ask for directions. Harrison had a pistol suddenly shoved into his face. Ordered to step down, Harrison complied and was forced to witness the thief ride off on his horse. On foot Harrison made it back home but almost immediately set out to track down his attacker. Although Harrison never had the satisfaction of catching the thief, he did eventually get his horse back but not before the animal had been "badly used."[2]

Harrison served with distinction in the Civil War where he first commanded a cavalry company assigned to the Texas frontier. Later, he achieved the rank of Brigadier General as a part of the celebrated regiment of Terry's Rangers. In July 1865 Harrison applied to Andrew Johnson for a special pardon to restore his citizenship rights, which was granted in 1866.

The following is a description of Judge Harrison printed in the *Waco Register* and reprinted in the *Dallas Herald*, October 11, 1865—

> *Gen. Thomas Harrison has resumed the practice of law at this bar. He is an eloquent advocate, and his legal acquirements and natural abilities are commensurate with any cause that may be submitted to him.*

Turning back to politics, General Harrison once again ran for district judge. This time he was victorious against a crowded field. On June 25, 1866, he became judge of the Nineteenth Judicial District. His nephew, C. B. Pearre, was elected District Attorney in the same district.[3]

A political enemy emerged when Nathan Patten—New York

born—initiated a campaign against Judge Harrison. Patten publicly accused Harrison of being part of a vigilance committee bent on hanging Patten for being a Union man at the beginning of the Civil War. This accusation reflected the Unionists' complaints that district judges with Southern sympathies were not carrying out justice in their courts where Unionists were concerned.[4]

Judge Harrison's first and only trip to Erath County was challenging. Besides Indians still posing concerns, most of the county's records disappeared in a courthouse fire in 1866. While the state legislature provided for the replacement of deeds through the General Land Office, the records of the district court were gone. Inside a small log building, Harrison conducted the first court proceedings for Erath in more than a year.[5]

The judge served for little more than a year before the Provisional Government of Texas removed him from office during Reconstruction for being an obstructionist to justice. Even so, Judge Harrison was noted for his candor, independence, and loyalty.

Judge Harrison returned to his private law practice in McLennan County. He died in July 1891 and was buried in Waco.[6]

The Texas **Sixteenth/Fifth Judicial District** between 1867 and 1870 was composed of the counties of Erath, Palo Pinto, Parker, Johnson, Tarrant, Hill, Ellis, Dallas, and Kaufman .

John J. Good
Sixteenth and Fifth Judicial District Judge
1866-1868

Elections held in June 1866 brought John J. Good to the bench of the Sixteenth Judicial District Court. He was 39 years old and a veteran of the Civil War. A native of Columbus, Mississippi, Judge Good was born July 12, 1827. Prior to studying for the bar, his father trained John as a shoe cobbler, but the young man had other ideas about his future. After studying at Cumberland University (Tennessee) and working for an attorney, John Good was admitted to the Mississippi Bar in 1849.

Not content to settle in his home state, John J. Good migrated to Texas in 1851. He traveled to Austin but drifted back to Dallas, a town he had passed through when he first arrived in Texas and liked. At this time Dallas had a population of less than two hundred. Good set up his law practice and married Susan Anna Floyd, originally from Kentucky, in 1854. They had six children.

Photo courtesy of Jamie L. Petty

In an effort to have a successful law practice, Good started following the circuit with the district judge who moved from county to county holding court in one-week or more sessions in Tarrant, Parker, Johnson, Ellis, Kaufman, and Van Zandt. He endured extended separations from his family and the rustic conditions on the road. He traveled mostly on his favorite horse, Roderick. He had to travel lightly with only what he could fit into saddlebags or tie to the saddle. To ease the long evenings, Good wrote letters home to his wife.

Staying in Dallas when he could, Good had an office close to the courthouse. Unfortunately, it was destroyed in a fire in 1860 that left a good bit of Dallas in ashes. Later, Good was a part of the law firm—Good, Bower & Coombes—known for having the best law library in Dallas.

True to his Southern roots John Good raised the first artillery company that entered Texas Confederate service. He was wounded at the Battle of Pea Ridge (1862) in Arkansas. Given the rank of colonel, Good finished the war as a presiding judge of a military court for Louisiana, Mississippi and Alabama.

Returning to Dallas, John Good reentered his former life as an attorney. He was also a member of the Masonic Lodge and the Odd Fellows. He decided to enter politics by running for judge of the Sixteenth Judicial District. A Democrat, he defeated his opponents for what looked like an eight-year term on the bench.[1]

Judge Good was faced almost immediately with calls for his removal by Unionists and Freedmen who stated that Good could not be fair to their causes. In the middle of this the state legislature changed the districts. Erath, Palo Pinto and Hill counties were added to the other six counties, and the Sixteenth became the Fifth Judicial District. The efforts of B. F. Barkley of Tarrant County and William H. Horton, agent for the Dallas Freedmen's Bureau, paid off when Judge Good, along with several other elected district judges, was replaced with an appointed judge by the U. S. Army Fifth Military District under the leadership of General Henry Sheridan.[2]

Judge Good settled back in Dallas and became an important member of the community. He served as the first president of the Dallas Bar Association in 1873 and also became mayor of Dallas in 1880. Judge Good died September 17, 1882, and was buried in Pioneer Cemetery.[3]

A. B. Norton
Fifth Judicial District Judge
1868-1870

Many men migrated to the new State of Texas but perhaps none more colorful than Anthony Banning Norton, born May 15, 1821, in Mount Vernon, Ohio. He arrived in Texas in the late 1840s or early 1850s, traveling the state extensively before settling in Austin where he edited the *Intelligencer*.

Prior to emigrating, Norton studied law at Kenyon College in Gambier, Ohio, and participated in politics. An ardent supporter of Henry Clay and the Whig Party, Norton exclaimed in 1844 that he would not shave until Clay won the presidency. He sported that beard all his life. Norton also treasured a walking cane carved out of a tree from Ashland, Henry Clay's home estate.

Norton quickly became involved in Texas politics, serving three terms as a state legislator and supporter of Sam Houston. He moved to Fort Worth in 1859 and established a newspaper, the *Fort Worth Chief*. This stint as editor did not last long, as Texas moved toward joining the Southern cause. Norton's strong Unionist sympathies did not match the local pro-South fervor.

Governor Houston appointed the newspaperman to the position of Adjutant General, but Norton resigned when Texas voted to join the Southern cause. Unable to support the rebellion, Norton left Texas and went back to Ohio. He used his resources to find Texans confined to federal military prisons, helping them with extra food and medicine. Few forgot his kindness.

Unable to stay away, Norton returned to Texas after the South was defeated. He settled in Jefferson. Miscalculating the anger and resentment of the former rebels, Norton started publishing the *Union Intelligencer*, a newspaper leaning toward conservative Republican ideas. He barely escaped when an angry mob showed up at his home. Hiding in the woods, Norton watched as his house and press were destroyed. Taking the hint, Norton moved to Van Zandt County to start again before migrating to Dallas.[1]

Not surprisingly, when the elected district judges were removed in 1868, Norton was tapped to sit on the bench of the Fifth Judicial District following the death of D. O. Norton from Parker County who died shortly after being appointed to replace John J. Good. Accepting the appointment was not for the fainthearted. The federally appointed district judges were faced with hostility and obstructionist behavior in many of the counties. Norton had to request a military escort to travel into Ellis County to hold court.[2]

A different problem faced Judge Norton when he arrived in Erath County. Because of the removal of Judge Good and the death of his successor, D. O. Norton, Erath had not had a district court session for a year. The actions of Sheriff Brumley indicate Norton's arrival was not welcomed. Brumley left the county shortly before Norton arrived. Other county officials had resigned including the district clerk. Holding court seemed to be out of the question. Undaunted, Norton went forward. He appointed a sheriff pro tem, W. L. South, and sent him out to gather jurors.[3]

Mat Tucker was installed as district clerk. Years later, W. H. Fooshee wrote that Tucker was illiterate and could barely sign his name. So, while Tucker was the "official" clerk, local attorney, H. L. Ray, completed the documentation. Norton shed light on the situation in his letter to Governor Pease written from Erath County. He told Pease that loyal men (Unionists) were afraid to serve or take appointments. Illustrating this, Sheriff South resigned at the end of the court session. Norton appointed G. W. Keith as sheriff pro tem to take South's place.[4]

Judge Norton left the bench in June 1870 after Texas adopted a new constitution and the state returned to the Union. He stayed in Dallas practicing law and publishing *Norton's Union Intelligencer* out of his home on Ross Avenue. He remained a staunch Republican.

Norton served as postmaster and U. S. Marshal to the newly established U. S. Circuit & District Court in Dallas. Over his lifetime Judge Norton wrote several books including *The Great Revolution of 1840: Reminiscences of the Log Cabin and Hard Cider Campaign*. While many disliked his politics, those who knew Norton remembered his kindliness, unflinching sympathy, quaint humor, and big heart. Judge Norton died in Dallas, December 31, 1893.[5]

The Texas **Thirty-Fourth Judicial District** between 1870 and 1875 was composed of the counties of Erath, Comanche, Bosque, Hamilton, Coryell, and Bell.

John Patterson Osterhout
Thirty-Fourth Judicial District Judge
1870 – 1875

Not many men could be described as both a Yankee and a Rebel, but J. P. Osterhout fits the description. Born the youngest of ten brothers in Lagrange, Pennsylvania, in 1826, John Osterhout moved to Texas in 1851 after being admitted to the bar to practice law.

Osterhout first settled in the town of Bellville, Austin County, located sixty miles from Houston. He taught school and practiced law. In February 1858 Osterhout traveled back to Pennsylvania to take a bride, Miss Junia Roberts.[1]

In addition to his legal career Osterhout started publishing the *Countryman*. As editor, Osterhout made clear his sympathies were with the South and states' rights. His correspondence showed a growing rift with his family in Pennsylvania.

Both a secessionist and defender of slavery, John Osterhout served in the Fourth Texas Regiment. When the war was over, Osterhout switched from being a staunch Democrat to the Republican Party. He sold his newspaper and turned his attention to getting a judicial appointment from the Republican-run state government.

John G. Bell, a state legislator, was a friend to both Osterhout and Edmund Davis, the newly elected Reconstruction governor in 1870. Through Bell's efforts Governor Davis named Osterhout to the bench of the newly created Thirty-Fourth Judicial District Court. With the appointment Judge Osterhout moved his family to Belton in Bell County, which was at the Southern end of the judicial district.[2]

Judge Osterhout's career as a jurist had a bit of a bumpy beginning when he arrived in Hamilton in December 1870 to hold court. Adam Witcher, a local resident, met Osterhout brandishing a six-shooter. Wisely, Judge Osterhout retreated into a home. Determined that no court would be held, Witcher yelled that the judge was to leave. The standoff lasted six hours and only ended when Witcher got so drunk he fell off his horse. The sheriff arrested Witcher but later resigned because of criticism of his non-action during the fracas. Judge Osterhout appointed a new sheriff and proceeded to hold court.[3]

Comanche County provided another memorable moment when City Marshal Jeff Green shot in self-defense an associate of John Wesley Hardin's named Davis who had been drinking. It happened outside the Fossett Building where district court was in session. The impaneled jury was considering a case against an alleged cattle thief. Suddenly, the air filled with the sound of gunshots from outside. Judge Osterhout, the jury and even the defendant (who was quickly found not guilty) stumbled down the stairs to see what was happening. The grand jury, also in session, quickly took up the matter and "no billed" Marshal Green.[4]

Evidently, Judge Osterhout did not encounter the same kind of resistance in Stephenville. While previous district judges such as N. W. Battle did not have a positive view of Erath, Judge Osterhout was of a different mind. He went so far as to write into the official record, the *Minutes of the District Court*, the following -

> The Court desires to bear testimony to the general good behavior and polite deportment of the citizens & people of Erath County, & the Town of Stephenville in particular, toward the Court...[5]

Perhaps by 1871 the wild and wooly frontier town had finally started moving steadily toward the use of "Judge Blackstone" to resolve their legal problems.

When the Democrats won control of the state government in 1873, they set about recalling many of Davis' appointments. In his letters home Judge Osterhout made note that he had enemies in Austin. It looked like his days on the bench had come to an end when the state legislators recalled his appointment. The residents of his district surprised Austin when they signed petitions asking for his reinstatement. The legislature complied.[6] Osterhout continued to serve as judge until 1876 when a new constitution once again reordered the judicial system, and Erath moved into a different judicial district.

Retiring from the bench in 1885, Judge Osterhout took on the position of postmaster of Bell County and farmed on the side. He also opened a store in Belton. Osterhout and his wife, Junia, had six children. She died in 1897, and Judge Osterhout passed away at home in 1903 at the age of seventy-seven.[7]

The Texas **Twelfth Judicial District** between 1875 and 1880 was composed of the counties of Erath, Brown, Coleman, Comanche, Coryell, Eastland, Hamilton, Hood, Jack, Palo Pinto, Shackelford, Somervell, and Young plus seven unorganized counties (Callahan, Haskell, Jones, Runnels, Stephens, Taylor, and Throckmorton).

James Richard Fleming
Twelfth Judicial District Judge
1876 – 1880

One of the youngest judges to take the bench, J. R. Fleming was born in Feliciana, Kentucky, but his family soon moved to Tennessee. He served in the Civil War under General Nathan Bedford Forrest. Not long after the war, Fleming (like many others) moved to Texas. In Colorado County he owned a newspaper, the *Columbus Times*, and studied law. By 1870 he had a law license and a new bride, Mary McLeary Grace.

Seeing opportunity further west, Fleming moved his family to Comanche County where he practiced law while also entering business and banking. Emerging quickly in the frontier community, Fleming was elected as a delegate to the Texas Constitutional Convention of 1875.[1] The *Dallas Weekly* noted, "Mr. J. R. Fleming...is probably the youngest member of that body, being only twenty-six years old."[2]

A rising star, James R. Fleming, was elected to the newly created Twelfth Judicial District. With twenty counties in this district, Judge Fleming had to travel much of the year. The fact that he lived at the southern end of the district did not help. At age twenty-seven the new judge was undaunted.[3]

A couple of years after becoming the district judge, the *Dallas Herald* on, June 23, 1877, had this to say—

> *Judge Fleming is highly spoken of by The Comanche Chief as an able, fearless and pure judge. Judge Fleming's path is not strewn with roses, because the bad men of the frontier have sworn eternal hatred to him. He, however, is not the man to back down from duty for such reason as this. The right man in the right place was never more applicable than to this instance of devotion to duty.*

Anecdotal evidence seems to indicate that Judge Fleming conducted a no-nonsense court. The Erath County *District Court Minutes* show a notation that District Attorney S. C. Buck was fined twenty-five cents for "whittling during court."

Many times Judge Fleming relied on the efforts of the Texas Rangers to help clear out nests of outlaws who roamed the western edges of his district. Walter Prescott Webb in *The Texas Rangers* noted that the judge regretted not being able to join the Rangers who were hunting down twelve men who had escaped from a jail in Brownwood. The judge also informed Ranger Jones that Comanche had a good jail worthy of any overflow from Brownwood or elsewhere in his district.

While serving on the bench, Judge Fleming received notoriety during a dust-up in Shackelford County. The citizens were reluctant to serve, much less pass down indictments, as members of the grand jury. Fleming stated that the citizens were attempting "the uncertain, precarious and very dangerous" practice of vigilantism. His entreaties to have the wheels of progress turn did little to quell the night time activities of locals bent on meting out their own brand of justice, such as the execution of John Larn, an accused cattle rustler—among other activities—while he lay shackled in jail and before he could be tried in court.[4]

On January 22, 1880, the following was stated in *The Comanche Chief,* "The friends and admirers of Hon. J. R. Fleming, district judge of the twelfth (the Comanche) district, will be interested to know that he has positively tendered his resignation," which took effect on April

1, 1880. By this time Erath County had been moved into the Thirtieth Judicial District and had not been in Judge Fleming's district for two years.

While his reasons for stepping down are not clear, Judge Fleming at age thirty-two, may have seen a better future practicing law and being a businessman. Not long after his resignation, the judge moved to Cisco, a newly created frontier town in Eastland County. From there, he moved to Albany to help start a bank. By this time the wild frontier town of Fort Griffin had calmed down and Albany, the county seat, was growing in population. Well regarded, Fleming was elected a state senator for the Eighteenth Legislative session in 1883-84.[5]

Proving his restless nature, J. R. Fleming moved to San Antonio where he continued his practice of law while dabbling in politics. In 1894 he relocated to Houston for a couple of years before moving to Spokane, Washington, dying there in 1904 at the age of fifty-five.[6] While Judge Fleming died relatively young, he packed a lot into his short life.

The Texas **Thirtieth Judicial District** between 1879 and 1888 was composed of the counties of Erath, Coryell, Hamilton, Palo Pinto, Hood, and Somervell.

Thomas Lewis Nugent
Thirtieth Judicial District Judge
1879 – 1888

Irish in heritage, Thomas Nugent was born on July 16, 1841, in Opelousas, Louisiana. He graduated with honors from Centenary College in Jackson, Louisiana, electing then to move to Texas. Although his health was always on the weak side, Nugent volunteered to serve on the side of the South and joined the Confederate Army.

Thomas Nugent was married three times. Not long after arriving in Texas, he married Clara Hardeman with whom he had three sons and two daughters. Clara died in 1880. Nugent's second wife, Martha Chamberlain, died shortly after they were married. Catharine Earl, his third wife, survived him.

After the Civil War Nugent settled in the Austin area. He turned to the ministry with thoughts of becoming a Methodist minister but changed his mind and studied law instead. Receiving his law degree in 1871, Nugent moved to Meridian but relocated to Stephenville in 1873 to work as an attorney. Local citizens recognized his abilities early and chose him as a delegate to the Constitutional Convention of 1875.[1]

To no one's surprise, Thomas Nugent was appointed as district judge by Governor Oran Roberts after the Texas Legislature redrew judicial lines in 1879 and created the Thirtieth Judicial District made up of the counties of Erath, Hamilton, Coryell, Palo Pinto, Hood, and Somervell.[2]

At the beginning of his judicial tenure as judge, Nugent was forced to recuse himself from many trials already on the docket due to conflict of interests and having been a practicing trial lawyer. J. L. Martin and William Kennedy were appointed as special judges to clear out the old docket.

Like district judges before him, Nugent lived much of the year on the road, traveling among the six counties in his district. His family lived in Stephenville and welcomed him home after weary weeks on the circuit. Living in Stephenville did not always mean he would arrive on time to hold court there. The *Dallas Morning News* noted in May 1888 that flood conditions along the Bosque River, whose course meanders through town, prevented District Judge Nugent from holding court, because he lived on one side of the river and the courthouse was on the other.[3]

Much in favor of prohibition, Nugent joined the temperance movement while living in Erath County. He once conducted a study of criminal cases in his district, proclaiming that 75% of crimes resulted from the consumption of whiskey.

Later in 1888 Judge Nugent made the decision to resign as district judge. In a letter to local attorney Lee Young January 11, 1892, Nugent wrote, "You will ... come to know how utterly dependent upon good lawyers a judge is."[4] His stated reason for resigning was his poor health. This led to moving to El Paso. However, his stay there was brief, and he then relocated to Fort Worth where he set up a law office in 1891.

Before moving to Fort Worth, Nugent and his family returned to Stephenville. The *Stephenville Empire*, in an article entitled "We Lose A Good Citizen" and dated in December 1891, stated that—

> *Judge Nugent has for years enjoyed the confidence and esteem of the citizens of Erath County, being regarded as a man of rare ability, and it will be generally regretted that he has decided to cast his lot elsewhere.*[5]

The retired judge quickly became involved in the Populist Party, which was growing in popularity across Texas especially in agrarian areas. Because of his ties to the powerful Farmers' Alliance, Nugent was chosen as candidate for governor for the Populist Party in 1892. Thomas Nugent was aware he had little chance of prevailing, but the political season afforded him the opportunity to spread many of the ideas of the populist movement.

Judge Nugent lost his battle with his chronic and failing health December 14, 1895. His reported dying words were, "I have tried to do my duty." A special train was commissioned to carry his body from Fort Worth back to Stephenville. A large crowd gathered to show their respect for the former jurist who was accompanied by his widow and sons. The local masons took over to convey the judge to his final resting place at the East End Memorial Cemetery. Judge Thomas B. King and T. H. Gooden from Comanche delivered the eulogies.[6]

The Texas **Twenty-Ninth Judicial District** between 1888 and 1903 was composed of the counties of Erath, Coryell, Hamilton, Palo Pinto, Hood, and Somervell.

Charles Keith Bell
Twenty-Ninth Judicial District Judge
1888-1892

Hamilton Record Apr. 24, 1913

Judge Bell started life in Chattanooga, Tennessee, April 18, 1853, born to Dr. William and Elizabeth Bell. His father served as mayor. Later Bell's father fought in the Mexican War and lost his life during the Civil War defending control of the Mississippi River. At a very young age C. K. Bell became the man of the family, a responsibility he honored for the rest of his mother's life.

In 1871 Bell at age nineteen moved to Texas, taking his mother and sisters with him. He settled first in Bell County where he taught school and studied law on the side. Ready to take the bar exam in 1874, Bell moved his family to Hamilton County. Since the area was sparsely settled, Bell had to take odd jobs besides practicing law to make ends meet.

Bell's first elected office was as county attorney for Hamilton in 1876. He was elected the district attorney for the Thirtieth Judicial District, serving in that capacity from 1880 to 1884. He was known as fearless and unflappable. One anecdotal story told about Bell as district attorney involved a desperado on trial. At one point in the trial, the defendant called Bell a "damn liar." The district attorney promptly knocked the man down, even though the desperado had several armed friends in the courtroom. Bell served as district attorney for four years.[1]

In 1884 Bell was elected as a state senator. At age 33 C. K. Bell was the youngest member of the Texas Legislature. He served for two sessions. Bell found time to run for judge of the Twenty-Ninth Judicial District in 1887.[2] He served in this position until he ran for Congress in 1892. He won this election and served the Eighth Congressional District in Washington D.C.

Returning from Congress, Judge Bell moved to Fort Worth. By this time both sisters were married, so only the judge's mother moved with him. They lived in a boarding house with other residents including a bookkeeper, grocer, shoe salesman, postal clerk, stenographer and saloonkeeper. The judge formed a law partnership with Judge Milam.

In 1901 Judge Bell was tapped by Governor Lanham to serve as attorney general for Texas when Thomas Smith died in office. Bell won the office in his own right in 1902. At the urging of many, Judge Bell threw his hat into the ring to run for governor in 1905. Unfortunately, his mother's health started failing and prevented him from campaigning statewide. He lost both the election and his mother in March 1906.[3]

September 12, 1906, at age 52 Judge Bell married for the first time to Florence Smith, daughter of John Peter Smith, lawyer and philanthropist of Fort Worth. She was twenty-nine. They were blessed with a son, John Peter Smith Bell, in 1908.

Wedded bliss was short-lived as Judge Bell died April 22, 1913, at age fifty-nine after a severe attack of kidney trouble that lasted several months. Lawyers and other notables from all over the state attended his funeral. Judge Lee Young of Stephenville served as an honorary pallbearer. Judge Bell was buried at East Oakwood Cemetery in Fort Worth.[4]

John Smith Straughan
Twenty-Ninth Judicial District Judge
1893 – 1900

Born in Indiana in 1849, J. S. Straughan emigrated to Texas as an adult. He was already a practicing attorney and a member of the International Order of Odd Fellows. He married Martha (Mattie) Caroline Cowden of Palo Pinto in 1878. The couple had four children: Fred (who died young); Gertrude; Lantham; and Posie.

J. Collin George, Erath District Attorney, remembered his first meeting with the future jurist and wrote, "He was a magnificent looking man, a splendid specimen of physical strength, and exceedingly handsome and portly in appearances."[1]

Straughan continued to make his living as a lawyer and later successfully ran for judge of the Twenty-Ninth Judicial District. He chose to run at this time because the previous district judge, C. K. Bell, vacated the position in order to run for Congress. Straughan was elected in November 1892.

In 1893 the newly elected district judge moved from Palo Pinto to Stephenville. He remained in Erath when not on the judicial circuit until his death. Judge Straughan ruled from the bench as a conservative jurist. In 1896 the Gatesville Bar passed a resolution commending the judge for being both wise and conservative. They endorsed him for a second term.[2]

Judge Straughan was re-elected in 1896 by a large majority. The newspapers noted that the judge presided over a district comprised of six counties and that he had to hold court forty-four weeks of the year to keep up with the crowded docket.[3]

J. Collin George in a letter wrote, "Judge Straughan was a good man in the true sense of the word. He was kind and considerate to everybody including young lawyers."[4]

Faced with several murder trials in his second term, Judge Straughan kept a pretty formal court and showed he was tough on those accused of felonies. Interestingly, he admonished a grand jury in 1897 to remember that perjury was the "all-prevailing crime of the age."[5]

All was not just business. The judge along with other town dignitaries was invited out to the farm of C. L. McIlhany ouside of Stephenville in April 1897 to see the famous airship that had landed on the property. He later told a reporter that what landed was a—"60-foot cigar-shaped craft and its two occupants, who gave their names as S. E. Tillman and A. E. Dolbear." The crewmen told the crowd that the project was backed by certain capitalists from New York. The crowd was not allowed to get very close to the astounding contraption before it lifted off and sailed away. Other sightings were recorded in other counties before the airship disappeared for good.[6]

Another story told how during one term of court shortly before an election, Judge Straughan made a concerted effort to clear his docket, but every case that was called for trial was continued by agreement or by application. Judge Straughan, seeing the entire docket unresolved, said, "Mr. Sheriff, adjourn court for two hundred years so that these damn lawyers will have time to get ready for trial."[7]

At the end of his second term, Judge Straughan's health prevented him from keeping his busy hectic schedule. Sometimes he appeared in one of the counties to hold court, only to ask the local bar to elect a "Special Judge" to finish the docket. His wife Mattie died in October 1899 at age forty-four. Saddened, the judge took her back to Palo Pinto to be buried.

In 1900 Judge Straughan decided not to run for a third term. He remained in Stephenville but was not seen often out and about. His ill health increasingly caused him to be bedridden. On August 30, 1907, J. S. Straughan died. He was not quite sixty years old and was buried at Palo Pinto.[8] The Erath County Bar issued a solemn resolution of respect. Judge Straughan was the last district judge for the Twenty-Ninth Judicial District during the nineteenth century.

End Notes

Jack of Many Trades
1. Pylant, James. "Some Erath County Prisoners In the 1880s." *American Genealogy Magazine.* May-June 1992.
2. *Criminal Minutes of the District Court.* Book D. Twenty-Ninth Judicial District. Erath County, Texas (1897).
3. *Minutes of the District Court.* Book A. Nineteenth Judicial District. Erath County, Texas (1867).
4. *Minutes of the District Court.* Book C. Twelfth Judicial District. Erath County, Texas (1879).
5. *Erath County Sheriff's Docket.* Nathan Shands, Sheriff, 1896.
6. Jack Shands to Norma Wilson. 25 Jan. 2001.
7. *State of Texas v Light Nowlin.* No. 96. Thirty-Fourth Judicial District Court. Erath County, Texas (1871).
8. *Erath County Commissioners' Court Minutes.* Book A (March 1871).
9. Webb, Walter Prescott. *The Texas Rangers.* Austin: University of Texas Press, 1865.
10. *Erath County Commissioners' Court Minutes.* Book A (July 1877).

Forced Accommodations
1. *Minutes of the Erath County Commissioners Court.* Book A, 7 June 1871.
2. "Saws & Files In County Jail." *Stephenville Empire* 2 Feb. 1884.
3. Pylant, James. "Some Erath County Prisoners in the 1880s." *American Genealogy Magazine*, May – June 1992.
4. Fooshee, W. H. "Reminiscences of Old Days." *Stephenville Empire* 6 June 1913.
5. "Some Erath County Prisoners in the 1880s." Ibid.
6. Blackburn, Jr., Ed. *Wanted. Historic County Jails of Texas.* Bryan: Texas A&M University Press, 2006.

Court Life
1. McClurrin, Brenda, "'My Dear Sue.' Letters of Frontier Lawyer John Jay Good." *Legacies: A History Journal of Dallas & North Central Texas.* Vol. 19. No. 2, 2007.
2. Ibid.
3. Oxford, W. H. Personal Interview, 15 Oct. 2008.
4. Campbell, Randolph. "The District Judges of Texas in 1866-1867: An Episode in the Failure of Presidential Reconstruction." *Southwestern Historical Quarterly.* Vol. 3, 1989.
5. *The State v Riley Majors.* No. 503. 12th Judicial District Court. Erath County (1878).

A Citizen's Obligation
1. "Permanent Jurors." *Galveston News* 16 July 1869.
2. "The Professional Juror." *Dallas Weekly Herald* 30 Jan. 1875.
3. Kicking Eagle. "The Professional Juror." Editorial. *Dallas Weekly Herald* 19 Feb. 1885.
4. Untitled. *San Antonio Express* 21 June 1891.
5. "Registration & Jury Duty." *Galveston News* 21 Nov. 1873.
6. *Minutes of the District Court.* Book A. Nineteenth Judicial District. Erath County, Texas (1866).
7. Ibid. Spring, 1867.
8. *Minutes of the District Court.* Book A. Thirty-Fourth Judicial District. Erath County, Texas (Fall 1873).
9. Ibid, Spring 1868.

10. *State of Texas v Tom Wood*. No. 1852. Twenty-Ninth Judicial District Court. Erath County, Texas (1891).
11. *State of Texas v Anna Williamson*. No. 800. Thirtieth Judicial District Court. Erath County, Texas (1881).
12. *State of Texas v Tom Wright*. No. 2729. Twenty-Ninth Judicial District Court. Erath County, Texas (1891).

Seat of Justice
1. Hale, Miley. "Pioneer Experiences." Centennial Edition. *Stephenville Empire Tribune*, 27 Oct. 1854.
2. *Gammel's Laws of Texas*. Portal of Texas History. Accessed 16 March 2009. <http://texashistory.unt.edu>.
3. *Minutes of the Erath County Commissioners Court*. Book A. Erath County, Texas (1867).
4. Ibid. Book B, 1874.
5. King, Richard. "Inferno On the Square." *Erath Observer* 4 Dec. 1875.
6. "Erath's New Courthouse." *Fort Worth Gazette* 14 June 1891.
7. "Local." *Dublin Progress* 20 June 1891.
8. "The Courthouse." *Dublin Progress* 11 July 1891.
9. Untitled. *Dublin Progress* 27 June 1891.
10. "Election Returns." *Dublin Progress* 1 Aug. 1891.
11. "Crushed to Death." *Stephenville Empire* 26 Sept. 1891.

Early Justice
1. Fooshee, W. H. "*History, First Hand.*" Reprinted in *Grand Ol' Erath* by H. G. Perry, 1974.
2. Sharp, Gary and Maurice. Personal Interview. Dublin, Texas. 4 Dec. 2008.
3. Britton, F. L. *Report of Condition of Affairs in Erath and Comanche Counties*. Dec. 4, 1872.
4. "*Owen West of Tolar Tells of Pioneer Days.*" *Stephenville Empire Tribune. Memorial Edition* January 1936.
5. Fooshee. Ibid.

The Lower Brazos Reserve Indians' Massacre
1. Wilbarger, J. W. *Massacres, Reliable Accounts of Battles, Wars, Adventures, Forays, Murders, and Massacres*. Austin: Hutchings Printing, 1889.
2. Richardson, Rupert. *The Frontier of Northwest Texas 1846-1876*. Glendare, Ca: A. H. Clark. Co., 1963.
3. Hughes, W. J. *Rebellious Ranger: Rip Ford and the Old Southwest*. Norman: University of Oklahoma Press, 1964.
4. Perry, H. G. *Grand Ole Erath*. Stephenville: Perry, 1974.
5. "Indian Disturbance in Palo Pinto, One Citizen and Seven Indians Killed." *Dallas Weekly Herald* 5 Jan. 1859.
6. "To the Citizens of Parker County and Weatherford!" Open Letter. *Dallas Weekly Herald* 12 Jan. 1858.
7. Ray. H. L. "Letter to the Editor." *Dallas Herald* 11 Aug. 1866.
8. "Latest News About the Difficulties in the Brazos Reserves." *Southern Beacon*. Henderson, Tx., 29 Jan. 1859.
9. "Capt. Ford, Defense." *Texas State Gazette* Austin, 30 April 1859.
10. Untitled. *Texas State Gazette* 9 April 1859.
11. "Mr. Gurley's Rejoinder." *Texas State Gazette* Austin, 21 May 1858.
12. "Neighbors, Robert Simpson." *The Handbook of Texas Online*, Accessed 23 Dec. 2007. <http://www.tshaonline.org/handbook>

13. "Battle, Nicholas W." *Biographical Encyclopedia*. New York: Southern Publishing Co., 1880.

Drink As Much Whiskey As You Want
1. Conine, Will. *The Memories of Will Conine*. Collected by Sharon Whitney. Waco: Texian Press, 1999.
2. *Minutes of the Nineteenth Judicial District Court*. Book A. Erath County, Texas (1866-1868).
3. Conine. *Ibid*.

Frontier Insanity Proves Fatal
1. "Horrid Tragedy in Erath County." *Flake's Bulletin*. Galveston 29 Sept. 1869.
2. "Horrid Tragedy in Erath County." *Galveston Tri-Weekly News* 27 Sept. 1869.
3. Ibid.
4. Untitled. *Galveston Tri-Weekly*, 1 Oct. 1869.
5. Ibid.
6. "Suicide of a Lunatic." *Flake's Bulletin* 13 Nov. 1869.
7. Ewers, Marilyn. *Some history of the Duffau community, Erath county, Texas*. Stephenville, Tx: Ewers, 1996.

A Wrong Move on the Texas Frontier
1. Crenshaw, Gary and Karen. Personal Interview. Stephenville, Tx, 10 Nov. 2008.
2. Crenshaw, Parks. *Texas Rangers Roll Card*. Texas Rangers Museum. Waco, Texas.
3. *Travel Voucher*. William Skipper, Sheriff of Erath County. For Transportation of Parks Crenshaw (1864).
4. Crenshaw, Gary and Karen. Ibid.

When an Overland Stagecoach Overturns
1. "Stagecoach Lines." The Handbook of Texas Online. 2 June 2008.
    <http://www.tshaonline.org/>.
2. "Giraffe Line." Editorial. *Dallas Herald* 17 Nov. 1858.
3. Editorial. *Houston Telegraph* 22 June 1859.
4. *Frederick P. Sawyer et al v. Nelson Dulany et ux*. 30 Tex. 429, Supreme Court of Texas (1867).
5. Ibid.
6. Hamilton, Theodore. *American Negligence Cases. A Complete Collection of Reported Negligence*. Albany: Renich, Schilling & Co., 1905.

Taking the Edge off
1. *State of Texas v I. W. Lacy*. No. 45. Fifth Judicial District. Erath County, Texas (1868).
2. "Allison, Robert Clay." Handbook of Texas Online. 9 June 2009. <http://www.tshaonline.org/handbook/online>.
3. Wagner, Edwin. "Coe Outlaws." 4 Nov. 1998. Rootsweb. 10 June 2009.
    <http://listsearches.rootsweb.com/th/read/COE/1998-11/0910203648>.
4. Colleen Fossum to Sherri Knight, 10 June 2009.
5. Wagner. Ibid.
6. "How Montgomery Got A Wife." *The New York Times* 16 July 1884.

Charged With Murder
1. *Convict Ledger*. Huntsville State Penitentiary. No. 2048. 30 Aug. 1871.
2. Untitled. *Galveston Tri-Weekly News* 27 Sept. 1869.
3. *Consolidated Convict List for Erath County, Texas*. Compiled by Texas State Library, 2008.

4. Untitled. *Galveston Tri-Weekly News* 8 Oct. 1869.
5. *Minutes of the District Court*, Fifth Judicial District Court. Erath County, Texas (1870).
6. *State of Texas v James Taylor*. No. 77. Thirty-Fourth Judicial District. Erath County, Texas (1871).

Marital Bliss
1. "Women and the Law." Handbook of Texas Online. 9 June 2009. <http://www.tshaonline.org/handbook/online>.
2. "A Case of Wife Beating." *Galveston Tri-Weekly* 28 Sept. 1872.
3. *State of Texas v Sarah Long & W. N. Dodson*. No. 53. Fifth Judicial District Court. Erath County (1868).
4. *Harley v Harley*. No. 53. Thirty-Fourth Judicial District Court. Erath County (1870).
5. *Holloway v Holloway*. No. 383. Thirtieth Judicial District Court. Erath County (1876).
6. Ibid.
7. "William Gunter." *Stephenville Empire* 31 Sept. 1882.
8. *Bagwell v Bagwell*. No. 547. Thirtieth Judicial District Court. Erath County (1881).
9. *Burnick v Burnick*. No. 546. Thirtieth Judicial District Court. Erath County (1881).
10. *DeLave v DeLave*. No. 572. Thirtieth Judicial District Court. Erath County (1882).
11. *Bishop v Bishop*. No. 1936. Twenty-Ninth Judicial District Court. Erath County (1897).
12. *Stephens v Stephens*. No. 1109. Twenty-Ninth Judicial District Court. Erath County (1891).

A Woman in a Man's World
1. *Gibbs v W. W. McNeill*. No. 35. Fifth Judicial District Court. Erath County, Texas. Transferred to Ellis County (1870).
2. *Gibbs v Peter Gravis, T. S. John, W. A. Shaw & Lewis Blalock*. No. 34. Fifth Judicial District Court. Erath County, Texas (1869).
3. *Gibbs v W. W. McNeill*. Ibid.
4. *Gibbs v Gibbs*. No. 55. Thirty-Fourth Judicial District Court. Erath County, Texas (1870).
5. *Ex Parte*. Phebe Gibbs. No. 85. Thirty-Fourth Judicial District Court. Erath County, Texas (1871).
6. Bicket, Cindy, Ed. *The Cage House Archives*. Stephenville, Tx: Ken Jones, 2004.
7. Fooshee, W. H. "History, First Hand." Reprinted in *Grand Ol' Erath* by H. G. Perry, 1974.
8. *Peacock v Haws*. No. 79. Thirty-Fourth Judicial District Court, Erath County, Texas (1871).
9. *Martin & Neill v Phebe Haws*. No. 303. Thirtieth Judicial District Court. Erath County, Texas (1880).

Bigamy Leads to Murder
1. *State of Texas v W. F. Holland*. No. 272. Thirty-Fourth Judicial District Court. Erath County. Texas (1873).
2. *Complaint*. Filed by John Hayes. Thirty-Fourth Judicial District Court. Erath County. Texas (1872).
3. *State of Texas v W. F. Holland*. Ibid.
4. *Holland v State of Texas*. 38 Tex. 474. Supreme Court of Texas (1873).
5. *Conduct Ledger*. W. Frank Holland. Huntsville State Penitentiary, 30 Oct. 1879.
6. *State of Texas v Joe Edwards*. No. 1171. Thirtieth Judicial District Court. Erath County, Texas (1885).
7. *Petition*. Citizens of Erath County to Gov. Culberson, 1896.
8. *United States Census*. Eastland County, Texas (1900).

Attempted Citizens' Arrest Ends In Deadly Force
1. *State of Texas vs William Barry, S. O. Berry, and John Shelby.* No. 446. Twelfth Judicial District Court. Erath County, Texas (1875).
2. *State of Texas vs James Mastin & P. T. McGinnis.* Complaint. No. 232. Justice of the Peace Court (9 Jan. 1877).
3. *State of Texas vs William Barry, S. O. Berry, and John Shelby.* Ibid.
4. Fooshee, W. H. "Reminiscences of Old Days." *Stephenville Empire* 6 June 1913.

Three Views to a Killing
1. "A Deputy Sheriff Killed by Desperadoes – The People Aroused and Eleven Thieves Shot and Hung." *Dallas Weekly Herald* 6 June 1874.
2. "Their Vengeance." *Dallas Weekly Herald* 6 June 1874.
3. "The Wild West. Texas Desperadoes." *Indianapolis Sentinel* 26 June 1874.
4. "Letter From Bell County." *Dallas Weekly Herald* 6 June 1874.
5. "John Wesley Hardin." *New Orleans Daily Picayune* 5 Sept. 1874.
6. *John W. Hardin v State of Texas.* 4 Tex. Ct. App. 355. Court of Appeals of Texas (1878).
7. Ibid.
8. Ibid.
9. Ibid.
10. "Dear Exponent." *Weatherford Exponent* 13 Oct. 1877.
11. *John W. Hardin v State of Texas.* Ibid.
12. Ibid.
13. "The Wichita Falls Affair." *Dallas Morning News* 28 Feb. 1896.
14. Hardin, John Wesley. *The Life of John Wesley Hardin by Himself.* Norman: University of Oklahoma, 1961.
15. Ibid.
16. Nordyke, Lewis. *John Wesley Hardin, Texas Gunman.* New York: Morrow, 1957.

The Bad Luck Horse Thieves
1. *State of Texas v C. E. Aiken.* No. 629. Thirtieth Judicial District Court. Erath County, Texas (1879).
2. Ibid.
3. *State of Texas v A. B. James.* No. 630. Thirtieth Judicial District Court. Erath County, Texas (1879).
4. *Conduct Ledger.* Huntsville State Penitentiary, 1880.
5. *Conduct Ledger.* Rusk State Penitentiary, 1881.

What's Yours Is Mine
1. *State of Texas v Jasper Reynolds.* No. 639 and 662. Thirtieth Judicial District Court. Erath County, Texas (1879).
2. *Sheriff's Docket.* Erath County, Texas, 1879.
3. *State of Texas v Jasper Reynolds.* Ibid.
4. *J. Reynolds v. State of Texas.* 8 Tex. Ct. App. 412. Court of Appeals of the State of Texas (1880).
5. *J. Reynolds v. State of Texas.* 8 Tex. Ct. App. 493. Court of Appeals of the State of Texas (1880).
6. *Travel Voucher.* Texas State Penitentiary. Receipt. No. 372, 1884.
7. *Erath County Criminal Indictments, 1866 to 1900.* Abstracted from Erath County District Court Records. 2009.

Revenge
1. *State of Texas v Morg McInturf.* No. 1041. Thirtieth Judicial District Court. Erath County, Texas (1885).
2. "He Unlocked it With His Little Key." *Stephenville Empire* 5 July 1884.
3. *State of Texas v Morg McInturf.* Ibid.
4. *Morg McInturf v State of Texas.* 20 Tex Ct. App. 335. Court of Appeals of Texas (1886).
5. *Conduct Ledger.* Ruak State Penitentiary, 1892.

Murder Near Rat Row
1. *State of Texas v Harry Barrett.* No. 608. Thirtieth Judicial District Court. Erath County, Texas (1879).
2. *Harry Barrett v State of Texas.* 9 Tex. Ct. App. 33. Court of Appeals of Texas (1880).
3. *Conduct Ledger*, Huntsville and East Texas State Penitentiary, 1880 & 1883.
4. *Petition.* From Erath County to Governor Ireland Concerning Harry Barrett, Dec. 1886.
5. *Silas Buck to Governor Ireland*, 14 Sept. 1886.
6. *Pardon.* Issued by Governor L. S. Ross, 25 Sept. 1889.

The Traveling Murder Case
1. *David Kemp v. State of Texas.* 11 Tex. Ct. App. 174. Court of Appeals of Texas (1881).
2. *State of Texas v David Kemp.* No. 708. Thirtieth Judicial District Court. Erath County, Texas (1880).
3. *David Kemp v State of Texas.* Ibid.
4. *State of Texas v David Kemp.* No. 873. The Thirtieth Judicial District Court. Erath County, Texas (1882).
5. Ibid.
6. *David Kemp v. State of Texas.* No. 1491. 13 Tex Ct. App. 561. Court of Appeals of Texas (1883).

Infanticide
1. *Minutes of the Commissioners' Court.* Book C. Erath County, Texas, 1882.
2. *State of Texas v Anna Williamson.* No. 800. Thirtieth Judicial District Court. Erath County, Texas (1881).
3. *Conduct Ledger.* Huntsville State Penitentiary, 1882.

Road Work
1. *Gammel's Laws of Texas.* Vol. 8, 29 July 1876. Accessed 19 Jan. 2009. <http://texashistory.unt.edu>.
2. *Road Minutes.* Commissioners Court. Erath County, Texas, 1882.
3. "Captured At Last." *Stephenville Empire* 4 Nov. 1882.
4. *State of Texas v John Henning.* No. 855. Thirtieth Judicial District Court. Erath County, Texas (1883).
5. "The Henning Trial." *Stephenville Empire* Apr. 28, 1883.
6. *State of Texas v John Henning.* Ibid.
7. Pylant, James. "Some Erath County Prisoners in the 1880s." *American Genealogy Magazine.* May-June 1992, pp 30-34.
8. *Conduct Ledger.* Huntsville State Penitentiary, 1898.

Murder After Dark
1. *State of Texas v Monroe Coldiron and Brink Favors.* No. 1004. Thirtieth Judicial District Court. Erath County, Texas (1884).

2. "He Unlocked it With His Little Key." *Stephenville Empire Tribune* 5 July 1884.
3. "The Jail Boys." *Stephenville Empire* 28 June 1884.
4. Family Records of Larry Gage, Lou Favor Urban, Favors Family, Coldiron Family, Stone Family, Wanda Harbert, Welch Family, and Audrey Favor Rankin provided by Hollice Favors. July 2009.

The Moral of the Murder
1. "Tom Putty." *Stephenville Empire* 28 May 1892.
2. *State of Texas v Tom Putty.* No. 1937. Twenty-Ninth Judicial District Court. Erath County, Texas (1892).
3. *Petition for Pardon.* Tom Putty. To Governor C. A. Culberson. Filed 1 Oct. 1895.
4. *Letter.* Thomas B. King to Honorable Governor Culberson. 24 Sept. 1895.
5. *Conduct Ledger.* Tom Putty. Rusk State Penitentiary, 6 May 1897.

Hate Crime
1. "Incendaries at Work." *Dublin Progress* 14 March 1891.
2. *State of Texas v Lauderdale.* No. 1803. Twenty-Ninth Judicial District Court. Erath County, Texas (1892).
3. Ibid.
4. Ibid.
5. "Examining Trial." *Dublin Progress* 21 March 1891.
6. *Lauderdale v State of Texas.* 19 S.W. 679. Court of Criminal Appeals. Texas (1892).
7. *Conduct Ledger.* Huntsville State Penitentiary. 1895.

A Knifing in the Side Room
1. "John Reed Arrested." *Stephenville Empire* 9 Jan. 1892.
2. *The State of Texas v Tom Wood.* No.1892. Twenty-Ninth Judicial District Court. Erath County, Texas (1891).
3. Ibid.
4. *Petition for Pardon.* Tom Wood. To Governor C. A. Culberson. 24 Oct. 1895.

When Adultery Leads to Perjury
1. *State of Texas v John Hull.* No. 2012. County Court, Erath County, Texas (1897).
2. *State of Texas v John Hull.* No. 2728. Twenty-Ninth Judicial District Court, Erath County, Texas (1898).
3. *John Hull v State of Texas.* No. 1836. Texas Court of Criminal Appeals (1898).
4. *State of Texas v John Hull.* No. 2728. Twenty-Ninth Judicial District Court, Erath County, Texas (1899).
5. *Conduct Ledger.* John Hull. Rusk State Penitentiary. May 1901.

The Sable King
1. Frank Lewis. *Record of Convict Labor.* Erath County, 1883.
2. Ibid. *1886.*
3. "Hit With a Spade." *Stephenville Empire* 20 Aug. 1891.
4. "Blood on the Moon." *Stephenville Empire* 26 Sept. 1891.
5. "Not Given Justice." *Stephenville Empire* 21 Nov. 1891.
6. *Lewis v Lewis.* No. 1495. Divorce. Twenty-Ninth Judicial District Court. Erath County (1893).
7. *State of Texas v Lewis.* No. 3033. Twenty-Ninth Judicial District Court. Erath County (1900).
8. Ibid.
9. *Lewis v State of Texas.* 59 S.W. 1116. Court of Criminal Appeals of Texas (1900).

10. "Negroes Ordered Out of Dublin." *Stephenville Empire* 1 Sept. 1893.
11. *Lewis v State of Texas.* Ibid.

"They Have My Boy in That Damned Hell Hole"
1. *The State of Texas v T. J. Wilson.* No. 2443. Twenty-Ninth Judicial District Court. Erath County, Texas (1896).
2. *T. J. Wilson v State of Texas.* 37 Tex. Crim. 64. Texas Court of Criminal Appeals (1897).
3. *State of Texas v Charley Wilson.* No. 2134. Twenty-Ninth Judicial District Court. Erath County, Texas (1894).
4. *State of Texas v Charley Wilson.* No. 2742. Twenty-Ninth Judicial District Court. Erath County, Texas (1898).

'Promise Me That You Will Let Liquor Alone'
1. "Election Returns." *Dublin Progress* 1 Aug. 1891.
2. "Local Option In Effect." *Dallas Morning News* 3 Nov. 1893.
3. "Local Option at Dublin." *Dallas Morning News* 20 Aug. 1894.
4. "Temperance Damage Suit." *Dallas Morning News* 9 Apr. 1895.
5. "Injunction Proceedings." *Dublin Progress* 7 Feb 1896.
6. "Local Option Campaign." *Dallas Morning News* 25 July 1895.
7. *State of Texas v Wright.* No. 880. Thirtieth Judicial District Court. Erath County, Texas (1882).
8. Petition. Erath County to Governor Hogg. Sept. 1893.
9. *State of Texas v Wright.* No. 2729. Twenty-Ninth Judicial District Court. Erath County, Texas (1898).
10. Ibid.
11. Ibid.
12. Ibid.
13. "A Fatal Tragedy." *Dublin Progress*, 24 Dec. 1897.
14. *State v Wright.* No. 2729. Ibid.
15. Ibid.
16. *Tom Wright v State of Texas.* 50 S.W. 940. Texas Court of Criminal Appeals (1899).
17. "Tom Wright Sentenced." *Dublin Progress* 6 Oct. 1899.
18. "Declined to Interfere." *Fort Worth Register* 10 Nov. 1899.
19. Petition. Erath County Bar to Governor Sayers, 4 Nov. 1899.
20. "Temple Times On the Execution of Wright." *Dublin Progress* 17 Nov. 1899.
21. "Into Eternity." *Stephenville Empire* 10 Nov. 1899
22. Ibid.
23. "Wright Pays the Penalty." *Dublin Progress* 10 Nov. 1899.
24. Ibid.
25. "Temple Times On the Execution of Wright." *Dublin Progress* 17 Nov. 1899.
26. *McMann, Warden et al v Richardson et al.* 397 U.S. 759; 90 S Ct. 1441. Supreme Court of United States (1970).
27. *Frank Leslie v State of Texas.* 57 S.W. 659. Texas Court of Criminal Appeals (1900).
28. *State of Texas v Leslie.* No. 2730. Twenty-Ninth Judicial District Court. Erath County, Texas (1900).

Nicholas William Battle
1. "Battle, Nicholas William." *The Handbook of Texas Online*. 16 Jan. 2008. <http://www.tshaonline.org>.
2. *Biographical Encyclopedia of Texas.* New York: Southern Publishing Co., 1880.

3. Ibid.
4. Davis, Jenny. "A Chief Justice, a Waco Cemetery and a Surprising Connection." *Texas Lawyer*, 12 May 2008.
5. Untitled. *Houston Daily Union* 7 Aug. 1876.

Wilson Yandell McFarland
1. *Story of Bell County, Texas. Vol. II.* Bell County Historical Commission. Austin: Eakin Press, 1958.
2. Tyler, George. *The History of Bell County.* San Antonio: The Naylor Company, 1936.
3. *Story of Bell County, Texas. Vol. II,* Ibid.

Richard Coke
1. "Richard Coke." *Justices of Texas 1836 – 1986.* Tarlton Law Library. University of Texas at Austin. 29 Nov. 2007. <http://tarlton.law.utexas. edu/justices/spct/coke.html>.
2. "Texas Intelligence." *Houston Tri-Weekly Telegraph* 27 Oct. 1865.
3. "Richard Coke." Ibid.

Thomas Harrison
1. D'Alaroone, De La Harpe. *A Memorial and Biographical History of McLennan, Fallas, Bell, and Coryell Counties.* Chicago: Lewis Pub. Co., 1893.
2. Wood, W. D. *Reminiscences of Reconstruction In Texas, and, Reminiscences of Texas and Texans Fifty Years Ago,* United States: Texas, 1902.
3. *Biographical Encyclopedia of Texas.* New York: Southern Publishing, 1880.
4. Campbell, Randolph. *Grass Roots Reconstruction in Texas, 1865 – 1880.* Baton Rouge: LSU Press, 1997.
5. *Minutes of the District Court. Book A.* Nineteenth Judicial District. Erath County, Texas, 1866.
6. D'Alaroone. Ibid.

John J. Good
1. *Biographical Encyclopedia of Texas.* New York: Southern Publishing, 1880.
2. Campbell, Randolph. "The District Judges of Texas in 1866-1867: An Episode in the Failure of Presidential Reconstruction." *Southwestern Historical Quarterly.* 1989, Vol. 3.
3. *Biographical Encyclopedia of Texas.* Ibid.

A. B. Norton
1. "Judge A. B. Norton." *Dallas Morning News* 1 Jan. 1894.
2. Campbell, Randolph. "A Moderate Response." *Legacies: A History Journal of Dallas & North Central Texas.* Vol. 5, No. 2, Fall 1993.
3. *Minutes of the District Court. Book A.* Nineteenth Judicial District. Erath County, Texas, 1868.
4. . Fooshee, W. H. "History, First Hand." Reprinted in *Grand Ol' Erath* by H. G. Perry. 1974.
5. "Judge A. B. Norton." Ibid.

John Patterson Osterhout
1. D'Alaroone, De La Harpe. *A Memorial and Biographical History of McLennan, Fallas, Bell, and Coryell Counties.* Chicago: Lewis Pub. Co., 1893.
2. Sparks, Randy. "John P. Osterhout, Yankee, Rebel, Republican." *Southwestern Historical Quarterly.* Vol. 90, Issue 2. Oct. 1986.
3. "Telegraphic From Austin." *Galveston Tri-Weekly* July 16, 1870.
4. Wells, Mrs. Eulalia Nabors. *Blazing The Way.* Comanche: Comanche Litho-Print, 1996.
5. *Minutes of the Thirty-Fourth Judicial District Court.* Book B. Erath County, Texas. 1873.
6. "John P. Osterhout." *The Bedford Gazette.* Bedford, Pa. Jan. 30, 1903.

7. D'Alaroone. Ibid.

James Richard Fleming
1. "Fleming, James Richard." *The Handbook of Texas Online.* Accessed 7 Aug. 2008. <http://www.tshaonline.org>.
2. Untitled. *Dallas Weekly Herald* 11 Sept. 1875.
3. "Fleming District Judge One Hundred Years Ago." *Stephenville Empire Tribune.* Undated.
4. DeArment, Robert K. *Bravos of the Brazos.* Norman: University of Oklahoma, 2002.
5. "Fleming, James Richard." Ibid.
6. Ibid.

Thomas Lewis Nugent
1. Nugent, Catharine. *Life Work of Thomas L. Nugent.* Chicago: Laird & Lee, 1896.
2. Nugent, Thomas Lewis. *The Handbook of Texas Online.* Accessed 8 Sept. 2008. <http://www.tshaonline.org>.
3. "Horses Struck By Lightning." *Dallas Morning News* 13 May 1888.
4. Judge T. L. Nugent to Lee Young. Stephenville: January 11, 1892.
5. "We Lose A Good Citizen." *Stephenville Empire* 26 Dec. 1891.
6. Wright, Earl. "Nugent's Premature Death Dimmed Political Career." *Stephenville Empire Tribune* 14 June 1964.

Charles Keith Bell
1. "Death of Judge Charles Keith Bell." *The Hamilton Record* 24 Apr. 1913.
2. "Don't Oppose Him." *The Dallas Morning News,* 8 Apr. 1888.
3. "Judge C. K. Bell, Prominent in Texas Politics for Years, Dies." *Fort Worth Star Telegram* 22 Apr. 1913.
4. Ibid.

John Smith Straughan
1. J. C. George to Honorable W. J. Oxford, 16 Dec. 1907.
2. "Judge Straughan Commended." *Dallas Morning News* 16 Aug. 1896.
3. "Court News." *Dallas Morning News* 8 Dec. 1896.
4. J. C. George to Honorable W. J. Oxford. Ibid.
5. "Stephenville Court." *Dallas Morning News* 4 Nov. 1897.
6. "The Great Aerial Wanderer." *Dallas Morning News* 19 Apr. 1897.
7. Coombes, Charles. *The Prairie Dog Lawyer.* Dallas: University Press in Dallas, 1945.
8. "Death of Judge J. S. Straughan." *Dublin Progress* 1 Sept. 1907.

Index

Adams, John C., 179, 181-182, 184-187, 193
Adams, W. S. J., 95
Aiken, C. E., 103-105, 227
Alabama, 74, 77, 203, 206
Alexander, 27, 136, 171
Allen, B. F., 8
Allen, Dr., 130
Allison, Clay, 64
Anderson, Ben, 145
Andrews, C. C., 150
Andrews, H. H., 183
Armistad, W. S., 77
Armstrong, Noah, 6
Arnold, Fount, 17, 44-47
Arnold, W. W., 88
Atchison, Topeka & Santa Fe Railroad, 134
Bagwell, John, 72-73
Bagwell, Margaret, 72-73
Baker, Will, 162
Baker, Winfield, 135
Baldwin, Major, 171
Barkley, B. F., 207
Barkley, Pless, 153
Barrett, Harry, 81, 117-120, 228
Barry, Dr. W. M., 5, 88-90, 226
Bates, W. B., 58
Battle, N. W., 31, 40-43, 197-200, 206, 211, 224, 230
Baylor University, 204
Baylor, John R., 38
Baylor, R.E.B., 31, 204
Bays, Tom, 185, 189
Beaver, Henry, 185
Bell County, 68, 180, 197, 199, 200, 210-212, 219, 227, 230
Bell, C. K., 121, 125, 147, 153, 157, 219-221, 232
Bell, J. R., 111
Bell, John G., 210
Bell, T. C., 56
Belton, 200, 211
Benche's Blacksmith Shop, 118
Berry, S. O., 88-90, 226
Bexar County, 117
Bishop, J. D., 74
Bishop, Joe, 185
Blankenship, A. J., 189
Blasingame, Gus, 182
Bogan, Dan, 122-125, 127
Boling, James., 115
Bosque County, 14, 31, 33, 48, 51, 107, 164, 170, 197, 202, 210
Bosque River, 217
Boucher, George, 10, 156
Boyd, J. H., 129
Boyd, James, 71
Bratton, Frank, 183, 185
Brazoria County, 203
Brazos River, 37, 39, 59, 201
Britton, Frank, 33
Brown County, 33, 91, 92, 95, 98-99, 146, 193, 213

Brown, Pompey, 70
Brown, Rev. C. E., 192
Brownwood, 94, 214
Bruington, Eugene, 169
Brumley, John, 21-22, 63, 209
Brumley, Sarah, 63, 65
Bryan, Terrell, 147
Buchanan County, 197
Buck, Silas, 94, 104, 109-110, 120, 182, 214, 228
Burdick, Mose, 170, 172
Burnes, S. P., 94
Burnick, Frederick, 73
Burnick, Sarah, 73
Burroughs, Dr., 89
Burroughs, J. R., 130
Bush, E. W., 120, 126
Butterfield Overland Mail, 57
Cabaniss, Mary Ann, 197
Cage, Jim, 45
Cage, Pearl, 80
Callahan County, 213
Calvert, 199
Camp Leon, 38, 41
Campbell, Thomas, 172
Carnes, James, 95
Carnes, John, 96
Carnes, Prior, 111
Center, Ely, 189
Chamberlain, Martha, 216
Chaney, Bill, 136
Chenault, T. J., 189
Chilton, Phil, 134
Choctaw Tom, 39
Cimarron, New Mexico, 64

Cisco, 82, 149, 215
Clay, W. J., 187
Coats, James, 34
Cochran, John, 42
Cochran, W. D., 191
Cody, W. E., 130
Coe, Frank & George, 64
Cohron, C. F., 159
Coke County, 12
Coke, Richard, 60, 61, 199-203, 230
Coldiron, Missouri, 138
Coldiron, Monroe, 6, 138, 140-144
Coleman, L. G., 45, 64, 213
Colfax County, 64
Collin, J. W., 186
Colorado, 12, 64, 65
Colorado County, 213
Colorado River, 12
Comanche, 2, 26, 34, 38, 91-99, 101, 102, 115, 147, 149, 211, 214, 218, 224, 231
Comanche County, 8, 14, 33-35, 37-38, 94-95, 97, 99, 105, 138, 143, 191, 193, 197, 202, 210-211, 213
Comanches, 37-38, 42
Coney Island Saloon, 156
Conine, Will, 44-46, 225
Cornett, Ed, 42
Coryell County, 14, 31, 60, 125-127, 197, 200, 202, 210, 213, 216-217, 219, 231
Cosper, J. H., 103-104

Court of Criminal Appeals, 23, 153, 171, 189-190, 192, 196, 229, 230
Cow Creek, 33
Cowan, Isaac, 129
Craig, Frank, 142, 151-153, 155-159
Crane, Mary Alice, 72
Crenshaw, Parks, 53-56, 225
Cresswell, Mack, 192
Crocket, William, 71
Cropper, W. T., 123
Cropper's Hardware Store, 122
Crow, Dr. M. S., 29, 89, 135, 167-168
Crow's Opera House, 174
Culberson, C. A., 147, 228-229
Cunningham, William, 95
Dallas, 206
Dallas County, 54, 68, 173, 205
Dallas Morning News, 180, 217, 227, 229- 232
Dallas Weekly Herald, 16, 20, 66, 92, 93, 223-224, 227, 231
Dalton, 33
Daniel, J. T., 190
Daniels, William, 188
Davidson, C. M., 111
Davidson, Tom, 11
Davies, W. J., 151
Davis, Edmund, 33, 35, 66, 199, 202, 210-212, 230
Davis, S. S., 189
Davis, Thad E., 161-163
Dawson, Bill, 13

Deaton, David, 195
DeHon, Joe, 156
DeLave, Marian, 73
DeLave, William, 73
Denton, 104, 115
Denton County, 67, 112
Desdemona, 148
Devil's Truck Patch, 143
Devine, W. H., 141
Dickerson, Thomas, 63
Dixon, Budd, 92
Dodson, W. C., 29
Dodson, W. N., 71
Dowdy, Jesse, 120
Dowdy, Nancy, 82
Dr. Perry's Drugstore, 122
Drysdale, J. E., 129, 130, 131
Dublin, 26-28, 134, 145, 149, 150-152, 154-155, 157, 171, 174, 178-185, 187-188, 194-195, 224, 228-230, 232
Dublin Drug Company, 186
Dublin Progress, 29, 149
Duffau, 48, 52, 84, 225
Duffau Creek, 48
Dulany, Lucinda, 57-59
Dulany, Nelson, 57-60, 225
Dunaway, Mrs. E., 88
Dunn, Crockett, 170
Dunn, R. H., 11
Eager, Mr., 28
Earl, Catharine, 216
Eastland County, 82, 115, 146, 148, 213, 215, 226
Edwards, Dr. William, 83-84

Edwards, Joe, 84-87, 226
Edwards, Martha, 87
Edwards, Mary, 83
Edwards, Nona, 160-163
El Paso, 57, 98, 102, 217
Elliott, J. C., 140
Ellis County, 79, 81, 205, 208, 226
Erath County, 1, 2-3, 5-8, 10, 12-16, 21, 22, 24, 26- 37, 39, 41-48, 53-54, 63-69, 71- 75, 77, 79-81, 89, 103-104, 106-107, 109, 111-112, 114-115, 117, 120, 126-127, 129, 132-134, 138, 141, 145-147, 151, 154, 157-161, 163-164, 167, 171, 174, 178, 180, 189-192, 195-200, 202, 205, 207-214, 216-217, 219, 221-231
Erath, George B., 40, 54, 200
Estes, Leno, 121
Farmers' Alliance, 218
Farris, T. Crowder, 151-153, 184, 185
Favors, Brink, 6, 138, 140-144
Favors, Mrs. Sallie, 143
Favors, William, 142, 143
Fifth Judicial District, 68, 205, 207-208, 225-226
Fleming, J. R., 3, 90-91, 96, 101, 213-215, 231
Floyd, J. Pink, 138-141
Floyd, Susan Anna, 206
Fooshee, W. H., 36, 80, 90, 168, 209, 223-224, 226-227, 231
Ford, Bob, 10
Ford, John 'Rip', 38, 40-42, 224

Forrest, Nathan Bedford, 213
Fort Belknap, 42
Fort Bend County, 169
Fort Griffin, 37, 117, 215
Fort Lewis, 65
Fort Worth, 2, 17, 30, 32, 46, 72-73, 152, 208, 217-218, 220, 224, 230, 232
Fort Worth Chief, 32, 208
Fowler, William, 46
Francis, A. T., 81, 117-120
Frank, L. N., 81
Franklin, L. O., 156
Freeman, Frank, 2, 177, 186
Frey, John, 29, 44, 67
Fugitives from Justice, 80
Fuller, John, 104
Galveston, 20, 78, 131, 223, 225-226, 231
Galveston News, 20, 223
Garland, Marion, 108-109
Garland, Peter, 39-42
Garrett, A. C., 74
Gatesville, 125, 128, 221
George, J. Collin, 147, 153-154, 157-159, 168, 221-222
Gibbs, John A., 77, 80
Gibbs, Phebe, 78
Gibson, James., 181
Giger, Arthur, 162
Gilbreath, Henry., 13
Gilbreath, J. C., 1, 4, 10-11, 13, 35, 114, 136, 141-143
Gilbreath, William, 174
Gillett, L. E., 8

Gillette, M. C. & E. B., 179
Golconda, 39
Good, John, 14-16, 21, 113, 205-208, 217, 223, 231
Gooden, T. H., 218
Goodman, Bud, 72
Gordon, J. Riely, 29, 30
Grace, Mary McLeary, 213
Gravis, Peter, 78, 226
Grayson County, 57
Green, Jeff, 211
Greenlee, B. E., 67
Griffin, Drew, 107
Griffith, I. A., 23, 189, 190
Groome, J. P., 115
Gunter, William, 72, 226
Gurley, E. J., 40-42, 198, 224
Hamilton, 60, 112-115, 122, 125-128, 155, 210-211, 217, 219, 225, 232
Hamilton County, 159, 193, 197, 202, 213, 216
Hamilton, A. J., 202
Hamilton, Alice, 112
Hamilton, Elizabeth, 112
Hamilton, James, 112
Hamilton, Robert, 112, 115
Handsel, Deputy, 5
Harbin, H. H., 27
Hardeman, Clara, 216
Hardin, George, 40
Hardin, Jeff, 99
Hardin, John Wesley, 91, 94-99, 102, 211, 227
Hardin, Joseph, 93

Hardin, Noble, 34
Harley, Mary, 71
Harley, William, 71
Harper, 84
Harrell, Joe, 179
Harris, Jane, 129
Harris, Willie, 6
Harrison, Green, 182, 185
Harrison, Sara, 174
Harrison, Thomas, 21, 45, 46, 184, 203-205, 231
Haskell County, 213
Hatch, 59
Haws, Phebe, 77, 80-82, 118, 120, 226
Hayes County, 71
Hayes, John, 83-84, 226
Hemming's Mill, 108
Henderson, James Pinckney, 201
Henning, John, 133-137, 228
Herring, Dr. S. L., 157
Hico, 155
Higginbotham Brothers, 187
Higginbotham, R. W., 187
Higgins, Janie, 170
Highly, John, 138
Highsaw, James, 126
Hill County, 204-205, 207
Hill, Asa Collinsworth, 35
History of Eastland County Texas, 82
Hitower, John, 189
Hitson, William, 46
Hogg, James, 154, 181

Holland, William Frank, 83-86, 226
Hollis, Jack, 12-13
Holloway, John Russell, 72
Holt, Bob, 189
Hood County, 8, 42, 103-104, 108, 213, 216-217, 219
Hopson, Belle, 170
Horne, Mary Evans, 201
Horton, William H., 207
Houston Telegraph, 58, 92, 225
Houston, Sam, 201
Howland, Big Dan, 65
Hughes, M. M., 156
Hull, Annie, 162, 164, 165
Hull, Edmund, 163
Hull, John, 160-166, 229
Hume, Kate, 195
Hume, R. T., 178, 192-194
Huntsville, 2, 11, 53-55, 68, 98, 101, 105, 110, 116-117, 119, 135-136, 142, 144, 147, 166, 169, 181, 196, 225-229
Hurley, Mose, 34
Hurley, Rev. Henry, 48
Hurt, Jack, 183
Hurt, James M., 196
Hyatt and Watts' Saloon, 130
Indian Territory, 1, 13, 42, 147, 160, 163, 198
Ireland, John, 120, 128, 228
Jack, William, 203
James, A. B., 6, 103-106, 227
Jamison Peak, 39

Jarrott, J. W., 161, 163-165, 176, 191
Jefferson, Wallace, 199
Jenkins, J. B., 177
Johnson County, 16, 64, 72-73, 205
Jones County, 213
Kaufman County, 46, 205
Kay, Billie, 173-176
Keith, Charlotte, 129
Keith, G. W., 67
Keith, Harve, 170, 192
Keith, J. B., 191
Kemp, David, 6, 122-128, 228
Kennedy, William, 217
Kerr, A. A., 189
Kimbell, F., 8
Kimble County, 107-108
Kimmell, Jack, 12
King, Sam, 189
King, Thomas B., 147, 160, 181, 189, 191, 218, 228
L. C. Cattle Company, 64
Lacy, I. W., 62-65, 225
Lafferty, Tom, 185
Lampasas, 154
Langsdale, George, 118
Langston, Mrs. George, 82
Lanham, Samuel, 220
Larn, John, 214
Latham, Fayette, 34
Latham, J. H., 187
Latham, James, 34
Lauderdale, Tom, 149, 151, 152, 153, 154, 180, 229

Law and Order Club, 187, 188, 189
Leon River, 30, 38, 143
Leslie, Frank, 178, 185, 187, 189, 190, 193, 196, 230
Leslie, Jack, 185
Lewis, Arizona, 167, 169
Lewis, Frank, 167, 168, 169, 170, 171, 172, 229
Lewis, J. B., 134
Lewis. J. D., 167
Lindsey, N. R., 94, 102, 147
Lingleville, 145
Lipscomb, J. A., 94
Locklin, W. L., 122
Long, C. B., 179
Long, R. T., 5, 26, 103, See
Long, Sarah, 71
Louisiana, 73, 202, 206, 216
Lucas, Harriet, 169
Lucas, John, 169, 170, 172
Mahan, Emily, 72
Maloney, Jesse, 186
Marlin, 59, 199
Marshall, John, 59
Marthel, Charley, 170
Martin, J. L., 217
Massie, Felix, 108
Mastin, James, 5, 89, 227
Maxey, Samuel, 198
May, Dr. J. L., 129, 135
McCain, Richard, 149, 182, 184, 185, 186, 188, 189, 190, 193, 195
McCarty, John, 193
McCarty, Jr. James M., 48

McCarty, Sr., James, 48, 50
McCleskey, J. E., 133
McCulloch County, 104
McDonald, Sarah, 204
McFarland, Mary, 201
McFarland, W. Y., 54, 199-201, 230
McGinnis, A. D., 80
McGinnis, J. T., 89
McInturf, Morg, 6, 112-116, 142-143, 227-228
McKenzie, J. D., 46
McLemore, Dr. J. J., 157
McLennan County, 8, 14, 29, 60, 67, 127, 197, 199, 201-202, 204-205, 231
McNeill, Dr. W. W., 39-40, 77-81, 135, 226
Mercer Creek, 38
Meridian, 51, 216
Milam, Ben, 42
Miller, Dr. S. L., 157
Mississippi, 77, 203, 205-206, 219
Mites, Joseph, 74
Mites, Mattie, 74
Monk, E. M, 89
Monk, James, 89
Monroe County, 197
Moore, Dick, 157
Moore, Ed, 185
Morse, Kate, 164
Moss, S. E., 25
Motheral, Sallie, 129
Motheral, William, 39, 54, 130
Murphy, J. W., 89

Murphy, S. N., 160
Murphy, Thomas, 23, 130
Nance, Lizzie, 75
Navasota, 57
Neighbors, Robert, 41
New Mexico, 1, 19, 64-65, 68, 128, 134
New Orleans Daily Picayune, 94
Nineteenth Judicial District, 14, 31, 43, 197-204, 223, 225, 231
Nolan County, 128
Northcutt, H. W. & W. M., 189
Norton, A. B., 21, 63-64, 67-68, 71, 207-209, 231
Norton, D. O., 208-209
Nowlin, Light, 5, 223
Nugent, T. L., 23, 27, 95, 104-105, 109-110, 115-116, 119-120, 125-131, 134-135, 141, 157, 171, 216-218, 231
O'Neal, John, 21
Oats, Charley, 183
Ogden, P. J., 85
Oklahoma, 1, 13, 42, 53, 56, 68, 134, 160, 224, 227, 231
Old Dublin Cemetery, 187
Osterhout, J. P., 8, 68, 79-81, 210-212, 231
Osterhout, Junia, 212
Owen, John, 33
Owen, John Thomas, 33
Oxford, John, 174
Oxford, W. J., 147, 151, 153, 157-159, 162, 171, 179-180, 232
Painter, Eliza Jane, 77-78

Palmer, Ben, 191
Palmer, N. W., 188
Palo Pinto, 39, 40, 221- 222, 224
Palo Pinto County, 5, 14, 32, 40, 46, 197, 202, 205, 207, 213, 216-217, 219
Parker County, 205, 208, 224
Parker, Buck, 179
Parker, Robert, 32
Parnell, J. D., 25, 119
Patten, Nathan, 204
Patterson, Green, 150-151, 153, 210, 231
Patton, Truss, 190
Peacock, Wilsen, 81
Pearre, C. B., 204
Pease, E. M., 209
Pendleton, George, 191
Penninger, Walter, 175-176
Perkens, Marion, 111
Perkins, W. N., 189
Phillips, Jesse, 186
Pierce, Sophie, 3
Populist Party, 218
Porter, J. J., 25
Prim, Sam & Jim, 179
Purvis, E. P., 140
Putty, Tom, 6, 145-148, 228
Radical Reconstruction, 16, 18, 20, 33, 63, 66, 202
Ranger, Texas, 87
Rat Row, 6, 117, 228
Rat Row Saloon, 118
Ray, H. L., 42, 209
Red Light Saloon, 73

Red River, 13
Reed, J. D., 155
Renick, S. H., 63, 94
Resley Creek, 107
Reynolds, Annie, 107, 109
Reynolds, Jasper, 6, 107-110, 227
Reynolds, T. D., 33
Reynolds, William, 108
Richardson, James., 155
Riddle, Lee, 164
Ringer, M. E., 115
Ritchie, Dr., 131
Roberson, Sam, 176
Roberts, I. N., 167
Roberts, Junia, 210
Roberts, Oran, 134, 216
Roberts, Phil, 12
Rodriguez, Julian, 149-152, 154, 158, 180
Rodriguez, Victor, 149
Ross, Fell, 4-5, 228
Ross, L. S., 120
Ross, Shapley, 39
Runnels County, 5, 213
Runnels, Hardin, 5, 38, 41, 201
Rusk Penitentiary, 2, 106, 111, 116, 119, 128, 136, 159, 166, 172, 181, 227-228
San Antonio, 20, 57, 67, 199, 215, 223, 230
San Antonio Express, 20, 67, 223
San Francisco Bulletin, 65
Sawyer & Company Stage Line, 57
Sayers, J. D., 166, 191-192, 230

Seattle, 199
Self, D. W., 46
Selman, John, 98
Shackelford County, 117, 213-214
Shands, Nathan, 3, 13, 28, 147, 157, 223
Sharp, Gary & Maurice, 32
Sharp, James, 103
Shaw, G. S;, 80
Shelby, John, 88-90, 226
Shellman, Henry, 57
Sheridan, Philip Henry, 202
Sherman, 152
Sherman, A. B., 171
Shofner, Bird, 151, 155
Shumaker, E., 123
Sikes, Perry, 103, 104
Silar, J. P., 22, 158, 176
Sixteenth Judicial District, 205
Slaughter, William, 12-13, 134
Smith, Annie, 169
Smith, F. A., 122
Smith, Florence, 220
Smith, John Peter, 220
Sneed, Bob, 186
Snyder, 6
Somervell County, 213, 216-217, 219
Southern Hotel, 157
Sparks, Captain, 5
Spear, A. M., 197
Spencer, R. B., 187
Spencer, Randolph, 67
Spokane, 215
St. Clair, J. D., 34, 108

St. Clair, Robert, 108
Stephen, John M., 24, 39-40, 81
Stephen, Samuel W., 40
Stephens County, 213
Stephens, John D., 94
Stephens, Mrs. B. M., 75
Stephens, R. C., 75
Stephenville, 4-6, 9, 11-12, 21-30, 32-34, 39-40, 44-47, 54, 63-64, 71-73, 77-78, 80-81, 88-90, 94-95, 103-104, 109, 114-115, 117-118, 129, 133-135, 142-143, 153, 157, 161-164, 167-169, 171, 173, 178-179, 182, 184, 186, 187-188, 192, 194-195, 198, 211, 216-218, 220- 232
Stephenville Empire, 28, 217
Stephenville Empire Tribune, 32
Stockton, Port & Ike, 64
Stone, Bill, 143
Straughan, J. S., 2, 74, 157, 159, 164-166, 171, 176, 189-191, 196, 221-232
Strawn, 12
Summers, Mary, 200
Tarrant County, 8, 46, 72, 103, 205, 207
Taylor County, 213
Taylor gang, 67
Taylor, James, 66, 96
Temple, 191, 195, 230
Tennessee, 77, 199, 200, 205, 213, 219
Test Oath, 15
Texas Central Railroad, 27, 111

Texas Court of Appeals, 63, 98, 101, 105, 141
Texas Criminal Court of Appeals, 165
Texas Rangers, 6, 39, 41, 43, 46, 80, 92, 93, 100, 200, 204, 214, 223, 225
Texas State Troops, 53-54
Texas Supreme Court, 131, 199, 202
The State of Texas v Anna Williamson, 23
The State of Texas v Riley Major, 17
The State of Texas v Thomas Edwards, 21
The State of Texas v Tom Wright, 23
Thirtieth Judicial District, 216, 219, 224, 226-228, 230
Thirty-Fourth Judicial District, 68, 210-211, 215, 223, 226, 231
Thompson, George, 184-185
Thompson, J. E., 5
Thompson, W. D., 114
Throckmorton County, 37, 213
Thurman, Baylor, 47
Tolar, 36, 224
Tomlinson, S. A., 30
Trammel, Barry., 187
Trout, Frank, 138-142
Tubberville, J. B., 186
Tucker, Mat, 209
Turnbough, J. W., 140
Turnbough, M. C., 140
Turnbow, James., 164
Turner, Titus, 130

Twelfth Judicial District, 91, 213, 223, 226
Twenty-Ninth Judicial District, 219-220
Tyler, George, 191
Tyree, Jim, 182
Upshaw, George, 109
Utterback, Bob, 183
Van Zandt County, 114, 208
Waco, 2, 17, 25, 31, 40-42, 57, 59, 67-68, 94, 127, 197-199, 202-205, 225, 230
Wade, Bob, 151-154
Waldrup ranch, 95
Walker, J. L., 131
Wallace, Jenks, 169, 170, 172
Wallace, William (Bigfoot), 57
Waller, H. G., 89
Waller, James, 39
Waller, John, 83, 85
Ward, Jack, 139
Ware, Henry, 93
Warren, Jim, 139
Wassen, W. J., 150
Weatherford Exponent, 92
Webb, Charles, 91-102, 223
Webb, Walter Prescott, 214
Wells, A. J., 189
West End Cemetery, 6, 40
Westbrook, Sallie, 129
Whisenant, John, 107-108
Whisenhunt, Noah, 107
Whitacre, Ed, 114
Whiteside, R. M., 16, 21, 45, 135
Whitney Saloon, 117-119
Whitney, Martha, 130
Wilkins, Henry, 29
William & Mary College, 197
Williams, W. C., 189
Williamson, Anna, 6, 129-132, 224, 228
Williamson, Dr. J. M., 130, 135, 176
Williamson, Temus, 6
Willis, Shedrick, 199
Wilson, Bone, 5
Wilson, Charley, 173-175, 177, 229
Wilson, Frank, 96
Wilson, Jake, 173
Wilson, T. J., 173-174, 176-177, 229
Windham, J. D., 33
Witcher, Adam, 211
Witcher, M. C., 187
Wood, Tom, 22, 155-157, 159, 223, 229
Woodward, J. H., 118
Wright Saloon, 95
Wright, C. O., 151
Wright, Katie, 191
Wright, Tom, 151-154, 178, 180-184, 187-192, 195-196, 224, 230
Yarbrough, J. M., 88-89
Young County, 213
Young, F. R., 130
Young, Gus, 6
Young, Lee, 37, 109, 115, 129-131, 157, 171, 217, 220, 231
Young, W. R., 187
Zimmerman, John, 23, 130

Author's Biography

A sixth-generation Texan, Sherri Knight grew up on a dairy farm in rural Erath County located in North Central Texas. She attended Lingleville and Dublin public schools before graduating from Stephenville High School (at age 16) and eventually Tarleton State University with degrees in English and history plus a Masters in Education.

Ms. Knight took her all-level teaching certificate throughout the State of Texas making stops at Houston, Mineral Wells, Callisburg, Childress, Tolar, San Antonio (17 years) and Mansfield school districts, completing 31 total years in the classroom. Her numerous awards include Outstanding History Teacher – UTSA Regional History Fair, Outstanding Teaching of the Humanities presented by the Texas Council for Humanities, Teacher of the Year – East Central High School (San Antonio), National Endowment for the Humanities Scholar, Fulbright-Hays Scholar, Fulbright Summer Abroad, and Texas Exes Award for Excellence in Education – University of Texas at Austin. Sherri Knight is a member of Women Writing the West and the Wild West History Association.

Since moving back to her hometown, Ms. Knight has become a member of the Board of Directors of the Stephenville Museum and has been appointed to the Erath County Historic Commission by Judge Tab Thompson. Her first book - *Tom P's Fiddle, A True Texas Tale* - was selected as a finalist in nonfiction at the North Texas Book Festival in 2008.

Ms. Knight is currently working on her next book, which will be a second volume of the history of the district court of Erath County, Texas.